MEETINGS OF THE MIND

We have more moral, political and historical wisdom, than we know how to reduce to practice; we have more scientific and economical knowledge than can be accommodated to the just distribution of the produce which it multiplies. The poetry in these systems of thought, is concealed by the accumulation of facts and calculating processes. . . . We want the creative faculty to imagine that which we know; we want the generous impulse to act that which we imagine; we want the poetry of life; our calculations have outrun conception; we have eaten more than we can digest.

Percy Shelley, *A Defence of Poetry*

Meetings of the Mind

David Damrosch

IN COLLABORATION WITH

*Vic d'Ohr Addams, Marsha Doddvic,
and Dov Midrash, D.C.A.*

PRINCETON UNIVERSITY PRESS

PRINCETON AND OXFORD

Library of Congress Cataloging-in-Publication Data

Damrosch, David
Meetings of the mind / by David Damrosch ; in collaboration with
Vic d'Ohr Addams, Marsha Doddvic, Dov Midrash.
    p.   cm.
Includes bibliographical references and index.
ISBN 0-691-05055-4 (alk. paper) — ISBN 0-691-05056-2 (pbk. : alk. paper)
Literature—Study and teaching (Higher)—United States—
History—20th century.   2. Criticism—History—20th century.
I. Title.
PN68 .D36 2000
801'.95'0904—dc21   99-087371

This book has been composed in Janson

The paper used in this publication meets the minimum requirements of
ANSI/NISO Z39.48-1992 (R 1997) (*Permanence of Paper*)

www.pup.princeton.edu

Printed in the United States of America

10 9 8 7 6 5 4 3 2 1

TO THE MEMORY OF

Charles Bernheimer

*Comparatist, co-conspirator,
friend*

CONTENTS

MEETINGS OF THE MIND

1 TOKYO

How Do Disciplines Die?

The Hakone region has aerial cable cars traversing the mountains, boiling hot springs, and lake cruises. . . . The most worthwhile attraction in the area is the MOA Art Museum, named after its founder, Mokichi Okada. While establishing one of Japan's new religions, the Church of Messianity, Okada was able to collect more than 3,000 works of art. . . . Located on a hill above the station and set in a garden full of old plum trees and azaleas, the museum also offers a sweeping view over Atami and the bay. *Admission: ¥1,500. Open 9:30–3:30; closed Thurs.* *Fodor's 91: Japan*

The projector, which was fitted with inadequate bulbs, threw faint images on to an over-large screen, and the lecturer, however closely he peered, could hardly discern their outlines, while for the public they were scarcely distinguishable from the damp stains on the walls. . . . To this mixture of moth-eaten ghosts and restless infants the lecturer was privileged—as the supreme reward for so much effort, care and hard work—to reveal his precious store of memories, which were permanently affected by the chill of the occasion, and which, as he spoke in the semi-darkness, he felt slipping away from him and falling one by one like pebbles to the bottom of a well.
Claude Lévi-Strauss, *Tristes Tropiques*

I ARRIVED at Narita airport, late in August of 1991, not knowing what to expect. Several hundred comparatists from around the world were assembling for the triennial meeting of the International Comparative Literature Association; this would be the group's first meeting in Asia. My uncertainty had partly to do with the conference's theme, if it had one; "The Force of Vision" was a pretty vague topic, though I'd certainly seen vaguer. My chief concern was with my fellow panelists. I knew none of them well, their work only a little better. As I waited for the airport train into the city, still groggy from a fourteen-hour flight, I wondered about the rationale for our having been lumped together on a panel entitled "Disciplinary Perspectives." Or were we the panel on "Perspectives on Disciplinarity?" Setting my suitcase down, I pulled the program out of my briefcase: there we were to be, two days hence, at nine o'clock on Saturday morning, in a session whose French title in our bilingual program, "Quelques perspectives disciplinaires," sounded almost apologetic to my ear. Who would have the energy to come? What would we have to say even if someone did show up? Here I was, prepared to talk about changes in children's literature, and the disturbing implications of those changes for future enrollments in English courses, while an independent scholar I barely knew, Vic Addams, was doing something on the discipline of Classics at the turn of the century, and Marsha Doddvic, a film theorist from Bennington, was going to discuss recent developments in feminist criticism. The Israeli semiotician Dov Midrash, of all people, would be a commentator on our papers, none of which, so far as I knew, he had yet seen.

Roland Barthes would probably have seen this concatenation as some Zen exercise in semiotic emptiness, but it looked to me like garden-variety disorganization, so typical of the pseudo-collaboration found in conferences when neither the organizers nor the participants are prepared to work together in any meaningful sense. Faced with hundreds of paper proposals from comparatists in dozens of countries, the conference's "organizers" had apparently resorted to some obscure stochastic principles in assembling the panels. Clearly, it would be a real challenge to the four of us to make something coherent of our manifestly unrelated disciplinary perspectives.

From what I knew of my fellow panelists' work, I wasn't optimistic. I had met and liked Marsha when we were both graduate students, and she'd come to a student conference I'd organized at Yale. At the time, her lively and open personality had seemed to contrast sharply with the dense theoretical prose of her dissertation on fetishism in the films of Buster Keaton. I'd never quite managed to understand her arguments, and I certainly didn't like the look of "scopophilia," for which Marsha was condemning—or perhaps praising—Keaton. Even granting that my problem lay in the gap between my capacities and Marsha's greater brilliance, I wondered just how we'd communicate to a common audience or even to each other. Still, those were old impressions, as we'd been out of touch for years, and I was curious to see how her thoughts had evolved in the meanwhile.

I have to admit that I was less eager to renew my acquaintance with Vic Addams, almost for opposite reasons. I loved his work—the impressive ease with which he could move from Sanskrit aesthetics to medieval mysticism to Aztec poetry; the resolutely untrendy aestheticism of his recent book, *The Utility of Futility*—yet I'd always found myself a little put off by Vic in person. Was it a certain superciliousness in his manner, or was I just envious of Vic's superbly tailored wardrobe, his places on the Vineyard and in Venice, his evident enjoyment of both the financial resources and the sparkling prose style that enabled him to spend his holidays doing articles for *Yachting Today*?

Most of all, I was apprehensive regarding the formidable Dov Midrash, whom I would be meeting for the first time. Readers of *Diacritics* may recall the controversy that swirled around Dov's major work of the mid-eighties, *Narrheit und Methode* ("Folly and Method")—an ambiguously ironic reconstruction of deconstruction that maintained that deconstructive insights are most profound precisely when they approach a state of pure self-parody. A wholesale attack on the book by E. D. Hirsch under the title "Darkness Risible" had only increased the book's cachet among those in the know. In a review essay in *Glyph*, the Turkish scholar Hymit Bathtöi had observed that even as Hirsch denounced Midrash's conclusions, he had grudgingly granted Midrash's major points, admitting the basic instability of poetic expression and the ultimate unknowability of an author's original intention. Bathtöi concluded that Hirsch's supposed attack was actually a covert defense of Midrash's position, promoting the very views it pretended to dismiss. Bathtöi went so far as to speculate that "Midrash" might be a penname for Hirsch himself, a charge which Hirsch indignantly rejected but which Midrash himself refused either to confirm or deny.

For my part, after reading several attacks and defenses, I only knew that I would never be enough in the know to know what Midrash was really talking about. And now the instigator of all this debate was going to be our respondent. Would we have to spend our time decoding Midrash's response, trying to figure out whether he was complimenting us or mocking us?

Actually meeting Midrash proved to be a relief. I found a message from him awaiting me when I arrived at my hotel, proposing that the four of us copanelists meet for breakfast the next morning at a nearby coffee shop. Dov and I were the first ones there; his stocky, bearded form stood out, the rest of the patrons being Japanese. Apparently the travelers in the surrounding hotels weren't venturing out so early, or if they did they may have been put off by the restaurant's English name—Snack Memory—and gone in search of more authentic cuisine. In fact, though, Snack Memory served standard Japanese fare to a clientele of office workers, and Dov and I settled down to a meal of miso soup and raw egg over rice. He proved to be a fascinating conversationalist, though at times he was a little hard to follow, speaking in low, gravelly tones punctuated by self-mocking interjections. He spoke English not so much with a pronounced accent as with underlying speech rhythms that reflected several different languages. As I later learned, he'd grown up speaking Russian with his father, Yiddish with his mother, and Hebrew in school, then had lectured in German for ten years at Konstanz, before assuming his new posts first at Geneva and now at Irvine as well. He had a keen ear for American colloquialisms, and at times he almost sounded American; then you'd get a glimpse of one or another linguistic layer beneath his command of English.

"Glad to meet you," Dov said. "This fucking architecture." He gestured at the bland office buildings outside, an unfiltered cigarette in his hand. "You see what happens when a culture gives up its own traditions? Food, no, thank God: here, we have a good breakfast." He used his chopsticks to stir his egg into his rice.

I could see that small talk was not going to be Midrash's strong suit. I decided to respond in kind. "But what are Japan's 'own' traditions?" I asked. "Do you mean the script they borrowed from China, or the metaphysics that came from India through Korea?"

Dov smiled. "Maybe you are right, it is just a matter of time. The import needs to put down roots, be corrupted or purified in local terms, so in five hundred years they will build remarkable skyscrapers here. We should maybe come back then and see."

I was about to point out the difficulty of doing so, when Marsha walked in. When I'd known her in her Berkeley days, we'd all been at the stage of androgynous jeans and tangled hair; now, though the hour was early, Marsha was wearing a suit, its black leather contrasting effectively with her pale skin and with the bright red of her nails.

"Don't you just love it here?" she asked, after I'd introduced her to Dov. "The energy, the electronic readouts in the subway cars, all that neon in overdrive around the train station!" She gestured toward the bustling boulevard outside. "Don't you think they do Paris better here than we do in America?"

Dov just shrugged. I decided to change the subject, and asked Marsha how she'd been in the last few years.

"Great!" she replied. "The Bennington students are a trip, and the department's a really collegial bunch. It's hard to get much writing done, but the whole atmosphere is wonderful, artsy, off-beat, intense, and they're putting me up for tenure in the fall. Everyone says it's a sure thing."

"So they have something so definite as tenure at Bennington?" Dov asked. "I thought they refused to play the usual academic games there."

"It isn't called tenure, that's true," Marsha replied; "it's kind of a point of pride in the campus culture to stay away from any hierarchy of power. So we have a permanent renewal of contract instead of tenure."

"It sounds like it's just the same thing under a new name," I remarked.

"Names matter," Marsha replied. "A symbolic change can have a ripple effect in reality—otherwise, all of us in literature might as well shut up shop. The proof comes in the performance. At Bennington, refusing the ordinary language of academic authority is a way we express an institutional reality. The power isn't held tight by our senior faculty at all—I chaired the department last year myself, even before the vote this spring. Of course, my case still has to go through the Trustees, times are tough, enrollment's been sagging some, but no one expects any problem. The administration has a long tradition of close consultation with the faculty, we've got a dynamic new president—a woman, no less—and she's sure to strengthen our collaborative culture. She wants us to have campus-wide discussions this coming year about the future of the institution. All in all, we're expecting good times ahead. If only I wasn't feeling torn in two so much of the time."

"What's going wrong?" I asked, alarmed.

"Nothing's wrong at all," Marsha replied. "Just too much good fortune all at once. Especially the arrival of Cassie, our daughter, she's thirteen months now. She's so wonderful! And *so* engrossing—I just don't know how I'm going to juggle everything when classes start back up next month. Last year I had a half-time deal, that helped a lot, but we can't really afford it this coming year. Anyway, I'm impatient to get back into things full-time, what with the promotion and everything. At least she stopped breast-feeding a couple of months ago, but even so—if only I had an 'insert paragraph' command in my life!"

"Is there a husband in the picture?" Dov asked. "Does he help?"

"You're damn right he does," Marsha replied, then paused. "I guess that came out sounding a little. . . . But I didn't really mean it that way. And he isn't exactly a husband, either, as far as that goes. Still, we've been together quite a while now, and we both wanted a child. Tom adores Cassie—he even *thinks* he does an equal share of all the work. I've never had to get up at night with her, which helps because I sleep like a rock. When I was nursing, we had this deal at night, I'd provide the food, he'd provide the transportation. But daytimes, I don't know, Tom can be kind of slow on the uptake, and half the time he's out in his greenhouses, or holed up in the study doing some gardening column on a tight deadline. A week can go by, and I've barely read a page. And as for writing. . . ."

Marsha's voice trailed off. She shook herself, and continued more positively.

"At least I feel I've earned this break. Ten days! I have to say, it's kind of nice to be footloose for a change."

Just then, a voice called out from the doorway:

"*David*, my dear, there you are!" Vic Addams never simply entered a room when he could make an entrance. Bending his head gracefully to avoid a hanging lantern, he came to our table, and draped his slender form onto a chair. Without waiting for introductions, he took a tourist brochure out of the pocket of his linen blazer.

"Do you see this?" he asked. We all looked: an ordinary promotional photo, showing the Tokyo skyline as seen from the bay.

"Look!" Vic said. "They're windsurfing out there, Mistral sails no less, right in front of the skyscrapers. Sublime! And think of the housing here— do you know what that means?"

"No, what?" I asked.

"Rentals! How many Tokyo apartments could have space for a board, not to mention the mast? My concierge informs me that the hot spot is a beach out at Tsudanuma, part way round the bay, where well-endowed young fellows rent well-equipped sailboards. Who's coming with me? I've hired a car for the day; my driver can run you by your hotels for your suits, and we're off."

"I thought we have a conference starting today," Dov said. "And our own panel comes tomorrow morning. I think we must plan it out, and I need to know what you will say so I can prepare my response."

Marsha and I spoke at the same time. "Dov's right," I said. "Let's go," said Marsha. "I've never been windsurfing."

"About the talk," Vic said to Dov. "I plan to extemporize; you can just disagree with whatever I say. People usually do."

"Here's my paper," Marsha said, handing Dov a folder. "All the panels today are pretty traditional source-and-influence things, so I think I'll get more out of some immersion in the culture."

"Immersion? Only if you're careless," Vic said. "The idea is *not* to fall in. But I'll show you."

I SPENT the next several hours in conference sessions. Marsha had been all too correct: a dutiful exposition of someone's influence on someone else, followed by a paper on the second someone's subsequent influence on some third someone, both presented by speakers who seemed to see life steadily, and see it in little pieces; a panel on that old chestnut, Ezra Pound's misunderstanding of Chinese script, the failure of all previous critics ever to say anything really interesting on this topic having inspired a new crop of earnest failures; and a depressing smattering of broader methodological papers, some presented by feel-good global-villagers who saw vague harmonies everywhere, the rest given by crypto-nationalists who emphasized the incommensurability of East and West and the implicit superiority of their own cultural system—unless, with an oppositional flourish, they demonstrated the superiority of any culture but their own.

None of the panels I attended had any internal coherence, except for the Pound panel, which had no variety; none of the conference rooms had any windows; none of the panels left more than five minutes for questions; none of the questions was audible; none of the replies was intelligible. Even so, I couldn't decide: were Vic and Marsha showing the only real sanity in the place by going off windsurfing, or was their escape act just another symptom of the problem?

As I emerged wearily from my third panel, I decided to find out. I walked up the street to get my bathing suit from my hotel. No concierge there, and the single desk clerk was absorbed in his comic-book novel, so I hailed a cab on the street. The driver spoke no English, and I had forgotten the name of the beach. Though I'd made an effort to learn some basic phrases, I hadn't thought to master any vocabulary concerning beaches and sailboards. After two or three minutes of fruitless non-communication, I let the cab go. Then it occurred to me that I might be able to pantomime my wishes, so I hailed another cab. Motioning for the driver to open his window, I made broad breast-strokes with my arms, pronouncing the words "swim, swim" and "beach, beach" slowly and distinctly.

The driver looked at me quizzically over the rims of his sunglasses. "You wish to go to a beach, sir?" he asked. "Would that be Tsudanuma?"

I got in, ignoring the looks of the passersby who had stopped to observe my performance. On the way, the driver taught me the Japanese term for windsurfing, which proved to be "windsurfering."

The beach was a broad arc of sand, bounded by a breakwater on the right and, on the left, a partially completed highway overpass surrounded by half a dozen construction cranes. I scanned the horizon for my friends. Japanese adolescents in Day-Glo bodysuits were zipping back and forth across the water, from the breakwater to the construction site and back, but Marsha and Vic were not among them. Probably they had left some time ago, I reflected; it was almost five o'clock by now. Then I saw them down the beach near the rental shed, their boards drawn up on the sand beside them. It seemed that they had forgotten to bring towels; Vic was drying Marsha's back with a tee shirt. Wearing only a skimpy black bathing suit, Vic somehow gave a more powerful impression than when clothed. His muscles had the fine but not bulky tone of runners and—as I could see, looking around—of windsurfing enthusiasts. His dark hair, neatly brushed as always back from his finely chiseled forehead, glistened in the late-afternoon sunlight.

I almost hesitated to disturb them, but as Marsha turned her head over her shoulder to say something to Vic, she caught sight of me, and waved cordially.

"It's been great!" she said, as I came up. "I only fell in a few times—I *hope* there isn't anything too toxic in the water around here. And I've even learned to tack!"

"A natural," Vic said approvingly. "Most people take far longer to get started. Care to take a turn, David?"

I contented myself with a swim, then joined the others at a beachfront snack bar where they were eating bowls of noodles.

"And now, what next?" Vic asked. "A stroll through some exquisite garden before we take in the play?"

"I'm afraid I missed my chance on that one," I said regretfully. "I didn't focus on it in the preregistration materials, and now I hear it's all sold out."

"So what?" Marsha asked. "My attitude's always been, these big corporate-sponsored events, I'll save my money for worthier causes."

"But Marsha, dear heart," Vic exclaimed, "this is not to be missed! *Hamlet* revised into Kabuki form, now being re-staged in a full-scale reproduction of the Globe theater?—To say nothing of the pleasures of the company," he added, with a smile that somehow seemed directed only at her.

"Oh, I'm going," Marsha replied. "I just don't plan to add to the take. They've already sold the seats anyway, but there's bound to be no-shows. You come too, David, I'll get us both in."

I found this hard to believe, given the precision with which everything seemed to be organized in Tokyo. Still, I had no other plans, and so I went along in Vic's car. We arrived at the Globe theater, somewhat incongruously set in a quiet residential neighborhood of single-story houses nestled among cherry trees and ornamental shrubbery. There was still some time until the show was to begin, so Marsha had us take a stroll.

"The trick's in the timing," she said conspiratorially, as we returned to the theater. "We waltz in thirty seconds before curtain time. You do have a ticket, right, Vic? Give it here—just follow me."

We went in behind Marsha as she strode purposefully into the crowd of last-minute arrivals, who parted before us. When we reached the ticket-taker, Marsha brandished Vic's ticket, tapping it significantly on her watch on her other wrist. She then pointed at Vic and me with the ticket as she held up three fingers of her other hand, smiling generously as she did so to indicate that we would spare the attendant the need to hold things up on our account.

The ticket-taker hesitated for half a second; it was enough. Marsha swept us in with her, as new people engaged the attendant's attention. Marsha cordially waved an usher away, and we settled into a half-empty row of seats.

"Do you think the ticket-taker really thought she saw three tickets?" I whispered.

"Are you kidding?" Marsha answered. "She thinks she *took* our tickets and gave us back the stubs! Stick with me, kiddo, and you'll do okay."

This was a side of Marsha I hadn't known about. Happily, no one came to demand our seats and have us ejected from the theater, and I gradually began to relax and enjoy the play. An unusual version of *Hamlet* indeed, written at the turn of the century by an early comparatist who hoped to reconcile East and West through creative dramaturgy. I had some difficulty following the action, partly because no translation was available, but also because the same actor played both Hamlet and Ophelia. Still, the play reached a forceful climax when Hamlet committed ritual suicide by ordering Horatio to cut off his head. I found myself moved by the solemn final scene, in which the new ruler, Fortinbras, set the severed head on a shrine in honor of Hamlet's dead father. Was the director making a subtle point, or simply saving costs, by having Fortinbras too be played by Hamlet-Ophelia?

As we left the theater, Vic proposed going out for sake. Jet-lagged, I declined. Tired though I was, I noticed that neither of my companions urged me a second time. Returning alone to my modest business hotel—a far cry from the Frank Lloyd Wright–designed Hilton where Vic was staying—I called my wife and children back in New York, now starting their day as I was ending mine. I then looked around my room. I could almost touch both side walls at once, and the room extended only a yard or so beyond the end of the narrow bed. Still, ingenious cabinets, trimmed in mahogany, ran under the bed to hold clothes, and compartments in the paneled end wall opened magically to reveal TV, VCR, CD player, and mini-bar. Perhaps under Vic's influence, I found myself thinking of my surroundings not as a budget single room but as sleeping quarters on a trim cruising yawl. Through my small, porthole-like window, I could see the stream of traffic eddying along the road below. It could be all right, exploring this new culture with my new friends, always assuming they could spare some time for me. But did we have enough in common ever to get beyond the transient intimacy of a conference trip? Could the conference itself provide a substantive counterpoint to our extracurricular activities?

I WAS still wondering about this the next morning, when I arrived for our panel a few minutes early and found only Dov in the room. He was already seated on the rostrum, scowling slightly as he jabbed at a draft (mine or Marsha's, I didn't really want to know) with a red felt-tipped pen. A handful of thrill-seekers wandered in over the next few minutes and subsided quietly into chairs. They almost disappeared from view, dotted about in a room meant to hold a hundred, their faces suspended in that strangely garish half-light peculiar to hotel conference rooms the world over.

I joined Dov on the podium, and then we waited. Finally, at ten past nine, in came a tanned Vic and a sunburned Marsha. "Sorry we're late," Marsha whispered as she settled down beside me. I gave a noncommittal smile and motioned to Vic, who went to the lectern. I could see in his hand some notes jotted on a sheet of Tokyo Hilton stationery.

"How do disciplines die?" he began. "Can any historical signpost point the way for the modern literatures as they plunge, lemming-like, down the steep slope of undergraduate enrollments, as business majors boom and literature falls off the charts? I propose to you the melancholy, monitory example of Classics, queen of the disciplines a hundred years ago—hated dominatrix of the college curriculum in the students' eyes, to be sure, but mistress of their professors' hearts. In those distant days, the study of the classics was the great source of mental discipline and of public morality alike. Not only could you not major in English, you'd be lucky to find a single course in English literature! This was the natural order of things, had been for the longest time, and no classicist in 1875 could have foreseen how swiftly the modern rabblement would dethrone their queen. The revolution took just a decade or two, and classics has declined from half the curriculum to a tiny fraction of it now. Blame the barbarism natural to American culture if you like, or take the classicists themselves to task for circling their wagons, for their defensive reliance on the greatness that was Greece and the glory that was philology. Yet know that the writing is on our own walls today, its message conveyed by the very fact that scarcely a soul in this room can read the Greek in which it is written!"

Rather melodramatic, I thought; still, he had gotten the audience's attention. Vic went on, leaning forward on the lectern, speaking more quietly now.

"I would not have you think I am here to mock Classics or even most classicists. If the signpost pointed only downward, what point would there be in pausing to decipher it? It took the classicists a long while to regroup, but regroup they have, and we should attend to the examples they are setting by their innovative efforts at outreach. They are far ahead of most modern disciplines in developing lively new grammars, interactive databases, links to high schools—not shrinking even from recourse to billboards and toga parties: methods not to be despised! There are lessons for us all in their current recovery; and there is a positive message in the long decline itself, if we can have the courage to face it. In many ways, that tectonic upheaval at the fin-de-siècle is the best thing that ever happened to Classics. How *ut*terly perverse it was, really, to enthrone classical civilization as the embodiment of nineteenth-century European values, once technology began to triumph over theology and the colleges decided to distance themselves from their sectarian roots! Bronze-Age warriors with Iron-Age values somehow magically preserving 'sweetness and light,' in between yesterday's rape and tomorrow's conquest? What would these slave-owning, pagan bisexuals have thought, if they returned to earth in 1890 and found themselves made into poster boys for the highest aspirations of a bourgeois, Victorian, Christian, homophobic, industrial capitalism? *Horribile dictu!*

"What a relief, really, for the committed classicist, to be freed today from the obligation to find sermons under every stone of the Acropolis. No need now to dress Homer and Euripides in proper Victorian garb, to fit them into patterns their limbs never knew, bending and folding them like paper dolls to serve—let's say, in honor of our hosts today—as the fons et origami of modern culture! No wonder the older classicists let their specious centrality fade away with little regret: devotees of the modern literatures should do so too, refuse any servitude to the *pietas* of state culture, whether the middlebrow moralism of the right or the middlebrow multiculturalism of the left."

Vic went on in this vein for several minutes more, in terms that will be sufficiently familiar from his book, especially the opening polemic on "The Futility of Utility." He argued that only in a marginal position can literary studies do justice to literature's paradoxical embodiment of cultural values and its dislocation of them, especially its undercutting of the cosy half-truths in which social values typically—I think he actually said "inevitably"—filter down into classroom presentations. On my right, Dov was shaking his head and writing furiously. To my left, Marsha seemed to be restraining herself from interrupting each time Vic made a disdainful reference to popular culture or cultural studies; I thought I even saw a flush spread across her neck, though this may only have been an optical effect of fluorescent lighting on her sunburn. Vic continued:

"Classics can point the way for the modern literatures, if only because the compromises that tempt all professors in search of an audience look so ludicrous in the case of antiquity. It is a mistake to make Milton popular, but it is a mistake that some cannot resist, trying to trade in the poet's 'fit audience, though few' for an unfit audience, but many. This is scarcely a good bargain, dear friends, and it is a game for which Theocritus and Anaximander make poor pawns. But do not suppose that I mean to evoke the classical writers as standard-bearers for an elite culture! Virgil may have been, Euripides most emphatically was not, but the ancients' values, popular *or* elite, only sporadically connect to ours in any event. We should not study such writers for their closeness to us and our egotistical concerns—their value lies precisely in their *distance* from us, their foreignness. Spare me the Christian reading of Aeneas and the feminist reading of Medea alike! It is not for us to appropriate such magnificent, enigmatic characters, it is for them to appropriate us. Ezra Pound had his reasons for urging us to 'make it new,' though his famous phrase looks less provocative now than he meant it to be, more in tune with the demands of a growing consumer capitalism." Vic cast a glance over at Marsha, who didn't look amused. He raised an eyebrow ironically, and went on.

"For us today, the challenge is quite the reverse: to make it *old*. We must allow the work the freedom of its *ut*ter estrangement from us, setting the stage for the liberation that comes when we are taken a while out of ourselves, disabused of our pieties and our vanities. We return to our world shaken, drained perhaps—surely the point of Aristotle's medical analogy to cathartic purgation. 'Be old! Anew!' as Joyce so beautifully says in *Finnegans Wake*: 'We are once amore as babes awondering in that chill childerness which is our true name.' A literature department must be more than a little inglenook where we sit and take the chill off our modern culture, dreaming of a nostalgic past—or else fantasizing the radical social change our young charges will enact just as soon as they finish their term papers on Fanon and graduate. We should resist the superficial satisfactions that come from acting the part of scholarly Jack Horners, pulling little social plums out of our textual puddings. The death of literature as an institution may mean the rebirth of a more vital literary experience; as scholars and teachers, it is our task not to mourn but to celebrate the death of Tim Finnegan the solid citizen, to assist in his resurrection as a shape-shifting, larger-than-life, life force."

Marsha leaned over to me as Vic sat down. "Mind if I go next?" she whispered. "I just can't let all that go by." I agreed, secretly relieved not to have to follow such a rhetorically charged performance. Marsha went to the lectern.

"What my esteemed panelist is peddling here," she began, "is the worst sort of retrograde bullshit."

Maybe I shouldn't follow Marsha either, I thought; maybe I should have stayed in bed that morning.

"If *I* was independently wealthy," Marsha continued, "I too could maybe afford to sit outside the institutional arena, making fun of the students who are looking to literature to give them some guidance in their lives, as they struggle to make sense of the racially and economically divided society around them. A society, after all, whose leaders would be quite happy to have all of us in literature confine ourselves to parsing grammar and syntax, topping our programs off with a little artistic polishing. Vic Addams may think he's taking a stand in favor of literature's lofty purity, but he's either kidding himself or he's kidding you. What he's really doing, like it or not, is playing into the hands of the right, the people who attack any questioning of the status quo as 'political correctness.' The idea of basing an appeal to artistic independence on Milton and Virgil! Can you imagine two more politically engaged writers? I'm happy to spare you the Christian reading of Virgil, and you can spare *me* the Christian reading of Milton too, as far as that goes. But I can't imagine a viable reading of Virgil that didn't begin from his celebration of the Roman Empire, or a reading of *Paradise Lost* that ignored Milton's despair over the collapse of the people's republic he thought Cromwell had created. Didn't he start that epic right after the restoration of the monarchy he hated so much? Doesn't that hatred fuel Satan's fury at the 'tyrant' in heaven?"

Vic was shaking his head; the corners of his mouth turned down in a fleeting smile at the words "Virgil's celebration of the Empire." On my right, Dov was writing as furiously as before. I could see a few words: "People's republic! Milton the Maoist?" Marsha went on.

"Literature deals in ideas; let's face it, it deals in ideologies. All art does, though you may not see this so clearly in the more indirect cases like music. With literature, it's as plain as the words on the page. Writers take positions in their works, and then their publishers and reviewers and readers put them into ideologically charged positions of their own. It's part of our job as critics to locate those positions, and take a stand toward them ourselves. If you want to persuade me otherwise, my dear"—Marsha turned and addressed Vic directly—"you'll have to give me some better examples than the ones you gave just now."

She turned back to the audience. "The most exciting thing in academic study today is the exploration of the social and cultural grounding of all forms of art, popular *and* elite, and part of the point is for us to clarify our own situations in the process. Let me give you a concrete case of what I mean. My example was supposed to introduce the topic I was going to present, before I was kind of derailed by Vic's presentation. I've called my talk 'Where in the World is Virginia Woolf?' The idea was to focus on Woolf to talk about the evolution of our discipline. If all politics is local, it's because it's localized in time as well as in place. The politics I want to reflect on is ours more than Woolf's, or rather, it's the way we keep reconfiguring Woolf's politics, and how our reconfigurings can give an index to our own shifting situations."

Marsha paused and put on the pair of purple-rimmed glasses that had been hanging on a cord around her neck. About to begin reading, she set her pages down and continued speaking directly to the audience, now with a hint of apology in her voice.

"I really don't object to aestheticism itself—who could fall in love with Woolf and not feel its attraction? When we read her, we get seduced by that dreamy language, that rolling swell of sentences with their whitecaps of semicolons. We do get caught up into her world, I'll grant Vic that. But I want us to remember that Woolf always attached her webs of words to the real world—'with bands of steel,' as she put it in *A Room of One's Own*. The detached aestheticism that Vic's proposing might be possible, who knows; it's just that in actual fact, that kind of 'detachment' has usually turned out to serve the politics of the status quo. Woolf is my example of this; again, I'm not talking about her own position, but about the politics her aestheticism was yoked up with until quite recently."

Marsha cast a look over at Vic, who seemed to be listening with interest, an impression not everyone could create while also using a bent paper clip to dislodge sand from beneath his fingernails. Marsha glanced at her own fingernails, and continued:

"But let me give you some of the actual talk you crossed all those time zones to hear." She picked up her papers, set a couple of pages aside, and began to read. "I'm sure that many people have become feminists by reading Woolf. Not me: what did the trick was reading the *article* on Woolf in the *Encyclopaedia Britannica*. This was in the late seventies, when I was a junior in college at Minnesota. I'd started doing a lot of literary theory, which meant structuralism, Freud, even some Lacan already—Minnesota was a pretty hip place—but feminism just wasn't on the map. This was still the Lacan of fathers and phalluses, 'Dads and Dongs,' as we called the course. And in my literature classes, you barely ever read a woman writer, and never, ever did you read her *as* a woman.

"That's just the way it was, and I wasn't the twenty-year-old who'd be savvy enough to see the problem on her own. It took the encyclopedia to teach me. I was trying one day to remember the dates of one of Henry James's late novels and one of Woolf's early ones—I was wondering if she could have read *The Golden Bowl*, I think it was, before she wrote some scene in *The Voyage Out*. So I checked into the *Britannica* in the reading room. This was when they'd just come out with their division into two sets of volumes: the 'Micropaedia,' for short entries, and the 'Macropaedia,' for the really major stuff.

"You can probably guess where this is heading, but believe me, I didn't have a clue in 1977; after I found James in the *Macro*, right where he should be, I innocently looked for Woolf there too. Nothing doing. But the real shock came when I tracked her down in the *Micro*. It wasn't just that Henry had *nine times* the column inches Virginia had: it was what those inches said. Everything in Henry's entry was about 'mastery'—I think they used that word about six times, all about his impact on the history of the novel, his cross-cultural insights, his elegant, ornate prose—the whole number. But Virginia? Weakness, insecurity, madness that her loving husband couldn't control; despair and suicide at the end, after which loving Leonard published her final novel for her. And her writing? Technical experiments with stream of consciousness, in between those bouts of madness. Every damn paragraph in Henry's article made you feel like an incomplete human being if you didn't go out and read six of his novels right away. Not one line in Virginia's entry would make you think you really needed to read her at all. Ever.

"I got mad, and I started looking around. I got myself over to the French department, and I got into film studies. In both places, a couple of un-tenured people were starting to teach things that could channel my anger and help me go somewhere with it. There was even a Marxist in Philosophy, though he was fired not long after that, and I started putting things together."

Marsha glanced at her watch. "I see I'm already running out of time. I was going to use this little story to set up a discussion of stages in postwar feminist criticism. As you can see, because of my age and the accident of where I was, I kind of missed the classic sixties and early seventies feminism that was working to redress the balance between Virginia and Henry. I went right into the high theory mode of late-seventies feminism, and that kept me busy for a good ten years. I was planning to go on to say something about the new stage we've entered now: less abstract and abstruse, more activist and angry—*Three Guineas* as our new model Woolf text, not *A Room of One's Own.* As my time's about up, though, I think it's just as well if I keep the focus on Virginia and Henry's adventures in the *Encyclopaedia Patriarchica.* The sixties generation began to set that balance right, and that work still needs doing today. It's no denigration of the beauty that Vic and I would both find in Woolf to say that the old stress on her style-for-style's-sake was one way of keeping her out of the Macropaedia."

Marsha looked over at Vic, who put a hand over his heart and shook his head, as if to assure her that he was certainly not trying to exclude Woolf himself. Marsha gave an impatient shake of her head and addressed him directly, apparently forgetting the audience in front of her.

"Look," she said, "the old high aesthetic line just isn't wearing too well these days, not even for James. He and Woolf are together at last in the latest edition of the *Britannica,* but not because we've gotten Virginia promoted to the Macro. No such luck! Poor Henry's been *demoted* to the Micro. Of course, he *still* has three times the space Virginia does, at least for now, but we're going to have to find more compelling ways to present all our favorite authors before they disappear altogether."

Marsha looked around, apparently remembering that she was standing at a lectern; she resumed speaking to the audience. "To read Woolf *or* James today, we need to do more than pile up more close readings of their novels, whether they're the earlier celebrations of *Mrs. Dalloway* or the more recent unpackings of deferrals and gaps in *Orlando* and *The Golden Bowl.* We need to read our authors themselves as social texts, with all the messiness that entails. Vic Addams is welcome to his catharses and his purifications, but if we leave Woolf floating in some exquisite stratosphere, she's useless to us here and now. The Woolf who struggled to make her way in the world, the Woolf whose books are still struggling to make their way, is the Woolf we can take our bearings from today."

She took off her glasses and sat down to scattered applause. As she reached her seat, she glanced over at Vic, who gave her a sweet smile. Or was I interpreting his expression too optimistically? Could a sweet smile really be sweet, as a matter of fact, under the circumstances? Probably Proust could have untangled this, but Proust wouldn't have been on a podium to begin with, needing to make his own point in the next twenty minutes. Could I find a positive way to build on both the earlier talks? This wasn't going to be easy. As I went to the lectern, I decided to pretend I knew Marsha and Vic better than I really did, hoping my assumptions wouldn't be too far off the mark.

"Vic Addams and Marsha Doddvic have more in common than you might think, and more than they may realize themselves," I began. "They were both passionate readers at an early age, and in college they gravitated toward the study of complex, demanding poets and novelists. Both also believed in the transformative role of literature, and they still believe this, though they may envision that transformation differently. Both began from a base in highly artistic works, more English and European than American. Each has broadened out from there, and yet neither really seems to have lost that early love of authors like Virgil, Milton, and Woolf. But as Marsha says, all these authors are now collectively an endangered species. Yet the problem goes beyond the issue of any given approach. I believe the real threat to literary study doesn't come from too much aestheticism, or from politicization either, but from broader changes in contemporary culture that endanger *any* study of great work from the past."

I turned to my topic proper, a discussion of the problems posed today by the changing cultural environment in which our children are now growing up. I began by citing statistics on the decline in English enrollments since the late sixties—a drop of 50 percent. "No doubt there are many causes for this decline," I went on, "from grim professionalism on the one hand to the excitement of new fields like women's studies on the other. But the cultural environment that children grow up in must be a major factor as well. Here the usual villain is television; it's often said that we've raised a TV generation that simply doesn't read.

"This claim is misguided, I think, for two reasons. First, it ignores the fact that the TV junkies of the fifties became English majors in droves in the sixties; if TV was so pernicious, we never would have had that boom to begin with. Second, the claim that kids no longer read is simply false. The problem lies exactly with *what* they read—not what they watch. The real culprit is a development that might seem like the best possible news for literary study: the contemporary boom in children's literature. This new wave of writing threatens to squeeze earlier writing—and especially earlier British writing—out of our culture altogether."

I looked out at my audience; no visible reaction, but at least they seemed to be listening. I continued.

"It was only in the early sixties that we began to see serious contemporary American literature being written for children and adolescents, a change that began with works like Madeleine L'Engle's Newberry-award-winning *A Wrinkle in Time.* That book, in fact, had been rejected by twenty publishers as too complex and troubling for young readers, before it was finally published in 1963. Until then, the available American choices had consisted mostly of cartoon-like works like the Hardy Boys adventures. For richer reading, kids would usually have to turn to imported British classics. From Beatrix Potter to A. A. Milne and Kenneth Grahame, then on to Dickens and Sir Walter Scott: a child was naturally led into classic British literature, given a taste for its cadences and its characters, its settings and its obsessions. Many an English major was born in this way.

"These books are still available, of course, but they no longer have the pride of place they still retained even thirty years ago, precisely because so much really good children's literature is being published in America today. My own children show more interest in the jazzy, ironic, postmodern children's books of Jon Scieszka than in any older British writer: Winnie the Pooh has been shouldered aside by the Stinky Cheese Man. Scieszka is an excellent writer: but he is likely to lead his readers forward toward Quentin Tarantino rather than back to Henry Fielding and Jane Austen. Children today have less and less need for anything written before 1960, especially for anything written outside America before 1960.

"Further," I continued, "the current generation of writers themselves work from a newly contemporary and American frame of reference. Madeleine L'Engle's pathbreaking work would have been impossible without a broad background in older British writers like George Macdonald and C. S. Lewis; Judy Blume's work would be impossible *with* such a background.

This shift is even clearer in the lighter literary fare with which adults relax. P. G. Wodehouse's favorite subject, in his British high school in the 1890s, was Greek verse composition, and he could compose Latin hexameters as rapidly as English iambics. And Wodehouse found his first and largest audience in America. Reading even an American humorist like S. J. Perelman in midcentury was like doing verbal gymnastics, keeping your mind in shape for reading a Joyce or a Laurence Sterne. A humorist today like Dave Barry doesn't have the same effect at all. Hilarious as Barry is, his jokes, and even his prose style, point toward Jerry Seinfeld and David Letterman, not toward Swift or Nabokov."

I concluded my presentation by calling for scholars to cooperate with teachers in elementary and secondary schools, to work together to achieve a better balance in the books students are getting as they grow up. "If we don't take steps soon," I said dramatically, "we won't have any students left to aestheticize *or* to politicize in our college classrooms."

I sat down, relieved to be done; I was also rather pleased to have been able to build out from concerns expressed by both Vic and Marsha, moving things to a broader plane and away from the personal invective they'd been courting. I just hoped that Dov would use his international perspective to carry the discussion further, and not simply go on the attack against one or the other of our copanelists.

I was half right. He didn't begin by attacking them: he attacked me.

"Damrosch seems to be groping at some institutional perspective," Dov began. "This could maybe be interesting, but so far his ideas remain superficial, thanks to his wish to please everybody. I think this is the problem of American liberals generally. No blame anywhere: teachers are not taking the path of least resistance, they are only swamped with too many excellent new books. Parents are nowhere to be seen and do not need to be. The poor little children are not ignorant and lazy, they merely need to have some old books thrown at them. They can even read them while they watch their daily dose of seven hours of TV: it's okay with Damrosch, *everything* is okay with Damrosch!"

I definitely should have stayed in bed that morning.

"This is really just a marketing problem," Dov went on, "if people used to read Wodehouse and now they read Dave Barry? I have to spend a lot of time on airplanes, and I have read this Dave Barry—the airline magazines seem to love him. This Dave Barry is a shitty writer! *That* is the problem: any society that abandons a Wodehouse for this Dave Barry is a society that is going to hell in the 747 where they read him just to forget the life they have only too briefly left behind them."

Dov took a handkerchief and wiped his brow. He then continued, more calmly now that he had disposed of me. "What holds my interest when I read Wodehouse are two things: his many-layered style and his *values*. Yes, Wodehouse has real values, and they give a true satirical bite to his ridiculous earls and their shiftless younger sons. You find in him lasting images of friendship, loyalty, and resilience; wittingly or witlessly, his Bertie Woosters and his Gally Threepwoods puncture pomposity, undercut class pride, and explode hypocrisy. *This* is real satire. But this Dave Barry, so far as I have read him, never rises beyond farce. Everyone's a fool, except Dave Barry himself, who only pretends to be a fool. In reality, Dave Barry means to manipulate us as much as any evil bureaucrat in his little chamber of horrors. There's no moral purchase for a reader anywhere in his work. He lacks a vital style, he just gives a series of one-liners, as they are called, with some minimal excuse of a theme for the day. I submit to you that this Dave Barry is morally and stylistically rootless, I might say ruthless, both at once. And I think this is not two problems but one." Dov cleared his throat and continued.

"I have a related quarrel with Dr. Addams's paper, too, if I should think in the contemporary terms that Damrosch invites us to use. Addams thinks aestheticism will rescue us from the old Victorian pieties. Oscar Wilde's dream lives on! Yet I fear that today aestheticism has become as debased as liberalism in modern culture: not even art for art's sake any more, just jokes for jokes' sake. I admire something of what Dr. Addams says, but he goes too far. I cannot agree that art has no necessary connection to life, still less that the great Greek classics are wholly foreign to us. Eliot was right that we know more than the earlier writers did: for they are what we know. There *is* such a thing as the Western tradition, multiple and various though it is. If you only ever live somewhere where people grow up in a different tradition altogether, you would see how deeply in our blood run Plato, Sophocles, the Bible, Milton. To deny this is to cut ourselves off from our moorings. This is a term, moorings, that I like better than 'roots,' and maybe Dr. Addams will like it too, since he is a sailor. Let's not insist on an organic connection to people and places thousands of years or miles removed from us. Even when there may really be some organic rootedness, this is a mixed blessing at best—the tyrants who rule Iraq and Syria today may justly pride themselves on their unbroken links to ancient Assyrian butchers like Shalmaneser the Third, who boasted of crossing rivers on bridges made from the skulls of his enemies. In Israel too, I think it is a dead end to look for God-given roots, to insist that Torah gives the coordinates for the eternal topography of Eretz Israel. Never mind the politics: this is shoddy scholarship! Sure, we can plot out the acreage that God gave to Abraham, and I for one do not doubt that God exists. But *Abraham* never existed, so he is a pretty weak link if you are trying to trace the deed to the territory."

Dov paused, as if listening to what he had just said. "*Deed*—a nice word in English, is it not?" he continued. "It can mean something that happened or it can be a piece of paper. A real Hebraism! Like our term *davar*, which means, indeed, both word and deed. But the fundamentalists have it backwards: yes, word and deed are inseparable, but this doesn't mean all those words really reflect actual deeds. It means all those deeds, whatever they were or weren't, are words and words only for us today. So let's not assume that we're rooted in or by our texts. We're at sea, and our texts are at once our vessels, our moorings, and the sea itself. Our traditions sustain us and guide us; they also can drown us unless we handle them skillfully, I would say with a skeptical piety. Indeed, the text as sea is a traditional idea itself: 'the sea of Talmud' is a phrase found already in antiquity. Maybe Keats spoke for all poets when he declared that his name was writ in water."

Dov paused, and looked out at the audience over the thick black rims of his glasses.

"So," he went on. "My caution to Dr. Addams is that we have less freedom than he suggests, in choosing the texts we use, and in the ways we use them. This is a fact that I personally do not regret: complete freedom is never achieved, it is only approached by madmen and by tyrants, but at a terrible cost—even, I think, to themselves. Now, if I heard Professor Doddvic correctly, she ended her talk by saying that she takes her 'bearings' from Virginia Woolf. This is what brought the nautical metaphor to mind, and so I endorse her view. At least, I endorse the view I wish she would have. But I suspect things are more solid for Professor Doddvic than they appear to me. She seems to be navigating between fixed positions, the Left and the Right, and even allying herself with one position against the other. But how fixed can they be, these points of reference? Suppose I come to meet Professor Doddvic half way, won't *her* left be *my* right, and her right, my left? Or worse yet, suppose her landmarks turn out to be wandering rocks, and we are the ones who are stuck in place? Either way, I sense a certain fixity in Professor Doddvic's position. This may hinder us to see the works we discuss in a full depth of perspective. Let us say that we do want to emphasize Milton's politics, for example, how far will we get if we begin by throwing out his Christianity, as she seems prepared to do? Are we left with some modern secular residue, Milton the Maoist? So I wonder if Professor Doddvic really does need Woolf so much to get her bearings, or is she going to end up giving marching orders to her authors?" Dov paused, looked over at us, gave a little shrug.

"Probably I have annoyed everyone enough by now, so I will stop." He sat down. Marsha was indeed looking annoyed; Vic was looking bored, which didn't seem much better. For my part, I was just wishing I'd never mentioned Dave Barry. I decided we'd better shift the discussion outward.

"Questions?" I asked brightly.

None were forthcoming. Of the dozen members of the audience when we began, three had disappeared during my talk, and several others had left as Dov began his commentary. Four people remained: two of them were studying the conference program together, the third was eating some kind of pastry, and the final person seemed to be asleep. I glanced at my watch, and was relieved to see that our time was almost up anyway. I announced my regret at this discovery, and closed the session.

THE four of us pretty much avoided each other for the next couple of days. Did we have any common ground at all, personally or intellectually? I thought there had been intriguing ideas in each of the papers, but the panel had unfolded in a depressingly familiar pattern of mutual incomprehension and disregard; the whole was noticeably less than the sum of its parts. We might never have resumed our discussion at all, had we not been trapped by Japanese hospitality on a day trip to Hell.

It seemed like a good idea at the time. Most of us conference participants were new to Japan, and probably only Vic and Marsha had yet ventured out of downtown Tokyo at all. All the guide books said that the volcanic mountains north of the city were spectacular, but it seemed difficult to negotiate them in a brief time if one didn't speak the language. So when our conference organizers gave us a day off, and offered us a blue-chip day trip complete with mountains, lake cruise, and a dramatic hilltop museum—all at a low cost heavily underwritten by the conference's twenty corporate benefactors—three hundred of the conferees signed on.

At the start, all was sweetness and light. As our eight plush tour buses pulled out of our host university in central Tokyo, we settled back with a collective sigh. What a pleasure to surrender, for a day, our fierce independence, our Western individualism, our adulthood itself—to be taken care of, each with a little pin on our lapel giving the number of our bus, nothing to do but glide out of the city past the press of inbound salarymen, sipping highly sweetened tea while listening to nuggets of Japanese history and culture from our resolutely cheerful tour guide.

The very absence of actual content from our hostess's patter was part of its charm. After days of abstruse analytical discussion, how nice to be asked the thorniest of questions only to receive the simplest of answers! ("Does anyone know the difference between a Shinto shrine and a Buddhist temple? No? The Shinto shrines are the ones with a vermillion gate in front.")

Even the first hints of a certain rigidity in the arrangements raised no alarm. We were repeatedly admonished that coffee, and only coffee, would be served with lunch; any other beverage could only have been ordered in advance. Even though I dislike coffee and never drink it, I found myself idly wondering why anyone would want anything other than what had been arranged for us. What embryo in its right mind would refuse its complimentary amniotic fluid, and churlishly insist instead on tea, Coke, or that best-selling Japanese sports drink, Pocari Sweat?

I had met Marsha on the line waiting for the buses, and we had agreed to sit together; we snagged Vic when he strolled up at the last minute, and he was sitting across the aisle from us. Seeing him roll his eyes at something the tour guide said, I expressed my surprise at finding him on a tour bus to begin with.

"For the MOA museum, my dear, I'd do stranger things than this," he replied. "They have three National Treasures, you know; but they're so far out of the way that I've never been."

"I understand that part," Marsha interjected, leaning over me to speak. "It's the tour bus I don't get. Why don't you just rent a helicopter or something and go direct?"

"And miss the sulphur springs and the lake cruise on the fake Man-o'-War? Not for the world—*ça vaut le voyage* for the ethnographic curiosity alone."

Marsha grimaced. "I think that's a pretty condescending way to talk about the Japanese, Vic," she said.

"The Japanese?" he replied. "I was talking about the conference-goers! When I want to see my Japanese friends, I don't come to a conference, certainly not one in Japan; we meet up in Hawaii if the surf's good, in Paris if it isn't. No, no, it's the professors I'm here to observe. As I am normally deprived of the dreary delights of departmental life, this is my chance to see the species up close."

If Vic regarded the rest of us as specimens, our guides viewed us as schoolchildren on holiday, a perspective that became clear at our first stop, an outcropping of sulphurous hot springs and volcanic vents in Hakone.

The area was lovely, apart from a pervasive smell like rotten eggs and the somewhat uncanny belching sounds that the earth periodically emitted, but here we encountered a problem: there was so much to see in the region that we weren't going to be allowed to see any of it. I had learned from Fodor's that the great treat in Hakone would be to take a series of cable cars over the hot springs in the valley. This, however, we didn't have time to do, as our guides were intent on showing us the famous Lake Ashino as well, in the next valley. As a result, we had only a few minutes to admire the belching sulphur and watch the cable cars disappear into the haze. Our chief discovery at this stop, in fact, was Dov, who had been on one of the other buses but now joined us as we boarded our bus for the trip to the lake.

There, we were hustled onto a ferry, for a brief ride on the splendid Man-o'-War, a full-scale neo-Portuguese mock-up, which brought us to a resort town at the other end of the lake. There, Vic persuaded Marsha and me (Dov declined) to sneak away from lunch and rent a rowboat, for a delightful hour on the water. On the water but not in it, for the man who rented us the rowboats had warned us that the sparkling lake was unsafe for swimming. Some lingering respect for authority must still have clung to us, for we heeded his words even though the evidence of our own senses, on this hot summer day, belied his explanation: "The water is too cold. You will die." So we returned to our bus alive, but also twenty minutes late, to find that men with walkie-talkies were combing the area looking for the lost Americans.

Chastened, we resolved to be better group participants during the day's culminating activity, the visit to the museum. A lecture on Noh drama, an after-hours tour of the museum's galleries and its gardens, followed by dinner in the museum: does this sound like an introduction to penal servitude? Yet from the moment of our arrival at the MOA Museum of Art, we could sense that things were getting a little bizarre. The museum was built by a department store owner who went on to found a new religion, the Church of Messianity. He then turned to art collecting and museum-building as the culmination of his life's work, and indeed the museum seemed to have taken inspiration from each stage of his career. Perched atop a steep hill, the museum was reached through a chain of long escalators buried in the hillside. Escalator after escalator flowed up to the heights above, while multicolored fluorescent lights bathed the rippling concrete of the tunnel walls and ceiling, and Muzak from hidden speakers soothed the ears. We were given complimentary copies of the museum's catalogue, which describes the effect perfectly: "The tunnel-escalator system does not simply convey visitors to the main museum building but, through its environment, prepares them for the experience of viewing beautiful art objects. . . . Together the shape of the arch and the form of the stairs produce the best acoustics and lessen any fear a visitor may have when looking down the stairway from above. The beauty of the rhythmic, continuous ripples which converge at each landing, creates the fantasy of a different world for the visitor." A different world indeed, or rather an amalgam of usually separate earthly elements: department store, temple, and airport terminal all rolled into one? A metro station that just wouldn't quit?

Dov escalated up beside me, scowling.

Our journey culminated in a final multimedia blitz in the Circular Hall, a cave with marble floor and sprayed-concrete ceiling studded with woofers, tweeters, and laser machines, which treated us to a half-hour sound-and-light show. Thus prepared for the viewing of beautiful objects, we were ushered up some final escalators to the museum proper. Here our troubles began in earnest. The four of us soon tired of the lecture on Noh Drama— most of us knew too little to get much out of it; Vic knew too much—and so we tried to go off to the galleries. Every way we turned, however, museum guards politely but firmly escorted us back to the lecture hall. No impediment stood between us and the galleries, so far as we could tell, but our schedule itself: it wasn't yet time for us to see the art.

Finally we were released to the galleries, where we would at last have time aplenty. We were slated to spend a full four hours at the museum before our buses would take us down to the bullet train for Tokyo. This newly relaxed pace was a relief, but there was a problem: the museum had hardly any art at all on display. Half a dozen huge galleries were sparsely dotted with lonely looking ceramics and screens, while a couple of smaller rooms held a random collection of European paintings. Two of the three National Treasures were in fragile condition, and were not even on display; the third, a small tea-storage jar of considerable technical interest to ceramicists, quickly exhausted its appeal for the uninitiated.

If there wasn't a lot to do indoors, at least it was a lovely late afternoon outside, and our thoughts soon turned to the verdant grounds stretching off toward bamboo and pine groves on both sides of the hill, looking out on a seaside resort town below. Going outside, Dov and I strolled off to the left down a curving dirt path. This, however, proved to have been intended only as a visual effect: within a few yards we were brought up short by a chain-link fence topped by barbed wire, barring our way to the bamboo grove. We returned to the museum and encountered Vic and Marsha, who had met the same fate in seeking the forest of pines off to the right.

There was nothing for it but to leave the grounds altogether, and go for a walk in the town. So we took the plunge down the escalators to the deserted Circular Hall, which was now murmuring a Mozart divertimento to itself in a dim pink light. Enchanted at the prospect of freedom—the outside doors were dimly visible in the depths below, and not a single guard could be seen blocking our retreat—Marsha and Vic paused for an impromptu waltz around the Circular Hall. We then completed our descent to the exit, but there was one detail we had not considered. We were special guests, viewing the museum after closing, and the doors to the outside had been locked. There was no way out.

When we again reached the top of the purgatorial stairway, we found that our fellow conference-goers had all arrived at the same conclusion. Little clusters of comparatists surged weakly back and forth, across the lawn, up the steps, into the galleries, and back out again. The tour organizers were nowhere to be found. What could we do? We tried a few sallies of pointed irony ("So when do we get our complimentary handcuffs?"), but even these witticisms began to wear thin after an hour or so, as the sun began to set and mosquitos (delicate, elegant Japanese ones) began to come out. Resigning ourselves to our situation, the four of us sat on a ledge and began talking.

"Doesn't this museum give you pause, Dov?" Marsha asked. "I don't really object on principle to your talk of tradition, but look *around* you. The po-mo escalator ride was great, but why not just come out on this incredible view? Do we really need this monumental mausoleum up here too? Art has a pious effect here, all right, but it's the piety of an invented religion. The effect is to trap us, not to guide our wandering feet."

"Look," Dov replied, "I dislike the architecture myself. Yet the man who built this museum devoted years to collecting great art. It is a sign of our own immaturity if we cannot look at twenty remarkable objects for more than twenty seconds each. One of these great works alone should suffice us for our entire visit here, if we were truly as cultured as the curators expect us to be. Perhaps they treat us like children in the process, but we do not need to prove them right by acting the part. We should slow down, look around, absorb the beauty of a few objects. Or simply sit here with pleasure and respect as we contemplate this magnificent view."

This was a new idea to me, and it also suggested more cultural flexibility than I'd realized Dov possessed. "What you're saying reminds me of a passage in Barthes's *Empire of Signs*," I remarked. "It's when he's discoursing on the Japanese love of packaging. If I remember the passage, it goes something like this: 'By its very perfection, the envelope, often repeated—you can be unwrapping a package forever—postpones the discovery of the object it contains. The object itself is often insignificant, for it is precisely a specialty of the Japanese package that the triviality of the thing is disproportionate to the luxury of the envelope. It is as if the object of the gift were the box, not what it contains: hordes of schoolboys, on a day's outing, bring back a splendid package containing no one knows what, as if they had gone very far away and this was an occasion for them to devote themselves in troops to the ecstasy of the package.'"

"What a memory," Marsha remarked. "You'd make such a good *hostage!*"

"Funny you should think of that analogy here," Vic interjected, "as we contemplate Dov's magnificent view across the barbed wire that keeps us trapped up here."

"But is entrapment really the right idea?" I asked. "Isn't Barthes's 'ecstasy of the package' more to the point? The Japan Travel Bureau simply couldn't imagine a greater pleasure for us than to conclude our tour contemplating an enormous *package*. Isn't the museum itself its own chief exhibit?"

"The hell with Barthes!" Dov cried. "This is not the Beaubourg—physical embodiment of Barthes's own prose on an off day, a series of self-referential gestures we enjoy for its own sake even if the content may be hard to find. I insist there is a real spiritual dimension here, not only some kind of self-display. It is different from Barthes's packages: the museum's layers of wrappings do not make up for some lack in what they enclose. They testify to its transcendent value, and this value would be decreased by raw, naked viewing. Atop ten flights of escalators, inside this gigantic sandstone shrine, in a nearly empty gallery ten meters high and twenty meters long, within a central display case, there rests the sole National Treasure we may see—an empty vase thirty centimeters tall. The museum does not display its art works, as we would think of display: it *enfolds* them. Most potent of all are the hidden National Treasures. These are truly enshrined, thus enhancing their invisible but radiant power. They are meant to share the glory of the emperor hidden within the Imperial Palace in the heart of Tokyo."

"And we're supposed to think of ourselves the same way," I added. "Not as truant adolescents, but as valued guests in a country that truly honors scholars. Think of the fact that the Crown Prince opened our conference, which wouldn't have attracted the notice of a Deputy Mayor in New York. Now they're giving us the ultimate privilege: to be *wrapped up* in this magnificent package. We ourselves are the exhibits for a few hours, free to contemplate our own enclosure both in space and in time. I have to admit I've been thinking of this as a day trip to hell, but in our hosts' eyes it was supposed to be a voyage to an earthly paradise, perfectly expressed in the founder's aesthetic mysticism. I shouldn't have been reminded of Dante's Inferno—where there's certainly more than enough to *do*. This is more like

Dante's Paradise, where circles of saints contemplate the endless son-et-lumière of the pulsating Celestial Rose."

Even Vic couldn't have turned a better phrase, I thought to myself.

"If you ask me, David," Marsha said, "I think you're starting to hyperventilate a little. For me, the kitschy effects neutralize the art, they just make it safe to consume. Busloads of office workers get sent here to get a controlled dose of transcendence, a little hit of aesthetic opium."

"*Please*, Marsha!" Vic interjected. "Would the world be a better place if these works of art were in storage somewhere and each clerk in the fellow's department stores had an extra twenty yen a week to spend playing pachinko? Do not misunderstand me—I favor an ethics of liberation as much as you do, it's just that we differ as to what that happy result would be. Your kind of liberation—forgive me, dear heart—is so *dreary*! So . . . *plodding*, even if it were possible, a most debatable idea. A bright-eyed, bushy-tailed, all-encompassing Respect for Everyone's Personal Values—who could disagree with such a program, really, if only it *were* possible, or even if it isn't? And yet, Marsha, such a sanitized set of virtues! Fine for Sunday School, I suppose, but why bother with art if a little political sermonette will do as well? Art as the vehicle of social progress, art as a forklift for moral freight—you're just so *American*, Marsha!"

"Oh, really? I'm the immigrants' kid, and your proper Bostonian background maybe makes you less American than me?"

"But of course, and not only if we compare your assimilationist parents to my loyally Belgian mother, not to mention her noble Luxembourgian ancestry. *I* am what I have made myself: a citizen of the world of art!"

Marsha bridled, started to speak, then checked herself for a moment. She began again, softly. "Vic, *dear heart*, I have to tell you, that kind of pomposity makes me puke."

Vic cast her a sharp glance; looked down, took a moment to examine the crease in his left trouser leg; replied with growing intensity.

"Imagine a childhood on Beacon Hill in the fifties, rattling around in a big house with a war bride mother who had, as a matter of fact, no reason *whats*oever to live in America except for an accidental husband with whom she had nothing whatever in common. Imagine, too, a father who knew it, who himself had been emotionally abandoned by a father whose footsteps he nonetheless followed into law. Who found success turn to ashes in his hands; who took to music as other men might take to drink. The *opera"*— Vic gestured expansively, as though we were now seated in an opera house—"was my parents' only common ground, and there they could witness, somehow share, the most exalted passions while also—best of all— remaining silent, *ut*terly alone together in their box. No need to say a word to one another for hours on end: Mozart, my father's favorite, Puccini my mother's, but they never missed Wagner though neither cared much for *him*."

"Why Wagner?" I asked.

"Length," Vic replied, suddenly subdued.

Dov broke in. "I have right here my violin, Vic," he said, "and I would be happy to serenade you if you like, but can we shift this away a little from the deprivations of your not so very deprived childhood? Or is ordinary unhappiness the only ground you give for your allegiance to art? Maybe you just need a good therapist?"

Vic smiled. "Don't get me started on therapists, Dov, though sometime I might tell you the tale of the cardiologist who broke my heart: not as far from the point as you might think. But you're right, of course, that I would be the last to rest my case on some insipid therapeutic view of art—all too close, to my mind, to a religious perspective, all very well for a rabbi manqué like Freud or for an ordained minister like Northrop Frye, hardly for me. My only point about my upbringing was that I was never drawn into the American worship of profit, gain, utility: when I look out at this sunset I don't see pennies but peonies in heaven. The most useless beauty is the best of all!"

"So then your art ends in nature after all?" Dov asked. "I thought I heard you opposing them in your talk."

"Only an analogy, Dov dear. And don't suppose that a sunset is just one thing. To the psalmist, it is the voice of nature echoing the voice of God—

'caeli enarrant gloriam Dei.' To the scientist, an optical effect of light striking atmospheric dust. To the divine Oscar, it is a second-rate Turner, a pale
imitation of the better beauties of art: a polemical exaggeration, of course,
but an exaggeration in the right direction."

"I don't know, Vic," I said. "Wilde himself couldn't pull off an entirely
asocial art. Would you really wish he'd finally found some refuge beyond
good and evil? Think of Mishima, endlessly contemplating the cold beauties of the craters of the moon. Even sunsets: do you recall that passage in
Spring Snow?"

"Oh, my God!" Dov exclaimed. "Another of Damrosch's little touchstones—I can see it coming!"

"I think it's kind of sweet David memorizes passages," Marsha said. "It's
so *literary.*"

"I happen to think it helps to keep as much poetry and prose in mind as
possible," I retorted. "But I shall spare you the actual Mishima quotation,"
I went on, putting a little asperity in my tone to cover a sinking feeling that
I really couldn't remember the passage after all. "The gist is that some of
Mishima's characters are viewing a gorgeous sunset, but then one of them
reflects that the beauty they are seeing has no meaning, no human content,
no vital connection to life at all. Mishima's sunset is anything but the guide
to life that Arnold wanted his touchstones to be. It's more like an invitation
to suicide, and to me it's a chilling reminder of the nihilism too easily en-
tailed in the worship of beauty for its own asocial sake. Is that what you're
advocating, Vic?"

"You're doubly wrong, David," Vic replied. "There wasn't an asocial
bone in Mishima's well-toned body, and my problem with his work isn't the
lack of a social meaning but quite the contrary. He makes a sweeping bid to
universalize an authoritarian social order, all the more perverse an enter-
prise as he knows perfectly well it's an illusion in the modern world, and yet
he won't forgive society for giving it up even so. Art, for Mishima, is a form
of masochism, a violent fiction to which he binds himself without even the
excuse of belief."

"You see all that in his sunset?" Marsha asked.

"All that and more, since he's playing on a thousand years' worth of symbolical clouds. You know I always see the ancient subtext when I look at anything modern, and Mishima's subtexts aren't far to seek in *Spring Snow*, beginning with his programmatic rewriting of *The Tale of Genji*. Recall, my friends, the old woodcuts reproduced in Seidensticker's *Genji* translation—you know it, don't you?—where clouds carry a double valence, both metaphysical and political. They suggest the transience of the floating world and also the divine elevation of the Emperor, the Son of Heaven, always shrouded from our view by radiant clouds. Mishima's suicidal nihilism has everything to do with the modern discovery that the Son of Heaven isn't behind those clouds after all. Not a necessary cause of grief, to me a cause for celebration even, but for Mishima the bitter paradox behind his insistence that we should set back up the pre-Meiji authoritarianism that the old metaphysics had justified, even though we now see that whole worldview for the fiction it was. Mishima resembles no one so much as the Baron de Charlus, in Proust—also echoed in *Spring Snow*—who knows that the boys he hires to whip him are innocent young things but who requires them to act the part of vicious thugs, hoping thereby to flog himself, so to say, into a belief in his own sordid play. Mishima's sunset has nothing to do with nature, everything to do with a twisted idea of culture that I reject."

"And so," Marsha asked, "what are sunsets to you?"

"They are nothing, literally nothing but a play of light on dust and vapor—and they are breathtaking. They are an emanation of beauty, somewhat as Suzanne Langer defined art, but on a different scale, in a different order of being: more ephemeral than art, also vaster, more securely permanent in their recurrence than any work of art will ever be: a summons, a reproach, a despair: a testimony to our own transience, a mockery of our will to impose meaning on ravishing beauty (is that one a duck? a *bunny*?), an affront to every idea of art as the pat little patterning of social data within the artist's soul: a revelation that art need not be egotism only but an escape from egotism, a dissolution that somehow we experience as freedom. What could be more liberating, what can be less neatly attached to some program of self-improvement or social change?"

Marsha shook her head, but didn't reply. The sun had set; it was growing chilly, and the elegant mosquitoes were now out in force. We all got up and went back into the museum, where dinner was now being served in an empty gallery.

I saw little of my friends in the remaining few days of the conference. I hoped we might have some further conversation once the sessions ended; perversely, perhaps, I was reluctant to give up on our discussions just when the deep fault lines between our views had come to light. As it turned out, though, Dov left immediately upon the conclusion of the conference, flying westward so as to stop off and see his sons in Israel en route back to California. Marsha and Vic stayed on in Japan but went off to Nara on their own, not thinking—or wishing?—to invite me along.

At loose ends, I joined up with a dozen conference-goers and went to Kyoto. Though they were congenial enough companions, they always seemed to want to rush from one important site to the next, just when I was ready to settle in for a while. Had I learned the spiritual lesson of the museum incarceration, or was I simply falling into a classic post-conference daze, the flip side of my companions' manic energy? Conversations among this group oscillated between guidebook recitations and well-worn academic shoptalk, and we were seeing so much that we were hardly seeing anything. Had we really come seven thousand miles to stand before a reclining Buddha and gossip about Harold Bloom? True, there was a certain similarity, but the quality of the gossip was hardly commensurate with the quality of the carving.

Breaking away from the group, I found myself almost alone at the Ryoanji temple at dusk. In the temple rock garden, miniature mountains of black stone rose from the carefully raked waves of white gravel lapping their shores. I had first heard of this rock garden early in my career, when I was an outside examiner for a dissertation defense in East Asian. Barely finished with my dissertation myself, I had shuddered inwardly at the two-hour grilling the candidate received from his own sponsor. The Ryoanji garden had provided one of the more memorable moments in this ordeal. "Now,

Mr. Konrad," the sponsor had inquired, pointing a slender finger at the page before him and shooting a penetrating glance at the hapless candidate; "you say on page three hundred that there are *several rocks* in the garden at Ryoanji. There are, of course, *fifteen rocks* at Ryoanji. Would you really call that *several?*" Sweat broke out on the candidate's upper lip; I don't recall his reply.

Seated in the twilit garden, I now saw that the mountain-rocks were arranged in three rhythmic clusters, of seven, five, and three rocks; clearly a significant ordering, a sort of visual haiku. The rocks were carefully placed so that some would always be hidden from any given vantage point on the wooden viewing balcony. Had Bashō written his tribute to Kyoto in this garden?

> At the cuckoo's cry—
> when in Kyoto
> I long for Kyoto.

Grateful though I was for this moment of reflective solitude, I found myself the next morning missing Vic and Marsha when I was struck by the enormous difference between the elegant golden shrine of Kinkakuji, made for aristocratic contemplation, and the messy, noisy, vibrantly populist Kiyomizudera, where at every turn one could ring a bell, decorate a statue, or buy an amulet guaranteeing good results on one's examinations. Marsha would have had interesting observations on the class issues, and Vic could have told us more than the guide books did about the temple architecture. He and Marsha might even have found common ground in discussing the two shrines' very different but equally creative modes of relating to their landscape settings.

I can't say that I missed Dov as such—or Dov *an sich*, as I thought of him—though I had a sudden wish for an argument about Middle Eastern politics when I bought a sports drink at a vending machine in downtown Kyoto. This was the summer just after the war against Saddam Hussein. The fighting in Kuwait had ended only weeks earlier, but at this vending machine I found a can of soda printed in a battle-fatigue pattern. Its name, given both in English and Japanese, was "Desert Storm: The Carbonated Beverage for Active People with Fighting Spirit." Not a drink to encounter on one's own.

Intimidating though my three Tokyo companions were, I wanted to see more of them. A full year went by, however, in which we only had sporadic contact by e-mail. Clearly, we would never get together again unless I made a deliberate effort. It occurred to me that the annual meeting of the American Comparative Literature Association would provide a good occasion, and so in the fall of 1992 I wrote to the others, proposing a panel for the next convention, to be held at Indiana University the following March. I was pleasantly surprised when they each accepted my invitation to join me in Bloomington. Our topic was to be "The Limits of Theory," and I hoped for a lively discussion. I was all too correct.

2 BLOOMINGTON

Traveling Theory Comes Home

The ideal conference setting provides for a variety of outdoor activities—walking, swimming, skiing, tennis, table tennis—suitable for various degrees of athletic enthusiasm. . . . If no relevant contrapuntal activities are provided for, various inappropriate and destructive things may happen, as a few members of the group think up pranks, engage in practical jokes, or emotions that could easily have been channeled into some cathartic and satisfying form . . . become diffuse and produce a sense of malaise and dysphoria.　　　　　　　Margaret Mead, "Conference Arrangements"

CYRIL (*coming in through the open window from the terrace*): My dear Vivian, don't coop yourself up all day in the library. It is a perfectly lovely afternoon. The air is exquisite. There is a mist upon the woods, like the purple bloom upon a plum. . . . You need not look at the landscape. You can lie on the grass and smoke and talk.
VIVIAN: But nature is so uncomfortable. Grass is hard and lumpy and damp, and full of dreadful black insects. . . . you had better go back to your wearisome uncomfortable Nature, and leave me to correct my proofs.
　　　　　　　　Oscar Wilde, *The Decay of Lying*

MY INTRODUCTION to Indiana was not auspicious. A long, dreary limousine ride from Indianapolis down to Bloomington, through long, dreary vistas of flat fields, empty crossroads, and more flat fields, still brown in mid-March after a cold winter; sitting wedged in among several auctioneers en route to their own convention: all overweight, great kidders all, retelling stories from past conventions that might possibly have been funny if you'd actually been there but had certainly gained nothing in the retelling. David Lodge, I felt sure, had never been to a conference like this. We'd had a few Lodge moments in Tokyo, no doubt, but a more typical conference scene was about to unfold in Bloomington. This is the truth those satirical novels repress, I reflected: the jet-setting theorist only rarely gets to explore unusual foods, strange ruins, unfamiliar bodies in some exotic locale in Israel or Italy. In real life, the locations are mostly far more ordinary, as are the interactions themselves, to say nothing of the food. What would it take to raise our discussions above the level of the cuisine?

I had done everything I could to see to it that my own panel, at any rate, would have some real coherence; I hoped that it would challenge the participants and the audience alike. I was nearing completion of my book on scholarship, and I'd come to feel that the alienation and aggression built into academic life are nowhere better reflected than in the sad parodies of collaborative work that conferences have become. Our own Tokyo panel had exemplified the problems of isolated production and indifferent reception so common in conference settings, and so I had determined to take some preliminary steps to promote interaction among the panelists this time around. The deep divisions among the four of us were clearly too great to be leapt over in a single bound, but I wanted at least to move in the direction of real collaboration. I had proposed that each of us should have a first draft completed a month in advance of the conference; I would send these drafts around for comments, and we could all revise our papers before the presentation. This proposal met with some success. Marsha and I actually did produce drafts on schedule; Dov at least sent me a letter outlining his argument. I circulated these materials, leaving out a postcard I'd received from the Seychelles, my only communication from Vic. The picture was pretty, and he did propose a subtitle for his talk, but the general effect seemed to detract from the seriousness of the collaborative process I was trying to inspire.

In all honesty, I must add that the results were rather more modest than I'd hoped, consisting mostly of several changes in phrasing that Marsha and I prompted in each other's respective accounts of Slavoj Žižek and Roland Barthes. Marsha sent Dov a long and thoughtful critique of his topic as outlined in his letter, to which he replied that she hadn't understood him and would see what he meant when she heard the full paper. Dov in turn wrote me only that he liked my paper, somewhat gratuitously adding that he didn't know—or care—enough about film theory to comment on Marsha's paper. I heard nothing at all from Vic in response to our drafts. As to his postcard, I was in something of a quandary concerning his new subtitle, for which I felt some responsibility. I had asked him if he could expand on his title ("The Afterlife of Mechthild von Magdeburg"), hoping that he'd reveal something about his subject, though I didn't admit in so many words that I'd never heard of her. As a result, Vic didn't get my hint, and the subtitle he submitted—"From the Platitudes of Piety to the Folly of the Feminists"—seemed likely to produce more heat than light. I never quite got around to sending in the subtitle to the conference organizers.

All in all, though, I'd done what I could in advance, and my spirits began to rise as we neared Bloomington. The bleak fields gave way to rolling, wooded hills, with the shrubbery showing the first signs of green, and I breathed easier once the auctioneers piled out of the car at a Marriott on the edge of town. I received a pleasant surprise when the limousine reached the campus: not the bland brick functionalism I'd somehow been expecting, but an imposing set of old stone structures, quasi-Gothic in style, set on a spacious campus crossed with winding paths and streams bordered with daffodils. Looking down a little later from the leaded glass window of my tower room in the campus hotel-and-conference complex, I concluded that we would certainly get more done here than amid the distractions of Tokyo, and we might even have an enjoyable stay as well.

I hadn't counted on the fact that my friends' lives were all, in varying degrees, falling apart. This began to become apparent at the opening reception that evening. The first thing I noticed when I came into the room was Marsha, talking with a mutual friend, Susan Suleiman; the first thing I heard, as I approached, was Susan exclaiming, "That's outrageous! How can they *do* that to you?" It emerged that Marsha had been turned down for tenure at Bennington; the trustees had overruled the unanimous recommendations in Marsha's favor by the literature department and the faculty personnel committee.

"I didn't have the heart to tell you when I sent you my paper," Marsha told me. "I just couldn't believe the trustees would turn down my appeal. I should have known better, though—they're in the president's pocket. All they did was offer me next year on paid leave, so I'd shut up and get out."

"But why'd this happen?" Susan asked.

"This new president comes in, Elizabeth Coleman, with all this talk about collegiality, using our financial problems as an inspiration to new thinking, we should all work together to restructure and return to our innovative roots. Turns out she meant corporate downsizing pure and simple, and 'working together' meant agreeing with her from start to finish. A bunch of us made the mistake of speaking up in the fall, and now she's firing just about all of us."

"Remember when sisterhood was power?" Susan asked. "And power would promote sisterhood?"

"That's what gets me," Marsha replied. "Coleman talks the talk, then she stabs you in the back. Sort of a cross between Mother Theresa and Pol Pot."

"So what are your plans now?" I asked.

"Everything's up in the air, and just when things were all coming together so well. My partner, Tom, has gotten his organic tool catalogue business off the ground, and Cassie's going into preschool in the fall. I was finally going to have a chance to finish my film book. Now I've got to spend all this time job hunting, and it's going to be tough with only a few articles out. Bennington just isn't a place where you get much time away from the students. And now our lack of 'productivity' is being shoved in our faces as the excuse for canning anybody with any independence of thought. *Productivity*, for Christ's sake!"

"I suppose Tom isn't wild about a move to some big city, either," I commented.

"That isn't the half of it," Marsha replied. "He's gotten into the Vermont climate in a big way, doing all this innovative stuff with cold frames on rails, he moves them across the field, different crops all winter long. Mass transit for veggies! He's the *real* organic intellectual in the family, and he just doesn't want to leave New England. I kind of enjoyed helping with the catalogue—"

"It's darling," Susan interrupted; "have you seen it? Those literary headings—'Mulch Ado about Nothing,' 'The Rake's Progress'. . . ."

"It was fun," Marsha went on, "but that's Tom's business, not mine. And the worst of it is, his name's *Coleman*. No relation, of course—at least, he'd better not be—but I'm going to be reminded of Miss Collegiality every time I have to fill in 'Cassandra Coleman-Doddvic' on some school permission slip."

"Where's Kafka when you need him?" Susan asked. "Speak of the devil," she added, waving to the Kafka scholar Stanley Corngold, who had just entered the room. He came over.

"Susan, how nice to see you," he said, giving her a kiss on each cheek. "And little Marsha!" he continued. "How *are* you, my dear? And who's your *friend*?" he asked, looking at me with an urbane smile. We had actually met twice before; was I not important enough to remember, or was Corngold merely suffering from a degenerative memory disease? I hoped the latter.

Marsha introduced me, adding, "but he isn't my 'friend' any more than you are, Stanley."

"But we're all friends here, I hope!" Corngold exclaimed genially. "Of course, all excepting that dreadful fellow Bathmat, I'm sorry to see he's here. Now I shall have to avoid him."

I had no idea who Corngold meant, until Susan corrected him.

"You mean Bathtöi, I suppose?"

"Yes, that's the fellow's name, isn't it," Corngold replied.

"You know, Stanley," Marsha said, "those of us with unusual names get pretty tired of jokey mispronunciations à la Letterman."

"But you mustn't take it *personally*, Marsha," Corngold replied. "It isn't boorish humor at all, it's pure Freudian slippage. You see, Bathtub and I go way back, too far back, and he wrote the most outrageous review of a book of mine a few years ago, all my friends called me up immediately to tell me about it. I had to write a novel about him to take my revenge. I called him 'Bahdaffi, the theory eraserhead,' and I felt better immediately. I'm perfectly serene around Bathysphere now. I just haven't forgiven my so-called 'friends' for telling me about the review in the first place."

What with Corngold's friends and Bennington's administration, I thought, maybe I should stop writing my book on scholarship. With colleagues like these, who needs collegiality? Turning these thoughts over in my mind, I realized what I needed for myself: a glass of wine. I went over to the bar, where I encountered Dov, deep in conversation with two young women. He greeted me—somewhat reluctantly, I thought. The women drifted over to what seemed to be a knot of fellow graduate students, and I asked Dov how he was.

"Shitty," he replied. "California is really getting to me. I took a two-year leave from Geneva to come to Irvine, and the second year is ending now. I have to tell Geneva if I will come back, and I don't know what to do. We in Europe have a kind of fantasy about California—what did Leo Spitzer call it, the Italy of America?—but the fantasy wears thin once you move in. Even the roads wear thin! I used to think the streets of California were paved with . . . pavement, but the cities are all short for cash. There are potholes everywhere. Crowds, pollution, fires, earthquakes, racial unrest, talk radio playing in the stores. . . . It is enough to make one long for the boredom of Geneva."

"So why don't you just go back?" I asked.

"My wife. She teaches at UCLA."

"I thought your wife and kids were in Israel," I commented.

"Other wife. Ex-wife, I should say. The big advantage of Geneva, it is not so far from Tel Aviv, though my boys there, they want me to stay in California so they can come for the summers. And Amy likes UCLA, she is pregnant also, so there we are."

"Congratulations!" I said.

"Sure, thanks," Dov replied, and turned to order another drink from the bar.

A funereal mood was settling over the reception as a whole. Perhaps this conference wasn't going to be the unrestrained orgy of intellectual exchange that I'd been hoping for. But things would probably brighten up once Vic arrived. Then I noticed him settling into a chair, rubbing his brow. Something must be wrong, I thought: he had actually come in quietly. I went over and greeted him.

"Forgive me if I stay seated, David," he said. "I have the most terrible headache, and I am simply exhausted. I can't seem to get used to it."

"To what?" I asked.

"I've been homeless for the past six months."

This sounded alarming, but further inquiry dampened my sympathies. It turned out that Vic was having his townhouse renovated and had quickly found that he couldn't take the dust. "So the Vineyard and Venice between them won't do?" I asked—a little regretting, even as I said it, the ironic edge I'd allowed in my tone. Vic didn't notice, however; he nodded wearily.

"The Vineyard is unspeakably dreary in March, you know, and the place I have there is astonishingly drafty. Promise me, David," he added, in the sorrowful tones of one who wished to communicate a hard-won wisdom: "promise me you will never build a summer cottage of steel and concrete, with walls of glass facing north, however fine the view!"

This was one of the easier promises I've had to make. "But Vic, there's always the apartment in Venice," I added, not quite believing I was having this conversation.

"Don't mention that disaster," he replied. "The city fathers dredged the canal last fall—not the city fathers in person, of course, but their brothers-in-law. A fine idea in theory, but they should have known better in fact: the brothers-in-law removed the protective layers of silt that were keeping everyone's foundations whole. The palazzo has been leaking all winter, and the wall along the canal is settling; the most amazing cracks have opened up everywhere. We can't get anyone to accept any responsibility, and I can't even get my apartment repaired. There's an endless waiting list for the good contractors—all the local families got to them first."

Vic looked so miserable that my initial Schadenfreude was short-lived, and I repressed a remark about deconstruction in action. It emerged, moreover, that an element of genuine distress underlay the façade of Vic's concern for his façades. When I asked where he was actually staying, he replied that he'd moved in with his mother, who had remained in the old family house after his father's death.

"I love my mother dearly," he said. "But I love her better when we're a few blocks apart. It's a little awkward, really. You see, I finally came out to her this winter, and I think it rather took her aback—it's clear from the way she's being so *noble* about it all, so deliberately unobservant about my comings and goings. I am starting to tiptoe in and out of the house, however mundane my purpose, as though I were indulging in a mad fling when I go out to read the newspaper over a cappuccino. Worst of all are the tactful silences. This kind of thing just wasn't talked about in mother's Belgian Catholic family, and all those avoidance mechanisms were only reinforced after she came to Boston in '46. They still work well enough for her now, I suppose, but her skin has taken on a translucent quality as she's aged: you can almost *see* the regret about grandchildren pass across her face on its way to being deep-sixed in her unconscious. If she *has* an unconscious," he added; then shook himself. "I shouldn't say that. You see, close quarters don't bring out the best in me. And I certainly shouldn't bore you with all this trivia. We should be talking about something of more general interest, like Proust's theory of metaphor. But probably all anyone here wants to do is gossip about Pierre Bourdieu's love life. If he *has* a love life."

I was still absorbing what I'd just learned. Vic had answered an inchoate question that I'd never formulated explicitly to myself; then too, I'd gotten a rather different impression in Japan. In any case, I still didn't know Vic very well, and he never seemed to want to talk directly about himself—or rather, he talked mostly about himself, but rarely on any truly personal level—so I was pleased that he would confide this much in me, and I didn't want him to regret having voiced such "trivia."

"Love lives aside," I said, "it can't be denied there's usually some deep link between one's scholarship and one's life. Given what you're telling me about your stay at your mother's, I expect there may be a real affinity between your talk and Dov's. He's calling it 'Traveling Theory Comes Home.'" Far from putting Vic at ease, however, my remark only irritated him.

"*Please*, David," he replied, "spare me the psychobiography! It is no concern of mine if Dov chooses to throw himself bodily into his topic, though I must say I fear a little for the safety of the poor topic. My own life is *ut*terly irrelevant to my talk—and life and talk alike are the better for it. So let's leave my private concerns out of it, shall we?"

Somewhat at a loss, I looked around. Never numerous, the crowd was now thinning out. I said something about looking forward to seeing Vic at our panel the next day, and left. I felt a fleeting desire to take a cab over to the Marriott and look up my auctioneer friends, all of whom had pressed their cards on me; by now, they'd be on their third round of drinks and their fifth round of war stories, doubtless having a better time than anyone at our reception. I resisted this impulse, and went for a walk in the gathering gloom. For this I'd left my wife back home to deal with our three small children at a hectic time of year? Not a total change, to be sure, if I were to compare my children to my fellow panelists, say in point of self-absorption; but at least my kids usually seemed genuinely glad to see me, which was more than I could say with any confidence here. What was I doing in this profession at all? Why hadn't I just taken the offer from the Foreign Service—I would still have been dealing with strange characters, but in more interesting places—or taken the fellowship for the trial year in divinity school? Maybe I shouldn't have tossed a coin to decide between seminary and graduate school after all; or I should have recognized that my willingness to treat chance as divine providence meant that I belonged in divinity school however the coin came up.

Whenever I start to slide into a deeply maudlin mood, I think of the Carter administration. True to form, my thoughts turned that way now, and I felt again the sense of futility I'd lived with in the late seventies: struggling with an intractable dissertation, renovating a cramped little house in a run-down neighborhood on Capitol Hill; trying to get the plaster dust off my suit as I went to my White House speech writing job, working for Carter's feckless health adviser; the relief when he had to resign after forging a prescription for Quaaludes for one of my coworkers; the depression when it sank in that the loss of the job left me no excuse but to finish the renovation and the dissertation.

Dissertation, job, book, tenure; a dozen years of teaching, grading papers, writing recommendations: all so I could come to Indiana, to be jostled by auctioneers, forgotten by Corngold, and rebuffed by Addams? And were my friends here doing any better, if "friends" wasn't too strong a term to use for any of them? I wandered into town for a solitary dinner, then returned to my solitary room, camping out unhappily amid a conference of unhappy campers.

THANKS to everyone's foul moods, however, our panel went surprisingly well. Our topic on "The Limits of Theory" had a naturally critical bent, and the speakers' edginess seemed to sharpen the focus and force of their analyses. Dov set the tone at the start by attacking our conference's location.

"It is appropriate," he began, "that I should take up the topic of homecoming here in the middle of America. I was even greeted at the airport in Indianapolis by a billboard welcoming me to 'The Gateway to America's Heartland.' Okay, this billboard wants to convey a reassuring truth—even I, a newcomer to this country, know that the concept of 'heartland' refers less to a location than to a history, a regional mythology, and a whole set of attending values the heartlanders pride themselves on. Yet an anxiety underlies this billboard's would-be banality. Even if we accept the metaphor of a country as a body, heart and all, how are we to overlook the desperate boosterism of the claim that it is Indianapolis, of all places, that should serve as its gateway? Chicago and Denver, they should shut down their airports, St. Louis should dismantle its triumphal arch? On the other hand, the billboard could mean just the opposite: maybe Chicago, Denver, St. Louis *are* the heartland, Indianapolis isn't, it isn't anything at all itself, just a gateway or a getaway, a point of transit or transition, a place you come home *through*, not *to*, as we did ourselves in coming to this conference." Dov paused for a sip of water.

"I do not mean to joke around here," he continued, "but to sensitize you to the instability of those always metaphorical terms 'Travel' and 'Home,' as I go to apply them, only a little more metaphorically, to our scholarly work. If our academic home is where the heartland is, we academics know what it should consist of, this heartland: the 'fields' we 'cultivate' in our scholarship and our teaching. For a generation now, the main alternative to staying at home in our academic field has been to take a ride on traveling theory, to use the term coined by Edward Said. As fields have multiplied and subdivided, it is theory that has promised to cross-fertilize, blowing where it will across the boundaries of our narrow plots of scholarly turf. By extension, it has been the theorist in person who has become the conference-hopping jet-setter par excellence. It was, of course, a theorist whose colleagues coined the saying, 'What is the difference between God and our colleague? God is everywhere; *she* is everywhere but *here.*'

"So theory travels abroad, but what will happen if it should one day reach a destination? This is my theme today: to suggest that it is time for theory to outgrow its transcendental homelessness—to paraphrase Lukács on the novel—and accept the responsibilities that come with a known address. As Gerald Graff argues in *Professing Literature*, scholars too gladly see themselves as some kind of exiles, maybe internal exiles from their own culture. To this we should add that theorists especially have often been actual emigrés. This is no coincidence: experiencing the clash of cultures, the differing dynamics of disparate literary traditions, they find themselves stimulated to theoretical reflection. Little wonder, then, that in their essays these emigré theorists have often personified theory itself as a fellow traveler, a figure of liberation from local confinement. Indeed, in one of his seminal articles on traveling theory, Edward Said seems almost to speak of himself when he concludes that 'the point of theory is to travel, always to move beyond its confinements, to emigrate, to remain in a sense in exile.'

"Now up to a point, all this travel is all to the good. It was the best thing to happen to me—and probably to my colleagues in Tel Aviv—when I got out of Israel, and my ticket out was not my biblical studies but semiotics. Yet we should not rest satisfied with an uncritical exaltation of theory as floating forever above time and space—a tendency often seen in the work of theorists less thoughtful than Said. All too easily, the image of the theorist as archetypal exile can degenerate. It gets romanticized, charged with a covert sentimentality disguised as world-weary rigor. The problem here is not so much the feeding of the scholar's vanity; vanity will always find ways to nourish itself, I think. The problem comes when the theorist uses his exilic theory as a diplomatic passport with which to avoid all scholarly Duties, all the mundane Customs to which more ordinary mortals must attend.

"This has always been a temptation; it is more and more a problem today. Erich Auerbach wrote his great book *Mimesis* in exile in Istanbul during the War, and in his epilogue he confesses with open relief that he lacked a good scholarly library. He goes so far as to say, and I quote, that 'it is quite possible that this book owes its existence to just this lack of a rich and specialized library. If it had been possible for me to acquaint myself with all the work that has been done on so many subjects, I might never have reached the point of writing.' Yet Auerbach's exile was an excuse not to read, not a compelling necessity: surely there were *some* scholarly books in Istanbul, but he avoided them. What is more, he only published the book after the war, when he could have gone back into a research library to verify and correct his observations. Yet he chose not to.

"Maybe Auerbach did not lose so much. His own ideas were original and profound, and the often narrowly positivistic scholarship of the thirties and forties would have had little to add to his topic. But is this still the case today? There has been an explosion of scholarship in recent decades. Few fields if any are uncharted territory now, and the heroic explorer-exile will lose more than he gains if his sole sustenance will be the freeze-dried theories he brings along in his knapsack."

My eye fell on the brown briefcase leaning quietly against the legs of Dov's chair. Squat, scuffed, overfilled, it had come to resemble Dov himself.

". . . to give you an example," Dov was saying, "from my own territory of semiotics. A few years ago, Tzvetan Todorov published *La Conquête de l'Amérique*, in which he proposed to account for the Spaniards' success by using the perspective of a cultural semiotics. According to Todorov, Cortés was a better master of signs than Montezuma, and so he outwitted the hapless natives and their gods. Todorov is not a specialist in New World cultures or even in Renaissance Spain, but he advances two qualifications for his task: his theoretical sophistication, and his personal sensitivity, as an exile, to issues of displacement and the clash of cultures. Near the end of his book, he displays the ideal of exile in its most ambitious form. He creates a little genealogy to link himself, through Said, back to Auerbach and even beyond, to medieval otherworldliness. Here is what he says: 'It is the exiled person today who best incarnates, though warping it from its original meaning, the ideal of Hugh of St. Victor, who formulated it this way in the twelfth century: "The man who finds his country sweet is only a raw beginner; the man for whom each country is as his own is already strong; but only the man for whom the whole world is as a foreign country is perfect." (I myself, a Bulgarian living in France, borrow this quotation from Edward Said, a Palestinian living in the United States, who himself found it in Erich Auerbach, a German exiled in Turkey.)'

"Todorov is entirely sincere in acknowledging his debts here. Yet I myself, an Israeli living in Switzerland and in California, am not impressed by this eloquent passage. Why not? Because in this book, Todorov reads the old sources about the conquest of America with only minimal reference to the scholarship of Mesoamericanists. Auerbach's exile did make it difficult, at least, to carry on his research, far from the excellent German research libraries: Todorov's exile, on the contrary, brought him from Sofia to Paris, with its great wealth of scholarly resources. In love with his own exile, however, Todorov shuns the library shelves where the works of mere specialists are to be found. He goes alone into the dark continent of the primary sources, and comes out with tendentious misreadings and oversimplifications that could readily have been avoided, as I have learned from correspondence with my fellow panelist Dr. Addams." Dov gestured toward Vic, then continued.

"A scholar of an older generation could maybe get away with this, to rove restlessly around the world of primary sources, a song in his heart and a theoretical skeleton key in his pocket to open the gate to every scholarly field. Lévi-Strauss, for example, actually boasts about his self-indulgence in *Tristes Tropiques*: 'I have a neolithic kind of intelligence,' he says. 'Like native bush fires, it sometimes sets unexplored areas alight; it may fertilize them and snatch a few crops from them, and then it moves on, leaving scorched earth in its wake.' The traveling theorist, I think, can no longer afford such primitive behavior. The scholarly economy is too highly developed, there *are* no 'unexplored areas' left to 'set alight'—a phrase whose ambiguity not everyone is able to appreciate as fully as was Lévi-Strauss. I do not mean that we must all bury ourselves in whatever local academic field we first begin to cultivate. I for one certainly have no plans to do so, any more than to settle back again in Israel. But like the contemporary anthropologist, we must recognize that when we carry our theories into some distant scholarly territory, that territory is already someone *else's* home. We have as much to learn from the specialists who cultivate the fields we visit as we have to bestow upon them in turn."

Dov sat down. I was intrigued by his argument, but even more by the news that he had actually been corresponding with Vic. Perhaps there was some chance after all that we could learn from each other, even though neither Dov nor Vic had bothered to clue me in on their exchange. Coming to the podium, I opened the floor for questions. Several slow seconds passed, the audience still in the grip of that ruminative or stupefied passivity that even good conference papers usually engender. I always feel personally responsible for these awkward silences, even when the paper is not my own—even when I am simply a member of the audience, in fact—and I found my palms turning clammy. Fortunately, Vic raised his hand beside me.

"While I admire the general tendency of Dov's remarks," he began, "I am concerned lest we minimize the necessary independence of the creative scholar. It would be a mistake to over-stress the pieties of professional courtesy to the local specialists; they may know more about the material, yet their thoughts also run in established paths—we could say, in the ruts their mental plows have dug over the years as they have cultivated those fields of theirs. I wonder whether Dov is not taking an extreme case, and then presenting it in an exaggerated fashion. I would not want you to think that Todorov was simply wrong, a brash interloper who should have kept quiet and listened to the experts. Quite the contrary: the fault lies more with the experts who dismiss his book in a footnote, blind to the fact that he offers a novel perspective from which they could learn." Vic looked over at me, as if to ask whether he could continue; I waved him on.

"You see, Todorov really was on to something: there truly was a semiotics of warfare, and the Aztecs did fail to control it. Not because Cortés mastered it, however, but because he was slashing his way through a delicate ecosystem and the complex civilization it supported. And Cortés cared not at all if his depredations wreaked havoc both with established customs and with the environment. By pure chance, for example, he attacked Tenochtitlán at harvest time. Moctezuma—to give his name more accurately than Todorov does—would never expect a serious attack in that season. The risk of starvation the next year would be too great, for the aggressors as much as for their victims. This was no canny calculation by a prescient Cortés; it was sheer luck, the product of blindness and ignorance. The specialists have this kind of information, and they are the ones who could make Todorov's argument really work. It is their own self-protective dedication to the values of their little in-group that has led them to turn their backs on a genuinely new way of looking at their own data."

"Perhaps you are expecting too much from human nature," Dov replied. "If Todorov ignores the Mesoamericanists, dismisses their lives' work in a few paragraphs, is it so surprising if they do not rush to accommodate him? Todorov is a guest in their house, so to say. If he comes in and shits in the hallway, should they give thanks for the gift of fertilizer for their kitchen garden?"

I spoke up now. "Surely we can move beyond the either/or choices the two of you seem to be assuming," I remarked. "Wouldn't an ongoing dialogue serve everyone better than endless fighting over specialized depth versus theoretical breadth?" Dov and Vic both shrugged. Was I hopelessly naive, promoting accommodationist views that could only produce bland and watered-down results? Or were Dov and Vic both so wedded to an aggressive and confrontational mode of work that no real dialogue would ever develop in any event? Rather than dwell on these questions, I turned back to the audience. Hymit Bathtöi's hand was now up, and I called on him.

"To Professor Midrash's penetrating observations," he said, "I would like to add that already Auerbach was exaggerating his exile in Istanbul—and poorly requiting my own institution's hospitality during the war, I may say. He was not trapped in some tent on the edge of a desert, after all. He had a chair at a major university, located in an ancient and cosmopolitan world city. More than that: his good friend Leo Spitzer had preceded him there by several years and had established programs of research and publication. Auerbach himself deigned to publish in our series on Romance philology. Would not his study of 'the representation of reality in Western literature' have gained a new dimension if he had taken a broader view of 'the West'? Ancient Israel and ancient Greece figure in his account, but not modern Greece or Palestine, still less the swiftly Westernizing land of Kemal Ataturk. How ironic it is that even as we sheltered him from the Nazis, Auerbach reinforced an ideal of European ethnic purity whose absurdity should have been visible every time he walked from his home to his office. Perhaps the idea of exile should be inverted: those who feel themselves at home are the ones most threatened by the repressed *unheimlich*, as Freud pointed out long ago. Conversely, the self-declared exile may always already be only too settled in a home away from home. Thank you."

Time was moving on, and so I took the opportunity to use Hymit's observation as a way into my own talk. I said that, in the spirit of his comment, I would present the converse of Dov's thesis: to argue that oppositional cultural theorists tend to be more closely rooted in their own cultures than they might care to admit. I organized my presentation around a case in point, Roland Barthes's savage attack in his book *Mythologies* on a traveling photo exhibition, "The Family of Man," an ambitious montage of hundreds of images of daily life around the world. In his introduction to the exhibition, Edward Steichen had described it as "a mirror of the universal elements and emotions in the everydayness of life," revealing "basic human consciousness rather than social consciousness." Viewing the exhibition when it came to Paris in 1955, Barthes would have none of this cozy universalism, which he saw as ratifying a repressive status quo. As he says in his essay, "this is the reign of gnomic truths, the meeting of all the ages of humanity at the most neutral point of their nature. . . . Everything here . . . aims to suppress the determining weight of History: we are held back at the surface of an identity, prevented precisely by sentimentality from penetrating into this ulterior zone of human behaviors where historical alienation introduces some 'differences' which we shall here quite simply call 'injustices.'"

I went on to say how persuasive I had always found Barthes's eloquent argument—until I chanced upon the published book version of *The Family of Man*. Barthes had responded to Steichen's treacly frame-tale, but he had missed the real drama of the exhibit, which devolved into an open advocacy of the social consciousness that Steichen had claimed to renounce. From the middle of the volume onward, page after page juxtaposes scenes in America with scenes in South Africa, Eastern Europe, and Asia, endorsing literacy, voting rights, and human rights generally. Far from accepting a repressive status quo in the name of universal values, the exhibit was actually doing the opposite: promoting an activist agenda of social change, aimed squarely against forces of political and economic oppression around the world.

Barthes may have had his fill at the start and walked out without even seeing these rooms in the exhibit; or he saw, but failed to comprehend their political point. Of course, the heartfelt liberalism of the exhibit's polemics would not have impressed him very positively either, if he had absorbed it, and he might well have written an essay condemning the bald attempt to export bourgeois American values under the guise of universalism; but this would at least have been a more accurate account of what the exhibit was really doing. Further, I argued, Barthes clearly had no interest in understanding the exhibit's strategy toward its primary and original audience: the isolationist American public of the early fifties. By insisting that "All People Are Created Equal"—a slogan that one photo showed painted on the side of a bus in Indonesia—the exhibit forcefully supported liberal efforts to channel billions of dollars into foreign aid, humanitarian assistance, and the funding of the United Nations. The Norman Rockwell framing of the exhibit was a calculated ploy, intended to tug the Americans' heartstrings strongly enough to pull their wallets right out of their pockets, and the exhibit probably had more real political effect than any sarcastic essay written by an openly activist cultural critic in the same years. Barthes, traveling theorist par excellence in Dov's terms, missed this; he failed to see what was before his eyes, because he failed to look across the Atlantic and consider the American cultural politics within and for which the exhibit had been created.

At this point I paused. Ordinarily, I would have felt satisfied to have done this much in a conference paper, and this was all I had brought to Bloomington. Ever since I'd finished my draft, though, I'd had a feeling that I hadn't really seen far enough into the topic, and knowing that I would be on stage with my high-powered friends, I'd had trouble sleeping the night before. Finally, around midnight, a passage from the final essay in *Mythologies* had come to me, and I realized that I could now conclude my argument. I sat bolt upright in bed, then in a fluid series of motions I switched on the light, dug my copy of *Mythologies* out of my briefcase, and took a pad and pen from the night table. As I wrote, the headboard behind me began to shake. At first I thought this was from my own energetic writing; I then heard muffled sounds coming through the wall, and realized that whoever was sharing the room next to mine was engaged in passionate activity of a rather different sort than mine. As my bed was one of those cost-cutting conference-hotel items designed with the headboard fastened to the wall rather than to the bed frame, the vibrations came directly through to my spine. Well, they might have each other, but I had an *idea*. I wrote for an hour, then switched off the light, settling contentedly back in my bed. As I did so, I realized with some surprise that I hadn't even noticed when the headboard had once again become motionless.

In the morning my jottings, while barely legible, still seemed to make sense, and so I was now able to present the fruits of my midnight inspiration. This involved reversing my own perspective on Barthes' limited perspective on *The Family of Man*. Barthes, after all, wasn't seeing the exhibit as an American in America, but as a Frenchman in Paris. The reason the exhibit's progressive political purposes failed to register with him was probably that the feel-good universalist frame was already being used to very different effect by the French government, which was trying to hold onto its colonial possessions in the name of "universal" values. Barthes brings forward this use of universalism in *Mythologies*' long concluding essay, "Myth Today." He begins the essay with the passage I had recalled at midnight. In this passage, he describes a visit to his barbershop, where he sees a copy of *Paris-Match*:

> On the cover, a young Negro in a French uniform is saluting, with his eyes uplifted . . . All this is the *meaning* of the picture. But, whether naively or not, I see very well what it signifies to me: that France is a great Empire, that all her sons, without any colour discrimination, faithfully serve under her flag, and that there is no better answer to the detractors of an alleged colonialism than the zeal shown by this Negro in serving his so-called oppressors.

Barthes, I concluded, was probably quite right after all to read the exhibit in the way he did, insofar as he was perceiving the impact the exhibit would likely have on an audience in France. His mistake was to present his reading as the whole truth and nothing but the truth, as though the exhibit had an essence, an inherent meaning that persisted unchanged as it moved from one cultural-political sphere into another and very different arena across the Atlantic. Thus Barthes himself universalized the exhibit's nature and meaning as much as the exhibit's own organizers were doing—an ironic result, in view of his ongoing efforts to deconstruct essentialist and universalizing approaches to cultural artifacts, and a warning to us all that the traveling theorist may find it harder to leave home than we might think.

I sat down; Dov actually nodded in my direction with something approaching approval, a new experience for me.

Vic now went to the lectern. As he began to speak, I realized that we hadn't stopped for questions after my paper. Would Vic's doubtless more dramatic performance put my talk out of mind by the time there was another break for questions? I was correct about this.

"I originally titled my paper 'The Afterlife of Mechthild von Magdeburg,'" Vic began. "More recently, I also proposed a subtitle, 'From the Platitudes of Piety to the Folly of the Feminists,' but this does not appear on the program. I shall prefer to blame the vagaries of the Pacific mail service rather than attribute any pusillanimity to our panel's organizer"— Vic cast a barely noticeable glance my way—"and yet my topic would be aptly illustrated if my title had indeed been censored in the interests of scholarly decorum. For my theme is the difficulty we all have in resisting our own will to power over our material, whether we are interpreting, editing, translating—or merely organizing a conference panel. It is all very well to say that every generation reinvents its past, in a creative interplay of old and new. What this means in practice, sad to say, is that each generation visits its own special pattern of abuse upon the defenseless texts in its possession. Ever new repressions and distortions are marshaled to avoid facing the radical otherness of the past." Vic paused, and came around the lectern with a handout.

"I have chosen to explore this problem," he said as he returned to the lectern, "with a writer you have probably never heard of. Mechthild von Magdeburg is one of the great mystical writers of the thirteenth century. A glorious writer, and a troubled soul! Yet her haunting prose-poetry has long been known only to specialists—and barely known even to most of them until recently, when feminist scholars began their intensive archival efforts in search of silenced voices. I myself would never have had the pleasure of encountering her work but for a brace of Belgian feminists, Emilie Zum Brunn and Georgette Epiney-Burgard. In 1988 they published an anthology called *Femmes troubadours de Dieu*. A properly poetic title for a lyrical scholarly endeavor of recovery and celebration—toned down, I regret to say, for the earnest American audience under the plodding title of *Women Mystics in Medieval Europe*. Let us grant the editors the passion of their project, and we are very much in their debt. Even so, dear friends, we should not congratulate ourselves too quickly on having overcome the repressive distortions of an earlier era. In fact, the process of distortion continues unabated today—and it does its dismal work more effectively than ever in the case of obscure figures like Mechthild. At least with a Shakespeare or a George Eliot, readers can assess a new interpretation in light of the knowledge they already possess of the author and the work. But few who read the bright new translations of Mechthild can have any idea how differently she is being dressed today for present consumption—and I use 'dressed' in the culinary sense." Vic gave a little laugh, more to himself than to the audience; he was always pleased to hit upon a bon mot in mid-flight.

"Mechthild provides a good case in point for other reasons as well," he continued. "She is a truly strange writer, and she offers stark challenges to the patriarchal order within which she had to make herself heard—and to the new feminist order that now wishes to ventriloquize its own concerns through her voice. The original of her book, moreover, is lost. All we have are later translations, beginning with early versions in Latin and in a German dialect called Allemanic, and more recently carrying on with translations into modern German, English and French. Thus we are denied the superficial assurance of returning to the original Middle Low German text that Mechthild herself wrote. *If* she wrote it at all; she may have dictated it to her confessor, a certain Brother Heinrich, who first edited and arranged her poems and visionary accounts—with what additions and alterations of his own, we can never know." Vic picked up his handout.

"I will spare you," he continued, "the tangled tale of the incestuous rivalry between the early Latin and Allemanic translations; my point about 'the limits of theory' can be made sufficiently if we just look at two modern translations: a pious 1953 English version by one Lucy Menzies, and then the vivid French rendering by Zum Brunn and Epiney-Burgard, translated into English within a year of its publication in 1988. Back in the dark days of the fifties, what did Menzies do? Programmatically, unabashedly, she assimilated Mechthild to the patriarchal tradition. She introduces Mechthild, for example, as an exemplar of 'the atmosphere of the Middle Ages'— 'the' Middle Ages being a unified historical space with a single atmosphere, you understand—and she presents Mechthild purely and simply as working in the the tradition of Bernard of Clairvaux and of early German mysticism, both 'pointing back to the Neo-Platonism of the fourth century.'

"So much for her editorial perspective; her translations make the same choices. Everywhere she can, she tones down Mechthild's opposition to the male hierarchy around her, and she systematically eviscerates Mechthild's stark sexual language. To take one instance, Mechthild has the Virgin Mary wrestle with God until he 'erupts' suddenly into her womb; this is too hot for Menzies to handle, and so this rousing passage becomes a chaste periphrasis:

> Love, thou didst wrestle long years
> With the Holy Trinity
> Till the overflow fell once for all
> In Mary's humble lap!

"When Christ brings Mechthild to the bed of love and asks her to undress, Menzies moves the bed out of the text altogether and replaces it with an ellipsis. Next, Christ's command to Mechthild to take her clothes off—*ir soent úch usziehen*—becomes 'Thy SELF must go!'"

Vic gave several more examples along similar lines, but I had trouble following the details, partly because of the fragments of archaic languages that kept cropping up, partly because of the difficulty I always have in concentrating on a speaker whenever I've just given a paper of my own. My attention returned when Vic read the riveting lines with which the new Belgian translators begin their selections from Mechthild:

> I have been warned about this book
> And this is what I have been told:
> That unless I had it buried
> It would become prey to fire!
> And so, as had been my wont since childhood,
> Being sad, I began to pray.
> I addressed myself to my Beloved
> And said to him: "Ah, Lord, behold me afflicted

For the sake of Your honor.
Will you leave me without consolation?
For it is You Who have led me here,
You Who ordered me to write this book."

"The stage is starkly set in these lines," Vic commented, "in terms drawn from courtly romance: Mechthild is surrounded by hostile men, enemies who want to burn her book. So she seeks succor from her lover, Christ himself. He comes through for her, a divinity in shining armor, carrying her book—the very book we're now reading—like a sword:

Then, without delay, God showed Himself to my saddened soul,
Carrying the book in His right hand.
He said: 'My Beloved, do not despair like that,
Nobody can burn the Truth.
He who wishes to take this book from My hand
Must be stronger than I am.'"

Vic read these lines in rousing tones, then went on: "Thus Christ warns the men that they can only get at Mechthild over his own—hah!—*risen* body. He proceeds to proclaim that Mechthild's feminine weakness is the true source of her strength, for she has not fallen into the sinful pride that grips the powerful men who would suppress her book. A stirring opening scene!"

Vic paused for effect, then went on, a finger raised in admonition.

"But this is not the opening to Mechthild's book. In anthologizing selections from her work, our Belgian friends begin with a passage fifty pages in; they then *double back* and give earlier scenes. Yet they still pass over the book's opening scene! This is a dramatic dialogue between the feminine Soul and Lady Love, in which it is Lady Love, and not any man, who has bereft the Soul of all earthly pleasure. Even before that scene, moreover, we have a long preface by the awestruck Brother Heinrich. He tells us that Christ appeared to him and ordered him to copy down Mechthild's sayings, urging everyone to read them nine times. How should we understand the good Brother's preface? Is the patriarchy already co-opting Mechthild's work, or is she playing her confessor like a lute in order to win an audience for her radical visions, enlisting Christ Himself as her publicist? I incline toward the latter view. Yet either way the book's multiple opening suggest a less confrontational—and more complex—politics of gender than our pious Belgians allow their readers to see."

As Vic went on, I felt a kick in my shin from Marsha next to me. I looked over; without making eye contact she angled toward me her note pad, on which she had written, "Pious, my ass! They're rocking the old boys' boat!"

"As with editing," Vic was saying, "so with translation. Like Menzies before them, the new translators consistently make choices that fit their own view of the world—whether we're talking more about the medieval or the modern world, I leave it to you to say. When Mechthild has the soul come to the heavenly court, she describes the soul as *wise und wol gezogen*. Menzies translated this in 1953 as 'discreet and modest'; the feminists now translate the very same words as 'wise and courtly.' In the same paragraph, the soul yearns for Christ, and 'desires his praise,' *gert unmesseklich sines lobes*, as the Allemanic text puts it. But who is the subject and who is the object in this phrase? By now, you should not be surprised to learn that each translator makes the choice that fits their pet Mechthild, or that keeps Mechthild their pet: in 1953, Mechthild's soul 'longs above everything to praise Him,' but by 1988, the soul is now 'intensely longing that *He* should praise *her*.'"

I took a pen and put a check mark on Marsha's pad, followed by three dots and a question mark, to ask whether she didn't think Vic was on to something. She tapped her index finger several times firmly on the pad, indicating that Vic had a point but needn't be so insufferable about it.

Vic then gave several more examples, then concluded:

"From the '53 translation, one would scarcely know that Mechthild was a woman; from the '88 translation, one would scarcely know she was a *Christian*. This is not much of an improvement, my friends, and I think we can do better. We must combat our narcissistic tendency to falsify our texts to suit our needs. Mechthild was no more a twentieth-century feminist than she was a fourth-century Platonist. We will do her more justice—and learn more from her—if we allow her the space of her irreducible difference from us."

Vic returned to his place on my left. I could hardly back up now for questions on my own talk, but at least I could deny Vic a question period of his own. I got up and introduced Marsha, who took the podium.

"It's easy to be smug in hindsight," she began. "Especially if it's a kind of short-sighted hindsight, talking about quite recent work that's gotten under your skin. Sure the Belgians are using Mechthild selectively, and probably further feminist work will deepen the picture in ways we'd all like to see. But they *are* on to real issues, things women really did face both then and now. I can't claim any detailed medieval knowledge, but I looked Mechthild up when I got word of Vic's topic. Even from the old Menzies translation that I got hold of, I see things a little less starkly than Vic does. I do accept the fact that Mechthild wasn't a twentieth-century feminist—and yet I also get the feeling she was a *thirteenth-century* feminist. So I don't have a problem with foregrounding the aspect of her work that's most significant for us today. I wouldn't call this 'falsifying' her writing at all, it's more a matter of highlighting what really is in the text that speaks to us now. What's more, I think things have improved since forty years ago, when even a woman translator couldn't see Mechthild's gender at all. So I can't go along with the easy cynicism of Vic's position that our distortions are as bad as ever."

"Not an easy cynicism," Vic whispered to me; "a *hard-won* cynicism."

". . . is at least partly right," Marsha was continuing. "Some of his points could be illustrated, in a modern context, in the creative liberties that feminists have been taking with older patriarchal theorists like Marx, Freud, and Lacan. This actually brings me to my topic today, 'The Hole Truth: Film Theory from P to Z,' P being Constance Penley, Z being Slavoj Žižek. Both of them dominant voices in Lacanian film criticism—starting twenty years ago, in Penley's case, and more recently with Žižek." Marsha put on her glasses and picked up a book she had brought to the lectern.

"The thing that concerns me," she went on, "is the status of European theory in the discourse of critics who want to talk about Hollywood film.

What are the limits of the foreign system, what are the ways you have to warp the theory in order to get at the realities? To me, the story of the past twenty years has a lot to do with a gradual move from a fairly literalistic use of the theory-model to a more constructivist stance. You could call this a move from a modernist kind of theorizing to a post-modernist one. Not that modernist and totalizing systematicity have lost all favor—you can still see an insistence on theoretical rigor in a number of people active today. Penley, for instance. She introduces her '88 collection *Feminism and Film Theory* by stressing the need to maintain an unyielding Lacanian line."

Marsha opened her book to a page tagged with a purple Post-it, ran her finger down to the lines she was looking for, and began reading: " 'To put it bluntly, none of these essays belongs to what could be called the "what if" school of feminist criticism: What if women had an Electra complex to complement the male's Oedipal complex? What if the crucial psychical relation were not to the phallus as a symbolic organ but to the real of the mother's body? What if there were no such thing as penis envy but, rather, "womb envy"? . . . These "what if's" are no more than the signs marking the well-worn dissident paths of reductive biologism, sociologism, or mysticism of the feminine; a kind of thinking, not solely confined to feminism, which sidesteps or dismisses years of reasoning and debate on the problematic status of these "alternatives." ' "

Marsha shook her head. "This passage makes my blood turn cold—for two reasons. First, because I think what I'm hearing here is the voice of the Patriarchy itself, rearing its blunt head where I least want to see it. Second, because this makes me recall how heavily I was invested in talking just this way, ten years ago, when I was working on my dissertation. 'The well-worn dissident paths'—isn't this the language Trotsky used to use when he was savaging the Formalists? Isn't Penley herself doing the very thing she mocks, sidestepping years of debate on the problematics of her *own* terms as well as of the terms she rejects? Her terms start to look like masculinity itself in patriarchal society—they get to be what's 'unmarked,' linguistically speaking, what's outside the debate, as if only the 'dissident' arguments *against* her normative views were somehow at issue.

"As I say, I pretty much started out keeping step with this kind of rhetoric, as you'd see it in the early work of Laura Mulvey, Penley herself, and some of the others who created such excitement around the new field of feminist film theory in the seventies. I wrote a Lacanian-feminist dissertation on the fetishistic gaze in Buster Keaton's films, and I'm not going to say there wasn't something there, even an absence there, a gap, the 'hole truth' that Lacan led us to look for—but gendered, like the burnt hole in the tablecloth that frames Buster's sweetheart's face in *The General*. But was the hole truth really the whole truth, even in a guy like Keaton, antagonistic to women though he was, and as hooked as he was into the Hollywood system he helped to build?"

Marsha set Penley down and opened a second book.

"This is what's refreshing," she continued, "in the work of Slavoj Žižek and his Slovenian sidekicks. He admits Lacan's work is a kind of sublime or ridiculous fiction, then he goes ahead and plays it for all it's worth. Here's Žižek in the introduction to his new collection *Everything You Always Wanted to Know about Lacan (But Were Afraid to Ask Hitchcock)*, just published by Verso: 'If, then, the pleasure of the modernist interpretation consists in the effect of recognition which "gentrifies" the disquieting uncanniness of its object ("Aha, now I see the point of this apparent mess!"), the aim of the postmodernist treatment is to estrange its very initial homeliness: "You think what you see is a simple melodrama even your senile granny would have no difficulties in following? Yet without taking into account . . . the difference between symptom and *sinthom*; the structure of the Borromean knot; the fact that Woman is one of the Names-of-the-Father, etc., etc., you've totally missed the point!"'

"The funny reversal in Žižek's title says it all," Marsha went on. "Now, studying Hitchcock is going to tell us everything we always wanted to know about *Lacan*. His theory is the real object of desire, not just a tool for revealing the sublime or sublimated Whole Truth about Hitchcock. In a way, the problem with Žižek and company is almost the reverse of Vic's theme: their Lacan seems all *too* grounded in his time and place. All too European, all too comfortably masculinist, even though the current recycler will usually make some gesture toward a feminist perspective. Probably we still need a healthy dose of Penley's insistence on truth. It does drive her and her friends at least to probe and revise Lacan's terms, even if they still insist on staying within the overall framework. At the same time, I want to hang on to Žižek's sense of play. It can help us move beyond the anxious worrying about whether the ideological apparatus of film itself is so totally masculine that women really don't have a chance to find themselves, as spectators or even as filmmakers. For a case in point, I'd like to offer one of my favorite recent films, *Virgin Machine*, by Monika Treut."

Marsha now passed out some handouts, showing several film stills.

"Interestingly enough," she said on returning to the lectern, "what brought this film to mind was Vic's heroine Mechthild. When I started reading her book, I nearly fell out of my chair when I came to the first scene, the dialogue Vic mentioned between Lady Love and Mechthild's own Soul. The Soul accuses Lady Love of robbing her of every delight, and Love replies by telling about the higher pleasures that await her in union with Christ. The reason this scene floored me is because Treut uses it, word for word, near the start of *Virgin Machine*. The film starts out in Germany, where the heroine is caught in an unhappy marriage. She's also been having an affair, off and on, with her half-brother. So she and this half-brother set up a little puppet theater and stage this very scene, with the heroine playing the Soul and the half-brother playing Lady Love. This brings the girl's unhappiness to a head. She makes a break and heads off to America— California, you'll be glad to hear, Dov—leaving husband and boyfriend-brother behind. There, she gradually comes to awareness of herself as a lesbian, and the film ends with a great performance in which she takes the stage in a women's bar, dressed as a man, moustache and all—looking now a lot like her brother—and does a triumphant strip-tease."

Marsha went on to discuss the film in some detail. She concluded: "My main point is that Lacanian theory was invaluable for me as I tried to under-stand Treut's film—invaluable, but also insufficient. Treut is playing the patriarchal norms of the Hollywood film as skillfully as Mechthild used to play the patriarchs of the medieval church. At the same time, she's moving beyond the Lacanian obsession with literal and metaphoric phalluses alike, and reinventing the gaze itself on her own terms."

Marsha's paper, with its effective links to Vic's preceding discussion, provoked a lively discussion. Marsha and Vic each received a spate of questions, which Marsha handled with her usual thoughtfulness and Vic with his customary aplomb. They even seemed energized by their disagreements, and each found opportunities to needle the other in a charged mode of affectionate polemic that both seemed to enjoy. The discussion spilled beyond the time allotted to our session, with many questions to both of them even if none to me; I finally had to usher everyone out, so that the next panel could begin.

As the session ended, Hymit Bathtöi came up and engaged Vic in an animated discussion; they left the room together, still talking. Dov turned to Marsha and me. "So what is to do in this Bloomington?" he asked.

"It's a beautiful day," I replied; "why don't we take a walk?"

"Sure thing!" Marsha replied. Dov shrugged. "I have been outdoors," he said.

"Last night?" I asked.

"No, it was ten years ago," Dov answered. "When I moved to Switzerland, my wife would not tolerate me any longer and she stayed in Israel. So when my boys were having their first visit, I thought I should find some Alps for them. It was sort of a disaster. Ben was only four years old, he couldn't walk too far uphill without being carried. His brother Ari was six, he did a little better, but all they really wanted was to go back to Konstanz and watch TV. Of course, they did not know German or French then, but that was okay, they could see all their favorite American cartoons anyway. But why am I telling you this?"

"I think the question had to do with taking a walk around campus," I replied. "It looks pretty nice."

"Besides," Marsha added, "if you come along, I can give you a hard time about your talk."

Dov smiled. "Now you are talking. Talking, walking, 'die reimt sich,' as Kleist's Amazon Penthesilea says about kissing and biting, just a phoneme apart in German: if they sound alike, they go well together. Nominalist humor!"

"I don't think everything's just words for Kleist," Marsha said. "I've taught that play in my 'Violent Femmes' course, and doesn't Penthesilea say it's true love that makes people confuse kissing and biting?"

"That is so," Dov replied. "'Wer recht von Herzen liebt, kann schon das eine für das andre greifen.' I allow that there is truth to the equation of kissing and biting. Especially in marriage. But I think the true nominalist always locates passion in language above all. Why do you think Penthesilea shoots Achilles in the throat, his organ of speech?"

"So you really think Achilles' throat is just his throat?" Marsha asked. "Isn't this a textbook case of a displacement upwards? Like Freud said, remember, when he got Dora to stop fingering that reticule of hers all the time, and she came down with the sore throat?"

Dov and Marsha began discussing castration as we strolled out into a beautiful spring afternoon. Only half-listening as we walked, I found myself thinking dreamily of Dora's reticule. Coming out of this revery—and feeling glad that my companions couldn't read my mind—I took advantage of a momentary lull in the theoretical discussion.

"It's surprising," I said, "to find such classic campus architecture here, after driving through all those miles of fields."

"It is okay, this campus," Dov remarked. "Mostly the big Midwestern state schools look more like the drab British red-brick universities, factories for the lower middle class. Here, they must have imitated Chicago's imitation of Oxford. I like to see the boldness with which the campus asserts its connection to European humanist tradition."

"That's just what's so irritating about it," Marsha returned. "It's all fake—like humanism itself! Who are they kidding? Really, Dov, you surprise me. Weren't you just going on about the need to relate old ideas to their new settings? Even granting that universities do partly exist to transmit older traditions, don't you think they could have come up with something a little more creative than this Masterpiece Theater stage set? It might be too much to expect them to hire Frank Lloyd Wright, but couldn't they have found a way at least to *gesture* toward the Great Plains? The landscape, the history?"

"But, Marsha," I remarked, "surely an artificial setting can have a real effect. Dov mentioned the University of Chicago. I have problems with Allan Bloom's ideas on education, but the best moment in *The Closing of the American Mind* is when he describes his arrival on campus, an immigrants' child encountering the grand cultural ambition of American higher education. He asks why he fell in love with learning, so instantly and irrevocably, when he started his freshman year at Chicago: 'It must have been the fake Gothic architecture,' he says. Even later in life, knowing it was fake, he still attested to its real power."

"If Allan Bloom is the best you can offer in defense of this style, I rest my case," Marsha replied acidly. "I'm glad at least to hear that you 'have problems' with Bloom, which is probably more than Dov would say."

Marsha seemed uncharacteristically testy. Would Dov take offense, or would he make allowance for the strain caused by her uncertain job situation? He did neither, but simply took up her challenge.

"I myself have little good to say of Bloom," Dov replied. "His idea of the classical tradition is so limited, and even his love affair with the architecture is absurd. He is just the sort of person I argue against when I reject the metaphor of 'roots.' You see, he bought into the empty fiction of rootedness that the Chicago system meant to instill through buildings and curriculum alike. Perversion of a noble ideal! Just as the secular humanists who built Chicago intended, Bloom accepted these new roots at the cost of tearing up his own. Look at his discussion of 'the Western tradition,' all Plato and no Hebrew Bible. Look at his university, 'a secular temple,' he calls it, not batting an eyelash at the contradiction in terms. What happened to his Judaism—his Jewish cultural heritage, let alone religion? He apostatizes from his own tradition and rents a new one, like the arriviste in Gilbert and Sullivan who buys the old manor house, chapel and all, and insists those are now his ancestors in the crypt, since he's bought and paid for them. This is not my goal!"

"I don't get it," Marsha said. "You were just admiring the architecture here, and now you're bashing the very same style up at Chicago."

"I like the setting better here," Dov replied. "Do not think that bricks and mortar convey some essential truth wherever they are: even concrete is partly abstract. We have to look at the entire semiotic system within which these architectural elements function. I admit the University of Chicago is a bête noire for me, because they really had a chance to create something innovative and they fell back on a prefabricated past. A bête accompli! I am a lover of tradition, and so I am outraged if it is domesticated, tamed, emasculated like our friend Achilles in your reading of Kleist. But how could it have been otherwise? The cultural gesture of a Rockefeller imbued with both the highest and the lowest aspirations of Protestant capitalism—aspirations only too fully shared by Robert Maynard Hutchins, who gave Chicago and the world his deracinated 'Great Ideas'—counterfeit cultural capital for the managerial class! They made their bête and now they lie about it, claiming *it* made *them*! If William Randolph Hearst had built a San Simeon University, the effect could not have been worse. Actually, it would have been better, at least he would have included a *zoo*. It would have been a more fitting embodiment of the ideals he and Rockefeller shared. Better a pet bête than a managerial menagerie!"

Dov's voice was raised, and his face was perspiring; his glasses were starting to steam up. Agreeing with him would only add fuel to the fire, so I decided to try the opposite tack.

"But isn't Bloomington just as bad?" I asked. "Isn't it even stranger, after all, to plunk down these Gothic buildings in a landscape of corn fields?"

"That is just what *is* better," Dov replied, more calmly. "In downtown Chicago, the danger is always that the fiction gets naturalized, taken literally: the campus ceases to be an alternate reality at all, it is just a fancier version of the banks and apartment houses lining Lake Michigan. But here is more like Las Vegas, a fantasy amid a cultural wasteland, in a setting that reveals the fantasy at every turn." He pointed to the football stadium that loomed in front of us. "Just look at this huge plaza de toros in the middle of the campus. The architects were not fooling anyone into thinking this campus is a medieval cloister, they did not even try. Willy nilly, they set up an irreducible tension of styles, eras, continents. I submit that the archetypal Chicago student is meant to come from his slum and be stripped of his identity, rebuilt, and installed as a cog in the managerial machinery, never to return home; the Bloomington students, I think, are supposed to return to their little hometown, get married, teach school and run the local bank. A true return to their roots, but enriched with a new perspective, an enlarged cultural awareness and an abiding love of the school teams. If I had to choose, I should rather teach here than at Chicago."

"I just don't see it that way," Marsha said. "You're trying to make Indiana University into some kind of Lacanian Imaginary, but I really can't buy it. I don't think it's a real Imaginary at all, it's more like an imaginary Imaginary, the worst kind of Deleuzian simulacrum."

My own secular temples were beginning to throb. Didn't these people ever relax? Could I contribute anything to this conversation? Fortunately, there was no need for this, as Dov and Marsha seemed to have forgotten my existence entirely.

"Fuck Deleuze," Dov was suggesting. "What does he know about the Great Plains? We need rather a Venturi to write a *Learning from las Vegas de Bloomington*."

"Oh, great," Marsha replied, with an impatient shake of her head. "Let's get a high-toned flak for corporate America to come to IU, so he can gush about how great it is to have a campus so big students have to *drive* just to get from one class to the next. And what are you expecting these kids to take home after graduation, when they drive back downstate to deposit themselves in that local bank? Some vague association between football and the *Iliad*? No doubt a committed teacher can do oppositional work even here, but only by working *against* the surroundings, not fitting comfortably into them. I don't see Indiana's all that different from Chicago in practice—and at least in Chicago there's the counter-story offered by the poor neighborhoods right around the campus. Here there's only fields, no real alternative to the official story at all, which is probably the same phallocratic Republican bullshit in both places anyway. Foucault would know what to make of a campus that's called Eye You, don't you think?"

"I think it does not strengthen your analysis if you see the same phallogocentrism under every George Bush," Dov replied. "This was the problem with first-generation deconstruction: Derrida, Lacan, Foucault were all so zealous to combat the enemy that they construed or constructed Panopticons everywhere. Phallocentrism-centrism! Philo-phallism! I think you yourself mean to get away from this, or that is how I understood your critique of Penley, but it seems to me you should read these institutional landscapes with more care. The stadium here is *shaped* like Foucault's favorite prison, but here you should sooner think of pentathlons than Panopticons. Chicago is a different matter, Michigan would be different again. We should attend always to significant variation between these differing systems."

"I worry about the result," Marsha replied. "Too much attention to teasing out exquisite variations and you can get lost in the pleasures of your own close reading. We're back to New Criticism, a New Criticism of institutions, debating the interior decorating when we should be tearing down the walls. Nietzsche was right: sometimes you have to philosophize with a hammer."

"I remember that Nietzsche said that," Dov replied. "Yet the same Nietzsche also said *Ich bin eine Nuance*, and I think he did his own deconstructive work better in his nuanced genealogies—his genealogies *of* nuance—than when he philosophized with the jackhammer of the *Wille zur Macht*."

Dov and Marsha began arguing about Leni Riefenstahl as we left the campus grounds and walked through downtown Bloomington. Ahead of us was a movie theater, which was playing the recently released *Pulp Fiction*.

"You speak of violence and film in the thirties, Marsha," Dov remarked. "But what of this Tarantino? His film brings to mind my question about your paper. All this colonization of Hitchcock by Žižek and his friends, this is fine with me, I think postmodern psychological theory was always a theory about modernist art to begin with. Hitchcock himself may not be so far in temperament from a Kafka or a Céline. But I wonder about today. Ideas that Lacan formulated in the fifties, based on his own experience in the thirties and the forties—I admire his polemics in the context of the time and the place in which he was advancing them, but must we drag him directly into the contemporary world?"

"Now you're echoing David's point about Barthes," Marsha replied. "As a local observation his argument was fine, but if you carry it to an extreme, you're left with nothing, just some antiquarian fussing over Barthes's or Lacan's place in the history of ideas. I really don't care that much about Parisian politics in the fifties. I love Lacan because I can use him here and now, even—or especially—when I apply his ideas to cultural material he wouldn't have given a shit about. I shouldn't even say 'apply': what I really like is setting up surprising juxtapositions and seeing where they lead. It's what my old Bennington hero Kenneth Burke called 'perspective through incongruity,' and it's a whole different ball game from the kind of appropriation David was talking about."

I was getting the uncomfortable feeling that Dov and Marsha were discussing my paper as though I myself had receded into the distant past. I decided to speak up before I disappeared altogether. "I know what you mean, Dov," I said; "I can already see the dissertation chapters being written about 'the mirror stage in Tarantino's middle period.' But can't we find some common ground in between the bandwagonism you're objecting to and the quietism that Marsha rejects in a purely historical approach to French theory?"

"Perhaps we can," Dov said, "but what do we gain if we do? Will one of those dissertations tell us one new thing about popular culture, or politics, or the American psyche? Hitchcock himself already confessed his love of building films around a meaningless object, his McGuffin, so now Žižek pats Hitchcock on the head and reveals that the McGuffin is 'really' Lacan's *objet petit a.* So what? Suppose it was, fifty years ago; who needs a McGuffin now in the age of the McMuffin? Let us grant that Tarantino is an artist for our times; why should we need to peer at him through lenses ground out by Lacan?"

"I'm not sure we really disagree," Marsha said. "I'm not interested in Lacan as an Authority, but he should be more than a museum piece. Myself, I'm not about to do one of those numbers on Lacan and Tarantino, because I don't see that either of them really puts much pressure on the other. Lacan and a lesbian experimentalist like Monika Treut, now, Lacan and the porno-theorist Annie Sprinkle—*that's* the sort of encounter I like. Žižek is half right: we need to see the game we play by bringing Lacan into a foreign cultural situation. I just think we have to go all the way and put Lacan fully into play with everything that resists his work."

"I suppose your on-line Fanzine would be an example of this," I commented.

"Oh, you've seen it?" Marsha asked, pleased. "Avital Ronell and I started it on a lark, we really didn't expect it to get many hits at all. But here we are on our eighth 'issue,' if I can use that term for such a fluid format."

"A Fanzine devoted to Lacanian theory?" Dov asked.

"Not Lacanian theory: Lacan himself. Or Lacanian theory *through* Lacan's own body. The 'Zine's called *Jacquesbaby*, you reach it on the Web at www.jacquesbaby.com."

"It's pretty funny," I said. "And I like the collaborative interaction in the chat forum, 'Dial-a-critic.' But I can't help wondering: can you really do serious work on Lacan in 'Zine format? I mean, those 'Jacques on Jacques' S-and-M fantasy scenarios are frankly so weird, I just can't see how they advance our understanding of Lacan *or* Derrida."

"I don't know if I'd try writing something like that myself," Marsha replied. "I can't speak about the intentions of the author of that series, whoever she really is; 'Orchid V. Saddam' has to be a pseudonym, probably for somebody who hasn't gotten tenure yet. Still, I think you could make a case for a real critique developing in that episode where Lacan's feeding francs into a telescope on the Eiffel Tower observation deck, spying down on Derrida having rough sex with a student in an alley behind Paris IV."

"It sounds a little derivative to me," Dov said. "My wife Amy brought home a magazine of this kind not long ago that her students were reading at UCLA. The entire issue had to do with imaginary sex scenes between Captain Kirk and Mr. Spock from the *Star Trek*."

"That's the point," Marsha replied. "Orchid's scenarios parody those stories, or they don't so much parody them as appropriate them. There's actually a sequel to the Eiffel Tower episode where the Jacques twins are called in as consultants for a TV movie that's being made about their careers. Starring Leonard Nimoy as Lacan and William Shatner as Derrida."

"I can see the resemblance," I remarked. "But what's the point, really?"

"The point is to have *fun*!" Marsha replied. Doesn't it strike you as weird that so many Lacanians have no sense of humor whatever? How'd they get hooked on Lacan to begin with, for Christ's sake? Lacan's the first great performance artist, he spent his entire career sending up his audiences, his settings, his career itself—and most people never got the joke! It's a shame, because Lacan's jokes were always serious, but they really only work if you keep the tension alive between their seriousness and their jokiness. Most of his disciples just suck up the seriousness, going around with the sticky fingers and the *longs visages* Lacan never tired of mocking among the orthodox psychoanalysts he was deconstructing."

"Probably the point goes farther than fun," Dov added. "What your Orchid is doing, if she does it well, should be to overlay Paris and Hollywood in an uncanny way, shake up our response to both. This could carry on Lacan's work more effectively than yet another scholastic disquisition refining his conceptual system. I must log on to this magazine of yours."

Marsha smiled. "Since you're being so nice, Dov," she said, "maybe I should lighten up a little about the campus here. I guess I'm just upset about not knowing if I'll have *any* academic home of my own come next year. And maybe I'm also replaying my ambivalence about my Midwestern background. Chicago's sort of a sore point—my parents were both raised there, poor, and no way were they going to make it to the University. Growing up in Flint, I was heading straight into union organizing like my dad. He finally persuaded me to go to college, but I was damned if I was going to take his advice and go to Chicago or even Ann Arbor. I convinced myself I'd be making some progressive statement by picking a less tony place like Minnesota. Then I got there, only to find Minnesota was doing its best to become the next Berkeley. On the other hand, at least that meant they were hiring the Ivy League types who introduced me to Lacan."

We were back at the campus. My headache had gotten worse, and I decided to go back to my room to catch up on the sleep I'd missed the night before. Marsha waved cheerily as I left; the walk and the talk had clearly done her good. Dov was in the midst of developing an insight about Hegel, and though he didn't say goodbye in so many words, a slight modulation in his tone accompanied Marsha's gesture toward me. Better than nothing, I supposed; then I caught myself thinking this, and wondered why I was so concerned to impress them. It wasn't as though I was longing to top their Hegel analysis with a Heidegger gambit, not that I could in any event. But I couldn't fool myself that my incapacity gave me any real moral superiority, as neither Dov nor Marsha showed any wish to play games of academic one-upmanship. They weren't even performing for the pure pleasure of the performance, as Vic would do. No, it was worse: they really *lived* "the life of the mind"—a cliché for most of us most of the time, at best an intermittent experience, hard to anticipate, impossible to sustain: those charged moments that sometimes occur in a seminar discussion, or in a conversation with friends dissecting a movie over drinks afterward; those moments when knowledge, life experience, and personal interaction suddenly, electrically, mesh.

As I was getting to know Dov better, I only found him more intimidating, but at least he was manifestly unhappy—a comforting realization, as it suggested that his intellectual attainments came at a cost not only to his wives but even to himself. Marsha, both happier and just *nicer* than Dov, posed a greater challenge. Somehow, everything seemed profoundly integrated for her: the organic life companion and elfin daughter, the interwoven feminist theory and substantive knowledge of film—an art form with a real connection to the contemporary culture she wished to influence. Probably I was romanticizing her holistic approach to her life and work, betraying my superficial liberalism by falling back on the stereotype of woman-as-organic-intellectual; but even if Marsha's life wasn't as holistic as it appeared, my own was certainly *half*-istic by comparison, split between impulses toward rootedness and restlessness: on one hand, twenty years of one marriage, an entire career at a single institution, but on the other hand, always another language to study and not quite learn, another discipline to try and assimilate, another shelf's worth of books to buy and mean to read one day.

Back at the conference center, I took the elevator up to my floor. Probably I was just projecting my own ambivalences onto both Marsha and Dov, exaggerating in both directions, failing to see the real conflicts in Marsha's life and the continuities in Dov's. Who was I to feel so downcast by these comparisons? Marsha, losing her job; Dov, torn between two jobs, three continents, any number of lives: it wasn't so bad, after all, to have a single secure job, a happy family, an office full of new books to read and old favorites all jumbled together. And wasn't I reacting perversely to the very success of our panel that day? We'd succeeded in reversing the conditions that had been so annoying in Tokyo: instead of isolated presentations to an indifferent audience, here we'd given coordinated talks to a good audience, with pertinent questions at the session and now an animated and substantive conversation during our walk. Was I just upset because I couldn't quite keep up? At least I'd engineered our reunion in the first place, and organized it to achieve the good effects it was having; was my vanity merely wounded because the others didn't seem appreciative of my efforts or bowled over by my talk? But then, they didn't waste time complimenting each other, either; they simply took it for granted that we were meeting on common ground, and high ground at that, then went on from there. Why couldn't I do likewise? If I'd had a less lonely childhood, would I have outgrown this need for constant approval? Then again, if I'd been more sociable at an early age, would I ever have developed the intensive reading habits that have been the foundation for my whole career, such as it is?

I am perfectly capable of going round in circles of this sort for hours at a time.

Fortunately, as I walked down the corridor to my room, fate intervened, towel in hand, in the form of Stuart McDougal. Professor of literature and film at the University of Michigan and president of our association that year, McDougal was coming out of his room as I passed by.

"David!" he exclaimed, beaming down at me. "Have you seen *Breaking Away*?"

"No," I replied; "is it playing?"

"I don't mean we should see the film; I want to see the reality. It was shot around Bloomington, you know. Remember those scenes where they go swimming in the quarries? I want to go swimming in the Empire State Building—they dug the limestone for it around here someplace. I'm meeting Emily Apter and Hymit Bathtöi in the lobby. Want to come along?"

This was an offer I couldn't resist. I'd met Emily when she gave an impressive talk at Columbia a few years before, seamlessly melding Freudian theories of fetishism, the image of the prostitute in Baudelaire, and an attack on the Reagan administration, and I looked forward to getting to know her better. While Hymit and I had never gotten along when we were in graduate school together, I'd been impressed by his cogent comments at the session earlier in the day. Looking back on the hothouse environment of comparative literature at Yale in the seventies, I reflected that it probably hadn't been easy being the only genuine young Turk in a program crowded with would-be young Turks.

I got my bathing suit and came down to the lobby. Hymit had brought Vic along as well; they had gone out for coffee while I was walking with Marsha and Dov. These latter came up just as we were piling into Stuart's beat-up Volvo. Stuart and Emily greeted Marsha warmly, having known her from film and fetishism circles, respectively.

"Grab your suits and join us!" Stuart urged.

"Are we not too many for your car?" Dov asked.

"Never fear!" Vic said. "I have rented a powerful roadster, as my childhood heroine Nancy Drew would say. Hymit and I can follow the rest of you."

We headed off. As we drove, I remarked that we'd forgotten to stop for Dov and Marsha to get their bathing suits.

"It is no matter for me," Dov said; "I shall prefer to sit and smoke."

"Bathing suits?" Marsha asked. "I teach at Bennington, remember? At least, I've *been* teaching there. . . . Anyway, old habits die hard. We usually wear clothes to class, but that's about it."

Stuart had gotten directions from a friend on campus. We drove first on back roads and then down a rutted dirt lane that ended at a clearing strewn with beer cans. We got out and walked through the woods, no quarry in sight, until suddenly we found ourselves, at the crest of a low rise, looking down thirty feet to the surface of a large pond, its walls rising sheer on three sides, with a grassy incline on the fourth side off to our left. Looking at the dark, still water below my feet, I felt a sense of vertigo, as though I were really gazing into the negative image of the Empire State Building, a water-filled shaft plummeting a hundred and ten stories straight down into the earth, our silhouetted heads floating far beneath us.

We clambered around to the grassy slope. In the end, most of us dispensed with the bathing suits, but our swim was extremely brief. Though the air was warm for an Indiana March, the water was still unbelievably cold, and I had only a few minutes to admire Vic's well-toned muscles and winter tan, which gave a very different effect from Marsha's slender form, her pale skin set off by her long, reddish-brown hair and the bright green of her nails. I noted as well that Stuart's angular body gave the impression that he was still wearing a bow tie even when naked.

He and Hymit were the only ones who seemed untroubled by the temperature, and they were still out doing laps when the rest of us were back on the grass, shivering and drying off our hair. Dov was smoking his pipe; he looked like he was thinking about Husserl. I decided to try and inaugurate a more relaxing conversation before he'd be moved to speak.

"I was interested in your middle name, Vic," I said, "when I saw it on the résumé you sent me with your paper topic. What kind of name is *d'Ohr*, anyway?"

"A hybrid," Vic replied, "a francophonic version of a Germanic original. You know that my mother is Belgian. Her own mother's family were von Ohrs, from Luxembourg. They altered the name after they moved to Belgium, so as not to appear overly Germanic during the First World War. They were a cadet branch of the great von Ohr family, hereditary lords of the eponymous village and its environs. If you don't know Ohr, it's just north of Esch, near the German border."

"I did not think any town in Luxembourg is exactly *far* from the border," Dov remarked.

"Come on, Dov," Emily said. "I'd think an Israeli like you would stay away from small-country jokes."

"I cover myself with ashes!" Dov exclaimed. "I bow before this new entry in the victim sweepstakes—*tiny countries*! God forbid we should admit that Luxembourg is barely a beauty spot on the cheek of Belgium, herself a poor step-sister to the great culture of France!"

"But Dov," I interjected, "surely you wouldn't speak so slightingly of your own native country, with its immense cultural and historical importance."

"And so why do you think I *left*?" Dov replied. "A tiny country that has persuaded itself, and tries to persuade the world, that it is the center of the universe! This chauvinism I can do without, and I am a little disappointed to hear Vic boast of his magnificent Luxembourgian family connections."

"You seem to have missed the irony with which I inflect the greatness of my lineage," Vic replied with a smile. "Yet my grandmother spoke of her family's long history without irony, and she made a point of passing her pride on to my mother. Call it identity politics if you like, but this pride helped my mother a good deal as she struggled to keep her bearings amid the disorientations of the War and her later move to Boston. Even today, when mother wishes to insist on keeping up some custom from the old country—attending Mass in mid-week, say, or cooking with glutinous syrups—she defends herself with the Luxembourgian national motto, *Mir Wellen Bleiwen Mat Mir Sin*: 'We Want to Stay As We Are.' It is no discredit to mother's faith in the power of this saying that most of the customs in question are Belgian in actual fact, and I have often drawn solace from the motto myself. Especially the 'sin' part."

Marsha looked up from drying her toes to come to Vic's defense. "I don't get it, Dov," she said. "Weren't you just doing this whole number with David and me about the importance of tradition and how Allan Bloom shouldn't have given it up?"

"You must keep in mind," Dov replied, "that I despise all essentialism. Family pride, national pride, they both suppose some organic continuity across time. This I reject. You must work with the tradition your culture gives you, but you must brew *your own* tradition from these not-so-raw materials—weighing, measuring, recombining the ingredients that have been handed down to you. You can and should take pride in the result, if you do it well. Yet too often, national pride, family pride, they serve as an excuse not to do this work to begin with."

"I wonder," I remarked. "What you're proposing sounds so much like scholarly research. Don't you run the risk of replacing nationalism with some kind of academicism? I've noticed that you always have your doctoral degree listed on conference programs, almost as though it's part of your name. Isn't this taking the pride of study a little too far?"

"I do not wear the D.C.A. as a badge of honor,' Dov answered. "It is more like a war wound. Or perhaps it is the badge that itself wounds the wearer."

"I can see why you were drawn to deconstruction," Emily commented. "But who even knows what your degree is? We don't have a 'D.C.A.' in this country; what's it stand for?"

"Doctorate in Critical Alterity," Dov replied. "Tel Aviv's pride and joy. The most rigorous theoretical program in the Levant, maybe in the world."

"What makes it so special, pray tell?" Vic asked.

"It no longer exists, actually—it self-destructed a few years ago. This was probably inevitable in a program that had the goal to carry to a new level the progressive alienation inherent in graduate school life, but too rarely embodied systematically and made intellectually valuable instead of merely emotionally destructive."

"So how did it work?"

"I will give as an example the way a student would complete the degree. We did not defend our dissertations in Critical Alterity: we attacked them. There would be a two-hour meeting with the sponsors in which the candidate himself—not too many women entered this program, for some reason—the candidate himself, I say, would begin by exposing every major weakness in his own argument, his methods, his evidence, placing particular stress on problems he could lay directly at his sponsors' feet. The sponsors would then defend *themselves*, first by counter-attacking the candidate's own intelligence and competence, then by shifting the blame onto their own teachers in turn. The most successful sessions would usually end with both parties agreeing to blame either the Likud or the Labor party, whichever was in power at the time."

"The whole thing sounds pretty harrowing," I remarked. "Still, I suppose the survivors came out with an exceptionally acute critical intelligence."

"Actually, only those who failed really benefited from the program," Dov replied. "This is why it has been closed down: it is hard to support a program solely by pointing to your drop-outs. Several of them went on to important positions in politics, investigative journalism, military intelligence. The few who actually got through the program were mostly good for nothing, except maybe for two or three of us, all of whom left the country as soon as we could. Still, I do not regret the experience. I can even say that my reaction *against* the program has been the basis of my later work."

I couldn't help feeling that Dov was exaggerating the distinctiveness of his program—it sounded a good deal like my own years at Yale—but at least the conversational ice had been broken. People began trading war stories of their own graduate years, emphasizing the indifference and egomania of their dissertation sponsors, always a delightful topic unless one is overhearing one's own students. Stuart and Hymit had come out of the water and dried off while Dov was talking, and Stuart joined in the conversation. A towel around his waist, Hymit took out a miniature silver comb and mirror and began combing his handlebar moustache with care.

The sun was nearing the treetops, and the tenuous warmth of the early spring day was fading rapidly. We left. The conversation as we drove back was relaxed and lively at the same time, and the good feeling persisted when we all went out for dinner at an Italian restaurant in downtown Bloomington. Vic commandeered the extensive wine list, refusing either to moderate the flow or to let us pay. As we ate and drank, Dov talked at length with Emily, asking her advice about long-distance commuting, as he was contemplating making a permanent dual arrangement with Irvine and Geneva. Emily had taught for a number of years at Williams while her husband was teaching at Princeton; they had recently moved together to UCLA, and Dov was sounding Emily out on how she thought his wife (and her new colleague) Amy might react to the arrangement. Emily gave an upbeat assessment of the viability of commuting and of Amy's ability to handle it.

I only heard snatches of a conversation between Marsha and Stuart, an extended technical discussion about the process of multiple exposures that enabled Buster Keaton to play all the parts in his short film *The Playhouse*. This ended when Vic and Hymit drew them into their own conversation; they were plotting the establishment of a new interest group within the American Comparative Literature Association, the ACLA/AAC or Aquatic Activities Caucus. They seemed to be quite serious about this, and Hymit waxed eloquent about "the mutual reinforcement of mentation and natation." By acclamation, Stuart was elected Beach Chair of the caucus. I was given the title of Navigator, duties to be determined by watching the Keaton film of that name, and Vic was put in charge of our floating membership. He accepted this responsibility with a fifteen-minute oration in which, not even seeming to pause for breath, he wove together references to gymnosophist philosophy, Aztec water gardens, floating signifiers, Herman Melville, swim-up palapa bars, the bodily-fluid photographs of Andres Serrano, and the relative merits of conference facilities in Bermuda and Guadeloupe.

As I finished my third or fourth glass of wine, I tried to remember why I'd felt discouraged earlier in the day. The panel really had gone well, and I surveyed my fellow panelists with genuine affection. Pig-headed, yes; full of themselves, mostly, but perhaps deservedly; fundamentally at odds on almost every question, to be sure, yet capable of genuine interaction; they even seemed to be modifying some of their views in the process. If a group as disparate as this could get along so well, there might be hope for the profession after all. I felt a sense of optimism and anticipation; we had laid a foundation on which we could surely build. If my own role would primarily be that of facilitator, it wasn't after all an insignificant accomplishment to bring together a group like this and foster productive discussions among them. As we gathered ourselves up and wove our way out to the street, I began casting about in my mind for good locales, good topics. Perhaps it was time to confront our differences head-on. A panel on the politics of cultural studies? I had no idea what a mistake I was making.

3 CHICAGO

The Politics of Cultural Studies

The MLA Annual Convention will be held in Chicago—a vibrant, world-class city located in the center of the United States on the shore of Lake Michigan. Chicago boasts nearly fifty museums—such as the Art Institute of Chicago. . . . Well-known shopping districts, each with a distinct style, feature famous department stores and specialty boutiques. . . . There will be 247 division meetings, 44 discussion group meetings, 267 special sessions, 214 allied and affiliate organization meetings, and dozens of social events. *Join your friends and colleagues at the MLA Annual Convention—and enjoy Chicago!*   Modern Language Association mailing

Q. But if academics cherish their isolation as much as you say, how could you hope ever to change things?
A. Academics are often tremendously ambivalent about "the pleasures of isolation" that they cultivate. Why else have academic conferences and symposia become so pervasive if it isn't that they answer to a longing for community that isn't being satisfied by their home campuses? You can sense this longing in the hyperexcited atmosphere at such events. . . .
    Equally pathetic is the abyss of local silence and indifference into which we academics send our publications. . . . when you go to a conference, your publication becomes a reference point, but to make it a reference point on your home campus would be like making one out of your sex life, or your religion.   Gerald Graff, "Self-Interview"

THERE WERE only three problems with my idea for our next panel, I later told myself: the timing, the topic, and the temperaments involved. Given the good feeling at the end of our meeting in Bloomington, I probably could have gotten somewhere with the topic and the temperaments if only we'd been able to reconvene fairly soon. With the lead-time for most conference proposals at six months or more, I was pressing my luck under the best of circumstances. As it turned out, the increasing instability of my friends' lives made it impossible to get together again even within two years, as Marsha struggled with temporary appointments, Dov began his trans-Atlantic commute, and Vic pursued an endlessly time-consuming new interest in competitive catamaraning, an avocation—almost a vocation—that always seemed to be taking him to Tortola or the Azores at just the wrong time.

Struggling over scheduling, I failed to consider the deeper problem of the potentially explosive mix of personalities, even though I might have known that a topic on the politics of cultural studies would bring out the sharpest differences among our group. We would be discussing work in an area, moreover, in which invective is more the norm than the exception. I somehow thought we would all offer trenchant commentaries on other people's polemics while remaining uninfected by the polemical spirit ourselves. At the very least, I assumed—in retrospect, naively—that we would treat one another with basic civility.

I should have taken the hint from fate when, having finally secured everyone's participation in a special session for the 1995 MLA, I submitted the proposal only to have it turned down. Doggedly refusing to leave well enough alone, I tried to persuade each of my friends that they should not take the rejection personally, though Dov's first reaction was that the cultural studies cabal would never allow someone like him to speak if they could help it, Marsha feared that a credentialist and textualist bias had weighed against someone with a temporary appointment and a slender publication record, and Vic spoke dismissively of the eunuchs in the harem of language who could never abide beautiful prose. I countered each reaction with my own enthusiasm for their abstracts, and tried to suggest that my own overall proposal must somehow have fallen short—an interpretation with which all three agreed rather more quickly than I might have wished.

There was one positive sign, or so I chose to take it. Though none of the three expressed any deep regret at the collapse of our panel, they were all still planning to come to Chicago: Marsha, to interview for jobs; Dov, so that Geneva would pay for his winter trip back to the United States; Vic, for unspecified personal reasons. I secured their agreement that those of us who did present at some session would at least attend each others' papers; we could then meet and talk among ourselves. In the end, all of them did give papers, Marsha at a session on ecofeminism, Vic on a panel on the modernist novelist Djuna Barnes, and Dov in a large session organized by some members of the National Association of Scholars, called "Reading: The Essential Gesture." It began to look as though only I would have no occasion to go, until I received an invitation from a friend of mine, Jennifer Wicke, to speak in a session on "Global Theory in the World-Wide Web," Homi Bhabha having canceled out after the session had been scheduled. I wasn't really sure what the topic meant, but I figured I could use the paper I'd planned to give at my own session. I was flattered, too, by Jennifer's assurance that she'd been torn all along between inviting Bhabha or me and was seizing the opportunity to invite me now.

I arrived in Chicago more than ready for some congenial intellectual exchange. Like many others, my university had been undergoing downsizing for several years. Our administration was not proving any more adept than most at handling this transition, and my colleagues reacted badly in turn as our numbers eroded, uniting only in despising the administration, spending most of their time mewling and puking at and on one another as they fought over the tough question of which fields would suffer the most. I knew enough not to be surprised at this phenomenon. I'd published my book on scholarly work that spring, and I thought often of an article I'd cited by Cynthia Hardy and several colleagues at McGill, who had studied the steady 3–4 percent annual growth in income and enrollments their institution had enjoyed all through the century. They had called this growth rate "the range of ostensible collegiality," the level of increase needed to support new initiatives without the sorts of hard choices that could only be made well if there were *genuinely* collegial discussion and compromise. Now the ostensibility was melting away everywhere as budgets shrank, and the underlying culture of alienation and aggression was coming ever more strongly to the fore.

My book, of course, was going to stem the tide. Amid all the polemics, mine would be a reasoned contribution—historically grounded, sociologically informed, and psychologically acute, offering a fresh perspective and some concrete steps that cumulatively could begin to make a real difference. By the time I arrived in Chicago, *We Scholars* had been out for six months, and while I could hardly expect a wholesale change in the atmosphere as yet, I looked forward to gauging people's reactions. I had in my briefcase the one review I'd seen so far, which my in-laws had faxed to me after they came across it in the *Washington Post*. Only in one of the *Post*'s occasional Education supplements, to be sure, essentially an advertising vehicle for continuing-education programs, but it was still a nice review, and I wanted to give it to my editor in case he'd missed it. I checked in at the hotel, a little disappointed to find that my "lake-view" room allowed a view only to contortionists with no fear of heights, neither of which qualifications I possessed. I closed the shades and went down to the hotel's fountain-bar-and-mini-mall area.

The lobby had been designed as a sort of Babylonian theme park, twenty stories high, with hanging plants cascading down from brass-trimmed marble balconies. Glass-walled elevators crept like snails up the moist walls. The effect was of being enclosed in a giant terrarium. Hundreds of anxious graduate students, earnest assistant professors, and world-weary tenured faculty mingled together, plastic cups of wine in hand. The networking was in full swing, something I despise and avoid whenever possible; I stayed just long enough to catch up with a couple of friends from the West Coast, introduce a student of mine to an acquaintance at a school with a job opening, and look around for my editor. Not seeing him, I decided to leave. As I approached the door, I observed Marsha in conversation with someone whose grizzled face I seemed to know from dust jackets. I went up, and Marsha introduced me to her friend, who proved to be Gerald Graff.

Graff's books had strongly influenced my own work on scholarship, and so I was pleased when he recognized my name and began telling me how much he'd liked my book. "The main thing," he added, "is, don't believe the reviews. Take Howard Lamar in the *Yale Review*—so what if he's president of Yale? He was so obviously defensive that nobody will think anything of those cheap shots of his."

"And anyway, Lamar's just the *acting*—" I was beginning to reply, when a beep came from inside Graff's jacket pocket.

"My cell phone," he said, with a half-embarrassed duck of the head. "Excuse me; I've got to take this." He took out the phone. "Skip? Yeah, Jerry," he said, turning away from us.

I asked Marsha how the job search was going.

"It's depressing as hell," she replied. "Everybody knows what a disaster it's been at Bennington, but they still look at me funny when they hear I only got a one-year replacement gig at Vermont last year. That's even before I have to say I'm only doing some adjuncting at a couple of places this year. It doesn't even seem to help that my film book's out now, it just lets people off the hook for looking at me for assistant professorships, for which I'm 'obviously overqualified,' but it isn't enough to put me in the category of Hot Young Theorist with Sexy Second Book Just Out from Routledge Whom We'd Better Grab before Duke Does." Marsha shook her head. "But I shouldn't complain too much, at least I've got a couple of interviews, Amherst, which would be fine with my partner Tom, and NYU, which is trickier for him but we could maybe live kind of far out in New Jersey somewhere. And I have a friend in film there, Bob Stam, who's been keeping my name alive, so we'll see."

Marsha seemed a little wound up. This was understandable enough, especially as she was giving her talk the next morning and hadn't yet finished it—a matter of concern, she indicated, as there was a chance that some people from Amherst and NYU would attend in order to assess her performance. Graff concluded his call and the two of them headed off to a publisher's party. I put on my coat and walked out into the frigid Chicago air, a refreshing change from the humid anxiety clouding the atmosphere in the hotel lobby.

I ARRIVED at Marsha's session early the next morning and found the room crowded; clearly, the people working on feminist ecology were committed to it. Dov was standing along a side wall, and I joined him; Vic never appeared. Marsha needn't have worried about her paper. In twenty minutes, she gave a brilliant critique of what she described as "techno-amateurism" in Andrew Ross's recent book *Strange Weather*, which she contrasted to the more challenging "post-masculinist scientism" in Donna Haraway's ecocritical work after her Cyborg Manifesto. The acuity and good-humored polemic of her talk stood out particularly strongly against a couple of the other papers in the panel. "The Prison-House of Landscape" sounded promising, but in fact it proved largely to be an obsessively close reading of Gramsci's passing references to neo-feudal land tenure policies in Sicily. A more interesting paper, on transgressive performativity in fem-inized spaces, was delivered in a hushed monotone by a young assistant professor who never looked up from her page. All in all, I thought Marsha's paper was a real stand-out.

I congratulated Marsha at the end, expecting her to be pleased and re-lieved; she wasn't. "Did you see the guy from Amherst?" she asked. "He actually came, and he's the chair there now. Did you notice how he left right after my talk? He didn't ask a question or anything."

"I don't know what he looks like," I said. "Where was he?"

"He was sitting right by where the two of you were standing," Marsha replied. "Older guy, you know?"

"Oh, the one who was nodding off at the end?" I asked, realizing too late that this was probably not the best way to identify him. "It *was* really early," I hastily added, "so I'm sure it didn't mean anything."

"Yeah, right," Marsha responded in a discouraged tone.

"I wonder if NYU people were here, what they thought of your attack on Ross," Dov said. "That was bold to do."

Dov's tone was complimentary, but Marsha flushed. "Thanks, Dov," she said. "Just help *David* here put me at ease. I really didn't want my talk to come out that way. I mean, I like Andrew, and I like a lot of his work, even *Strange Weather* has some really good stuff in it, but I didn't get that across. It's so frustrating! I didn't want to make him the fall guy for Haraway, but I just didn't have time to pull it all together. If only Cassie hadn't been sick last week, if I even hadn't gone out *dancing* last night, but by the time I got down to wrapping up my argument, it was sometime after two, I thought it would have to do. You heard that hostile intervention in the question period, I think it was from a friend of Andrew's, and here I've got to go interview with them this afternoon."

I assured Marsha that Ross could certainly take some criticism in stride, and would probably even welcome her analysis if he heard about it.

"Perhaps so," Dov said, "though I doubt the willingness of people like Ross really to entertain divergent views. This you will see from my paper this afternoon."

This comment was hardly likely to cheer Marsha up. Was Dov needling her, or was his focus on his own upcoming presentation merely overriding his interpersonal sensitivity, what there was of it? I cast a glance at Marsha, rolling my eyes to convey the feeling that I certainly didn't condone Dov's tactlessness but hoped she wouldn't take his self-absorption personally. Marsha pursed her lips in reply in such a way as to indicate that she'd overlook the comment this time for my sake but that I shouldn't expect her to let Dov try her patience indefinitely. On this uncertain note, we parted.

GIVEN the tension between Marsha and Dov, I was pleasantly surprised to see her in the audience at Dov's session that afternoon. Vic had never appeared that morning, and I couldn't detect him now, though it was hard to be sure amid the crowd filling the ballroom. Roger Shattuck, the panel's organizer, began with a brief diatribe against feminism and gay studies for replacing literary values with a social agenda. A somewhat surprising pair of targets for a Proust scholar, I thought; apparently Proust wasn't supposed to actually *see* anything through the famed "optical instrument" of his novel. In any event, Shattuck then turned the floor over to Helen Vendler, who offered a more nuanced argument that the opposition between literary analysis and cultural studies was a false one, as close reading of literature had always provided a privileged access into a culture's self-understanding; she illustrated this with an illuminating discussion of poems by Wallace Stevens and Seamus Heaney. Richard Rorty then went back on the attack, arguing that the cultural studies movement was not at all concerned with the study of culture as such but was promoting the deconstruction of culture, a debunking of idealism and individual creativity in the name of a tired collectivism dressed up in an exaggerated epistemological skepticism. "History is 'the record of the individual thinking,'" he concluded, "as Harold Bloom puts it in *The Western Canon*. I hope you won't let the nay-sayers take over in literary studies the way they have in philosophy. We need skepticism, but we also need inspiration, too, if we want to envision a real future, not just debunk the past. So we need to hear the voices of the inspiring geniuses who shape a culture's aspirations." He sat down to sustained applause.

Dov was next. "I guess you know a person by the company they keep," Marsha muttered, but Dov began his own critique of cultural studies by taking issue with the other panelists.

"I cannot agree with my respected colleagues," Dov began, "that the work currently called cultural studies must toe the line of traditional scholarship, or else must be indefensible insofar as it differs from it. To the contrary, I am impatient with the new cultural studies precisely because it too much *resembles* business as usual. Unlike Professor Rorty, I see all too little serious deconstruction, rather than all too much, at play in this work, or at work in this play. My wish would be for a cultural studies that would genuinely offer an alternative to the scholarly practices it hopes to displace. I should say I have little hope that my wish will be granted. But perhaps we will gain some understanding of our situation if we explore both the difference I could wish to see and the reasons why we are unlikely ever to see it." Dov growled softly, and continued.

"To my eye, neither the focus on mass culture nor the leftist political orientation per se differentiate cultural studies sufficiently from the older liberal humanism. Too often, there is only a modest difference in degree, not the radical departure that both its enthusiasts and its detractors perceive. Let me take Professor Rorty's lead and say that the key issue is the question of history as the record of 'the individual thinking,' above all the great individual, let us say the poet or the philosopher. This is precisely the view I *wish* the cultural studies scholars would abandon. At least as the dominant mode of work, though I hope we will always leave room for an individual reader as perceptive as Professor Vendler to think so deeply about her favorite poets. Professor Rorty wishes to return to individualism. I, however, wish to move beyond it—I would even say, move *back* beyond it to a more collective social experience. The cultural students mean to do something like this, yet as regards their own movement they retain all too much reverence for the heroic individual." Dov paused for a sip of water, then went on.

"Let me give an example to show what I mean. I will take the programmatic introduction to a book that *Lingua Franca* recently called the leading compendium of cultural studies work. This is the big collection entitled *Cultural Studies* edited by Grossberg, Nelson, and Treichler, published by Routledge not long ago. You will note the ambition implied by the absence of a subtitle or any modifying adjective: this book does really mean to present to the world cultural studies *tout court*, if one can use this phrase of a book that is six hundred thousand words long. 'A detailed and authoritative map,' as the cover tells us, 'capturing cultural studies in all its rich diversity.' In keeping with this ambition, the editors' synoptic introduction endeavors to define—even police—the field. They mean to weed out inadequate definitions and inauthentic work, to outline the history of true cultural studies, to suggest the main directions for the future that are implied by the current work they anthologize. The 'special intellectual promise' of cultural studies, the editors begin, lies in the fact that 'it explicitly attempts to cut across diverse social and political interests,' interests which 'can combine and be articulated in all their dazzling plurality.' This social reach requires, and inspires, an intellectual and an institutional diversity as well. Cultural studies, we are told, is resolutely interdisciplinary, and—relatedly—it is highly collaborative, qualities that the editors celebrate in outlining the history of the foundational program in cultural studies, the Centre for Contemporary Studies at Birmingham in England." Dov looked over at Rorty, and smiled.

"I use the word 'foundational' advisedly in the present company," he continued. "Though I will not criticize Nelson, Grossberg, and Treichler for their failure to abandon foundationalism, a quixotic effort at best, in my opinion. What I find ironic is the persistence of this foundationalism in the midst of their claim to eschew the old essentialisms in general and the Great Man view of history in particular. Not only is this a logical contradiction, it means they can avoid examining and refining this ongoing force in their midst. Woven tightly into the editors' rhetoric of dazzling variety and rich diversity there can be found a counter-rhetoric of centrality and of ideological purity: it is 'the new politics of difference'—note the singular formulation—whose 'dazzling plurality' will be embodied by cultural studies. Cultural studies, it seems, has as much to do with enforcing its own norms, patrolling its own borders, as with wider social change. 'Cultural studies requires us'; 'cultural studies must constantly interrogate'; 'cultural studies would agree'; 'cultural studies cannot be used': all these formulations appear in the space of just two paragraphs, and they have many equivalents throughout the introduction. Indeed, the social healing promised by cultural studies seems at times secondary to the more pressing task of uniting the left itself. It is, as the editors' opening paragraph tell us, 'within *the fragmented institutional configuration of the academic left*' that cultural studies 'holds special promise because it explicitly attempts to cut across diverse social and political interests.' Dov raised an ironic eyebrow over the dark frame of his glasses.

"You know the etymology of *supercilious*?" Marsha whispered to me, but Dov was already continuing.

"This is interesting," he said. "To the outsider, after all, it might seem that cultural studies is problematic to the extent that it embodies a single political outlook—denying admission, for example, to students of culture who might vote Republican, or who prefer capitalism to socialism. To the insiders, however, it is the fragmentation and conflict *within* their own movement that are paramount, while the wider society outside the movement is often described in strikingly monolithic terms, in phrases such as 'global imperialism' or 'late capitalism.'"

Dov paused, running his tongue probingly around the inside of his lower lip as he turned a phrase over in his mind. "*Late* capitalism!" he exclaimed. "How the hell do these writers *know* if it is late or not? Maybe we live now in the age of *early middle* capitalism—who can say? How absurd that historical materialists, of all people, can think to stand outside history itself, proclaiming in advance the senescence of the economic system they hope to defeat by endless exegesis of the minor works of Marx!"

He smiled genially. "I like endless exegesis myself, and I too hope it will make a difference in the world. Yet to make this difference, our analysis must be at once rigorous and modest. Modest in not overstating our claims; rigorous in recognizing the complexity of the situation we would understand. In the conservative attacks on cultural studies and in the culturalists' self-defenses as well, each side is right to see the diversity it recognizes as its own, and wrong to reduce its opponents to a single entity. In this, the editors of this anthology seem to me to reproduce one of the least attractive features of the 'Reagan-Bush right' that they believe to be everywhere around them. But I do not exactly accept the critique of leftists and rightists that David Bromwich advances in his recent book *Politics by Other Means*, in which he claims that left and right alike favor the collective over the sovereign individual. The problem is just the reverse: 'progressives' and 'conservatives' alike too often hold to a sentimental nostalgia for the heroic individual. As we read on in the introduction to *Cultural Studies*, for instance, we find in full flower the old foundationalist emphasis on the few seminal thinkers, in this case the founders of the Birmingham program. Even among the Birmingham group, our editors single out two super-heroes, Raymond Williams and Stuart Hall, who figure on *every page* of the introduction. In sixteen pages, Williams's name appears sixteen times and Hall's name, no fewer than twenty-one times. This is the problem, to put it in deconstructive terms: cultural studies' oppositional founders—originators of the movement's most powerful insights—have bred a kind of blindness in their followers through the very strength of their example, perpetuating the individualism they critique in others."

Dov took off his glasses and rubbed his nose in a meditative way. He replaced his glasses and continued.

"Okay," he said. "So what do we do now that we have had our little deconstructive insight? If we oppose the tendentious triviality of our modern academic and commercial cultures alike, we have the intellectual and ethical responsibility to find some better basis for our own work. This basis may actually be possible to find within cultural studies itself, if we can look further into the movement. Were cultural studies subject to a single or simple blindness, there would be little more to say. I believe, however that cultural studies in fact struggles with a double blindness, and this is a more interesting situation: a blindness not only to their lingering individualism but equally, *per contra*, to the underlying basis of their genuinely communal activity. What becomes repressed, I believe, is awareness of the deep continuity between their movement and its closest social equivalent: not a political party, not a trade union, but a religious community.

"I would say that religious community is the repressed Other of cultural studies: tolerated perhaps in the case of certain minorities, caricatured when it is not ignored outright in the wider society. In the *Cultural Studies* volume itself, in fact, Cornel West pleads for cultural studies to take religious organizations seriously as venues for social change, not simply to write religion off as the playground of conservative fundamentalists. His is a lone voice, however. The collection as a whole regularly illustrates the casual dismissal of religion that West tries to combat. Thus Constance Penley, for example, criticizes anti-addiction and self-help groups, 'which seem to encourage religious and highly individualistic ways of thinking that lead to social and political disempowerment.'"

Dov took off his glasses again, thoughtfully bit one of the earpieces, then leaned forward and spoke directly to the audience. "Do you see what concerns me here? If I read Penley's apposition correctly, she appears to equate religion with individualism, and both in turn with social disempowerment. Secular academics often make this mistake, and not only leftists: I think of Harold Bloom, to whom my fellow panelist Professor Rorty just alluded. Bloom's new book, *The American Religion*, suffers from its heavily individualistic orientation, his inattention to congregational life. Truly to comprehend religious experience, we must do more than merely read a sect's scriptures."

Dov paused. "Okay," he continued, putting his glasses back on, "I return to my own sermon." He resumed reading from his text. "Deeply wedded to the individualist bias they believe themselves to have rejected, the cultural students honor their pantheon of inspiring leaders just as Professor Rorty would have them do. But truly collective work remains stunted in much cultural-studies practice; this is why interdisciplinarity receives more lip service than real attention, if by serious interdisciplinary work we mean collaboration between people of different disciplinary expertise. It is rare even to find a coauthored essay in the *Culture Studies* volume, and I see no instance in which a pair of authors develop their topic by confronting genuinely different disciplinary perspectives, let alone differing ideological presuppositions.

"So I think," Dov concluded, "that cultural studies should pay serious attention to religious experience: both for its own sake and for the sake of the goals it hopes to accomplish. Religious organizations are the only true alternative in America to the look-alike Democratic and Republican parties, apart from the impossible dream of a leftist political movement winning a majority at the ballot-box. But more than this, if cultural studies is to carry out its first task, as the Routledge collection's editors define it—to heal the divisions within the movement itself—it would do well to attend to the structural homology between its own practices and those of religious sects. Now, many sects in history have arisen only to fail, or to survive in a weak and marginal position; others have prospered only by selling their souls; a very few sects have really achieved something new in society, and cultural studies should devote an intensive study to those successes if it is ever to wean itself of its own coterie or cult status. It is hard to create a movement *ex nihilo*, unwise even to try: better to build on some existing base. If one wishes to begin from a better model than some Maoist daydream, or some Stalinist nightmare, the best real-life models of collective action will be found among religious organizations."

Dov sat down. All the speakers had run over their allotted time, and no time remained for questions, so Shattuck brought the session to a close.

"So what did you think?" Dov asked Marsha and me, as we left the ballroom together.

"Very interesting," I said.

"Total bullshit," Marsha said. "Cultural studies isn't a cult!"

"It's an intriguing analogy, though," I added.

"Analogy, my ass!" Marsha retorted. "Dov means it *literally*. Don't you, Dov?" Not waiting for a reply, she went on. "I think you're the one who's being contradictory here. First you claim we worship Williams and Hall, so you can tell us to give them up because hero-worship's bad—and then you tell us to start going to *church* again! Apparently it's better to worship some fantastic Holy Trinity than draw inspiration from two or three real people. It's enough to make Christ weep, as my mother would say."

"Did I speak of any Holy Trinity?" Dov asked, as we crossed the hotel lobby. "Where are your multicultural sensitivities, my dear Marsha? Do they apply only to a short list of telegenically oppressed minorities?" Marsha bristled, but now it was Dov who continued without pausing for a reply.

"Look, I am Jewish. The only Holy Trinity I recognize are Thesis, Antithesis, and Synthesis, and I have even doubts about Synthesis. To me, Jesus was a great rabbi, nothing less but nothing more. After his death, his disciples did just what you in cultural studies are in danger to do. You deify the seminal thinker, his pronouncements become articles of faith, and so you blunt the edge of your critical faculty."

"So orthodox Jews don't do just that, in spades?" Marsha asked. "Anything Moses handed down on Sinai, you still do thousands of years later, and you lecture *me* about *my* critical faculty?"

"Firstly, I am not Orthodox," Dov replied, with an exasperated patience. "This you could have deduced simply from the meals we have taken together. Secondly, you do not know what you are talking about in any event. Yes, I accept the fundamentals of Jewish tradition, but this is the expression of the life of a whole people over centuries—in mainstream Judaism, we do not worship any one individual. This is all the more true for those of us who take seriously the findings of biblical scholarship. Moses is a fiction! A sublime fiction, I would say, a fiction that conveys truth, precisely because already in antiquity his name became a place-holder, an open site in which new material could be inserted and endlessly reinterpreted. Real people too, even major figures like Akiba and Hillel, did not speak on their own authority: they were consciously part of a tradition, even as they engaged in shifting elements of that tradition. When you Christians were writing your gospels to deify your founder—never mind that you couldn't even agree on a straight story—the rabbis were collecting the *Pirke Avot*, 'Sayings of the Fathers.' A much more modest document, more dialogue than hagiography."

"Okay, okay," Marsha replied. "I'll make allowance for your Judaism, just as long as you don't make me out to be a Christian. It's my mother who's an Irish Catholic, not me. My dad was a Trotskyite, and even that's too much belief for me. I just don't think anything religious is going on in cultural studies, and if it is, I don't want any part of it. I left the church for good when I was sixteen, all right?"

This conversation didn't seem to be going anywhere, or at least not anywhere I wanted to go, so I was relieved as we emerged from the hotel to see Vic standing on the sidewalk just ahead of us, studying the convention program.

"Greetings, all!" he exclaimed. "Sorry I missed your talk, Marsha, but really, I will never understand why they schedule sessions before noon. And when do you enthrall your grateful public, Dov?"

Dov didn't deign to reply. I indicated that the session had just ended.

"What a pity," Vic said. "I'm famished," he continued, and gestured toward a coffee shop across the street. "Shall we go in there?"

I glanced at my watch. Three o'clock; I certainly felt a need for caffeine. Marsha was amenable as well. Dov looked as though he wanted to be elsewhere, but then he was hailed from across the street by a Geneva colleague, Wlad Godzich, who was also about to enter the coffee shop. "Come on in, Dov," Wlad called over; "I'm meeting a friend, and I know he wants to meet you." We crossed the street.

"So you're going to get some lunch?" I asked Vic as we all went in.

"Breakfast," he replied.

It turned out that Wlad's friend was Lindsay Waters, the editor of my scholarship book; they'd become close friends when Wlad was at Minnesota and Lindsay was running the press there. Lindsay was already seated; he greeted us, or at least Wlad, warmly, his incisive moustache cutting the air as he spoke. Glad that I happened to have my good review with me, I gave it to him. "Very nice, David," he said, scanning it rapidly. "This might help make up for that hatchet job in the London *Times*."

"Oh?" I asked, but Lindsay was continuing with his train of thought, as usual speaking at double speed.

"And why'd the *Times* even give it to that Oxford guy to review? So he's eminent! At least he could have the good grace to admit he doesn't know baked beans about the American system. And that snotty donnish dismissiveness! 'Vacuity,' for crying out loud! Don't give it another thought, David."

"Well," I commented, but Lindsay had already turned his attention to Dov.

"Finally we meet," he said. "So when are you going to do a book with us?"

As the tables in the coffee shop were small, Dov sat down with Godzich at Lindsay's table; Vic, Marsha, and I sat down nearby.

"Don't worry about those reviews," Marsha remarked; "you'll never please everybody."

"Don't insult the poor boy with platitudes, Marsha," Vic interjected.

"You talk about collaboration, David, working across different viewpoints. It will never happen, my dear! And if it ever does, don't worry about not pleasing everyone—you'll never please *any*one!"

Had Vic forgotten our own plan to work up our discussions for publication? Or was he hinting at withdrawing from the project? I hesitated to ask, not sure I wanted to learn the answer. Fortunately, Marsha kept the conversation going.

"Come on, Vic," she said. "Aren't you at least going to learn something from the other speakers on your Djuna Barnes panel?"

"*Beh*," Vic replied. "The other papers sound worthless. The first person is going to be nattering on about 'crypto-racism' in Barnes's portrayal of Jews and blacks. Crypto, my foot! Djuna was as racist as the day is long, and a snob to boot, and her work's the better for it! As for the other two papers, I fear we are in for a brace of disquisitions on apparitional lesbianism. It was bad enough in the old days, when critics would belittle Barnes for being a Sapphist. Now they attack her for not being enough of one!"

"Well, it *is* a little weird that she'd never openly admit to her basic orientation," I said.

"It isn't weird at all," Marsha said. "She was struggling to make her way as a serious writer, not to mention as a human being. It's kind of patronizing to look back and expect her not to have felt the weight of everything the patriarchy was sending down on her."

"Isn't that line a little shop-worn by now?" Vic asked. "I think you're patronizing Barnes yourself, if you insist on seeing her concern for her own privacy simply in terms of patriarchal oppression. I would call it tact!"

I was afraid another argument was brewing, so I tried to divert Vic onto his favorite subject, himself.

"Even if their own papers aren't so good," I asked, "don't you expect your fellow speakers are going to learn something from you? Otherwise, why come at all?"

Vic frowned. "Why indeed? Mostly, I've come to Chicago to see a friend. . . . A former friend, I should say. Not a happy situation, actually, and so I suppose I imagined the conference would provide comic relief. As for learning anything, you can hardly expect the speakers themselves to cast aside their deeply held views and embrace an incompatible perspective. I may reach a person or two in the audience, *if* we get an audience, but I have no illusions that my fellow speakers will give a fig for what I have to say. Whether they praise Djuna or condemn her, all three of my honored co-panelists are committed to heavily biographical approaches to Djuna's Tragic Life and Her Triumph in Art. My paper runs directly contrary to this sort of bilge: I insist it is Djuna's astonishing command of metaphor that makes her a great writer. Her themes are of secondary importance at best, and her life is *ut*terly irrelevant to themes and style alike."

"Maybe to you," Marsha said. "But a lot of us really respond to her portrayals of marginalized figures, and she certainly drew on her life in creating them. I'd even say her luxurious language itself expresses the unstoppable energy of her characters, as they struggle against the dead hand of the decaying aristocratic order around them."

"Sentimentalism, my dear Marsha!" Vic exclaimed. "The one vice in which Djuna never indulged! *Nightwood* is a gallery of grotesques: Robin, the passive-aggressive somnambulist; Jenny Petheridge the harpy; Matthew O'Connor the alcoholic kleptomaniac—to speak only of Djuna's *major* characters, leaving aside Nikka the Nigger and his tattooed penis! Do you really mean us to take these paralyzed melancholiacs as *role models*?"

"But Nikka's quite a pos—" Marsha interjected, but Vic was continuing without paying attention.

"Perhaps Barnes molded her own life on her characters," he went on. "But what was the result? Forty years as a wine-soaked recluse! 'They say that life is nasty, brutish, and short,' she told one of her few visitors in those late years; 'but mine has only been nasty and brutish.' Barnes made her art from the wreckage of her life, I grant you, but the wreckage as such can command only our pity. It is her art that compels our admiration and merits analysis."

Marsha looked as though she was about to make a sharp reply, but I tapped her knee with a forefinger and raised an eyebrow to suggest that she shouldn't take umbrage at Vic's angry tone, as something personal was clearly bothering him. Marsha picked up a spoon, examined it briefly, and put it decisively down on the table, signifying her willingness to drop the subject if we could leave the coffee shop without further ado. This we did, each heading off in a different direction for separate appointments.

Vic's panel was scheduled for the shoulder period starting at 7:30 that evening, never a popular time. The session was sparsely attended, and even the speakers, Vic included, seemed listless. First came a high-minded and yet oddly tepid critique of Barnes's racial views. This was followed by a paper on Barnes's repressed lesbianism—not the attack that Vic had expected, but a painfully sincere celebration that was somehow more depressing than an attack would have been. The third speaker gave an extended account of her own adolescent years as a circus acrobat; though this was interesting, I missed a payoff in terms of new insights into Barnes's writing. Even Vic's paper failed to live up to the promise of its title, "'As Common as Whale-shit on the Bottom of the Sea': *Nightwood*'s Metaphoric World." He clearly hadn't done the detailed work that would have been needed to elucidate the obscure logic of Barnes's prose style, and his mind seemed elsewhere as he spoke in an uncharacteristically flat delivery. A couple of perfunctory questions were asked, a couple of perfunctory answers were given, and everyone filed out.

THE idea had been to have a festive dinner after the day's sessions. No one was looking too festive when we reassembled, though, and it occurred to me that some music might help. I began to sing the praises of a blues place I'd heard about: not one of the touristically famous spots, but (the tourist's perennial dream) an undiscovered little hideaway, known only to those in the know. I ignored my friends' hints that they were tired, whether of the convention or of each other I didn't want to find out; indeed, just because I feared the worst, I was bent on providing a social situation that might impel everyone to relax, loosen up, become civil again.

This might actually have worked, if only I'd gotten the address right, and it didn't help matters that I compounded the error by misunderstanding the directions. As it was, I promised everyone a short walk to an address on Grant Park, when I should have been arranging for a cab ride to Grand Street, some distance away. So we all set off by foot from the hotel at half past nine that night. Marsha and I walked together, with Dov and Vic gradually falling a little distance behind us.

Marsha was not in a good mood. "If I hear about 'imbrication' one more time, I'm going to implode!" she remarked, as we headed down Michigan Avenue toward Grant Park.

"But I always used to think you ate that kind of vocabulary for breakfast," I replied.

"Maybe that's why it bugs me so much. I've finally outgrown that compulsion to come across as more scientific than the scientists, au couranter than the French, or show that my syntax is bigger than the big boys' is. When I hear other people doing it, it drives me up the wall."

"But it's fine when it's done well," I said. "I remember that great article you had several years ago on 'The Specular Jouissance of "Dick" Deadeye'—Lacan would have been proud!" I was stretching the point a little, since in fact it had only been the title that I'd enjoyed; I hadn't been able to make heads or tails of Marsha's actual argument about Gilbert and Sullivan.

"Lacan would have been proud—that's just my point!" Marsha replied. "Why on earth should we be writing now just to please some dead French father? That's not using his theory, it's being used by it! This is what I meant before about missing the whole game if you take Lacan straight. You can deconstruct *le nom du père* without having to turn your own signature into the *nom de plume du père!*"

"So how are the interviews going?" I asked, searching for a more congenial subject. This wasn't it.

"They went. At least they're over. The Amherst one—what a disaster! They had about eight people there in this stuffy room, two or three young hotshots they've hired recently, then all these old guys who got their degrees at Harvard in the fifties. They were all nice enough, but I kept feeling I had to apologize to the old guys for being so theoretical. Then I had to field potshots from the hotshots, who obviously didn't think I'm theoretical enough for them."

"How about NYU?" I asked.

"Well, it was all right, Andrew was fine, he kind of teased me about my talk, which of course he'd heard all about. But even with that, I couldn't help wondering if he'd have taken me on directly if I'd been a guy, and not just teased me. It could have cleared the air some." Marsha paused. "But I'm being unfair to Andrew—it's just the paranoia you get into when you're in this weird situation. Really, the interview went okay, Bob Stam was asking lots of friendly questions, but he took me aside afterward to warn me there's an inside candidate. A visiting professor from Hong Kong, Comp Lit's eager to land him too, they can maybe get the line to be incremental if they do a joint appointment."

"But didn't they specify film theory in their ad?" I asked.

"Oh, the guy's a Lacanian," Marsha replied. "Half the Chinese comparatists are these days, and of course there's the whole wide-open field of Chinese cinema, Beijing and Taiwan as well as the Hong Kong scene. Somebody who really knows the stuff can probably make quite a splash."

She sighed. "It looks like another year of adjuncting, and it's really getting me down. You know what they call us, 'freeway fliers'? But in Vermont, there's hardly any freeways to fly on, just icy state roads to slide off of as I race back and forth across the state. I like the students fine, especially the ones at U of V, but let's just say the salary's commensurate with the prestige of the gigs. And the benefits? Maybe I'll become a union organizer after all."

I turned up my collar against a chilling breeze that had begun to blow off Lake Michigan. We were nearing Grant Park now, and I hoped we'd come to the club soon, but all I could see were banks and sports paraphernalia stores.

"At least we can relax a little once we get to this club," I remarked.

"I suppose so," Marsha replied. "I'd like to find out what's eating Vic, but I've got to tell you, Dov's charm is wearing pretty thin."

"I didn't think his talk was all that unreasonable," I said.

"It isn't just that! It's the whole context, not that he'd say anything about it openly, of course, but what do you think this line about a people's collective traditions *means* in Israel? Don't you see how it goes hand in hand with *suppressing* the cultural life of the Palestinians, not to mention their political rights? I overheard him at that coffee shop talking Mideast politics with Lindsay and Wlad. The dirt isn't dry on Rabin's grave and Dov's dancing on it! He was saying he'll be going to Israel just to vote for that jerk Netanyahu, when they have the election in the spring. The little prick!"

Suddenly I heard Vic's voice just behind us: "Marsha," he said warningly. He and Dov had caught up to us without our noticing. There was a moment's awkward silence, and then Dov spoke.

"Leaving my genitalia to one side," he said slowly, "I would ask you to try, if you can, to modulate a little your stereotypical thinking. Not every Likudnik is intent upon suppressing Palestinian culture, and as a matter of fact I myself am deeply concerned about the xenophobic elements in the party. I vote Likud despite this xenophobia, not because of it. In the real world, or at least in the reality of the Middle East, there are no choices that are simply good."

"Right," Marsha answered, unabashed. "So you really think this guy Netanyahu's the best hope for peace?"

"No, Netanyahu is not the best hope for peace, but I shall vote for him all the same. This is because I do not believe there *is* any hope for peace in Israel—or more precisely, such hope as there is seems to me pure fantasy. Look, my brother Ari fought in the '67 war, and I think he did have some romantic idea that he was 'fighting for peace.' Like fucking for virginity! When he was killed, my sister and I were quite young, adolescents really. Ari's death affected us profoundly, but very differently. She reacted by joining the Peace Now movement. I joined Likud. My parents were shocked, but I was looking for some middle way in between their European socialist vision of universal harmony, and the old, chthonic Levantine dream of regional domination by the strongest tribe. Some in Likud may actually want just that, I admit. Yet the Ottoman Empire is forever gone, however much it is mourned by the Arafats and the Ariel Sharons who imagine they would become Pasha if it could return. So peace is not the issue, in my view. It is a question of managing an endless conflict. Better that it should only simmer and not boil over, and I think Netanyahu may be the best one now to keep the lid from blowing off altogether. Maybe I am a Lidnik, not a Likudnik."

Marsha said nothing in reply. Vic spoke up next:

"And so where is this little *boîte* of yours, David? The chill is starting to sink in."

Department stores, fashionable shoe shops, more sports outlets; not a blues club in sight, and the few people we passed were hurrying along, muffled in scarves, their collars turned up and their hats pulled low against the wind. We walked on.

"I've been in Vermont so long I actually like cold weather by now," Marsha remarked. "The air's so lucid. But I can imagine, Vic, you'd rather be back in Boston by a warm fire."

"Not just now," Vic replied. "Too much disruption from the plasterers and paperhangers."

"Not really?" Marsha asked. "You were griping about the renovation two years back, and it's still going on?"

"Oh, that was finished a long time ago," Vic replied. "But I decided this fall that the parlor floor really wasn't working for me, so I'm having it redone."

"Good God!" Marsha muttered, though Vic apparently didn't hear this.

"It's nothing like the disruption I had two years ago, to be sure. And I can always use the sitting room up on the guest floor—"

"For Christ's sake!" Marsha burst out. "Homeless people are freezing on the streets of Boston, and you're redecorating *again*? Does the term 'conspicuous consumption' mean anything to you, Vic?"

"Most certainly it does," he replied, drawing himself up. "My favorite opera heroines usually die quite conspicuously of consumption, their vocal capacities strangely enhanced by the disease."

"Don't be an asshole, Vic," Marsha said pleadingly. "You know perfectly well what I mean—and that's even before we say anything about your new toys."

"But, Marsha!" Vic replied. "Catamarans are *ecologically correct!*"

"That's a laugh and a half!" she retorted. "You spend a quarter million dollars on one of those things, with God knows how many toxic compounds in the fiberglass and the varnishes, then you have some freighter burn a shitload of fossil fuel to ship the damn thing halfway around the world to some atoll somewhere—just so you and your little buddies can race back and forth and degrade the coral reefs! And you have the *gall* to say this toy of yours is 'ecologically correct,' as you put it, just because it doesn't use a motor?"

"It does have a motor, actually a pair of motors," Vic replied. "So we can make our moorings without damaging those precious reefs of yours. Would it help if we ran the engines on ethanol?"

Marsha was clearly about to make an angry retort, but she checked herself, and spoke quietly.

"You know, I actually used to like you, Vic," she said.

"I used to like myself," he responded, unexpectedly subdued in turn. "I know I'm getting more and more restless, jumpy even. I'm not going to try and justify the catamaran, either, unless perhaps as therapy. Poor therapy at that. No sooner do I manage to project myself into the experience than the boat becomes an alter ego, and it's all too similar to the original me: finicky, high-strung, always threatening to capsize when the wind's up, then getting becalmed when things . . . die down."

He gave special emphasis to the word "die." Less tactful than the rest of us, Dov remarked on this.

"Always the reader of inflections," Vic replied. "I would prefer to spare you the whole sad story, and I'm sure you'd prefer to be spared as well. I'll just say that this is why I'm here this week. A hospital visit I've been putting off for some time now. A year ago, things were looking rather different. I was finally in a serious relationship, I'd even brought Bill to Boston to meet my mother; they got along splendidly. His architectural practice is here, and I was actually contemplating a move. Then he got sick. I blame myself, I blame him, it doesn't even help if I say no one's to blame, but things fell apart."

"An architect?" I remarked. "Interesting that you'd react by redoing your house."

"Such insight!" Vic exclaimed. "Have you thought of becoming a talk show host? But *please*, David, don't patronize me by calling my reaction 'interesting.' See it for what it is, a futile exercise in sympathetic magic. As Bill's health worsened, my interiors began to oppress me. In the last renovation, I'd played up the front parlor as a Victorian fantasia, the walls hand-stenciled, vases of flowers.... Odette de Crécy could hardly have done better. Then you'd come into the art-nouveau music room—but you were there last winter, David, you know how it was."

"I hope you're keeping the dining room intact," I said. "It's not often you get such comfort out of a striking visual effect."

"No, the plush velvet barber's chairs are going too," Vic replied. "They looked lovely around the carved oak table, but it was just too much. Now I want everything uncluttered, spare, a little hard-edged. I even thought of giving up the table altogether, as I hardly feel in the mood for large dinner parties these days. Perhaps just have a few dentist's chairs here and there; one's plate could go on that little tray that swings around from the side, and the little tools would work so well for lobster. In the end, I rejected the idea as somehow rather assaultive.... But I won't bore you with the details, and really, this is irrelevant to our discussions here. Apart from the fact that it may explain why I'm *not* all here just now."

"Vic, I'm sorry," Marsha said. "And I'm sorry I gave you such a hard time before about your reading of Djuna Barnes. If her metaphoric world gives you refuge, I'm glad, and at least it doesn't take a lot of fossil fuel to get you there."

"So where *are* we?" Dov asked. We'd certainly come farther than we should have, and no blues bar was in sight. We saw a cab cruising by, and hailed it. Fortunately, the driver was able to untangle my garbled version of the name and address, and took us there. Joe's Be-Bop Café was packed, filled with smoke and the smell of beer; the crowd was hot and boisterous; a one-armed harmonica player went on for hours, backed by what Marsha called "a killer band." It was just what we all needed.

I<small>T</small> was long past midnight when I returned to my room, and I'd gotten a headache from the smoke and the noise. I slept poorly and woke very late, realizing with a guilty start that I had neglected to call home the night before; now my wife would be on the road with the kids, heading to Bethesda to visit her family. I took a long shower; not feeling like seeing anyone, I ordered some breakfast from room service and spent a couple of hours trying to unravel Richard and Sally Price's *Enigma Variations*, then just out. An intriguing blend of fact and fiction by a pair of anthropologists on the theme of originality and forgery, and quite effective in detailing the interactions between themselves—or their fictionalized selves—and Monsieur Lafontaine, their mysterious art-forging interlocutor. Oddly, the only scene that didn't seem to work was the one closest to home, a faculty seminar at Princeton—why didn't the Prices just give their research straight and cut out the middlemen? And they couldn't resist giving a stagily stilted manner of speech to a visiting German professor; but here I shut the book. No doubt the problem was with me. My head was still aching and my mood was too testy to read as actively as the Prices' experimental form required.

What to do? I looked with distaste at the telephone-book-sized conference program lying on the night table. Seven hundred sessions, and I couldn't recall having noticed any I'd want to attend that afternoon. Chatter, chatter everywhere, and nary a thought to think! . . . Was it just my foggy brain today, or were my witticisms always so witless? At least I was alone, so I wouldn't have to put up with Vic's pointedly pretending not to hear it. But after all, I couldn't just hide out all day in my room. I heaved myself off my bed and went down to the lobby.

I was in luck: right away I stumbled on my panel's organizer, Jennifer Wicke, in conversation with one of our fellow-panelists, Bruce Robbins. They seemed surprised to see me, but I greeted them warmly.

"I'm really looking forward to our session tomorrow," I added. "I actually think Saturday morning is one of the best times to draw an audience."

"But David," Jennifer said, "*today* is Saturday. You really *forgot?*"

I blanched. Not for the first time, I had fallen into that blurring of days so common in Las Vegas casinos and MLA conventions. This was, however, the first time that I'd ever missed my own talk. I definitely should have gotten out of bed that morning; if only I'd gone downstairs for breakfast, some conversation or some newspaper would have clued me in. As the session hadn't even begun until eleven, Jennifer obviously had reason to doubt my explanation, and I certainly looked like a fool in any event.

Seeing my discomfort, Bruce kindly intervened. "Not to worry, David," he said. "The rest of us had lots to say. And even though the room was crowded we had quite a lively discussion afterward. As it was, they had to shoo us out just now, so the next session could begin."

"That's right," Jennifer added, "and actually Homi was in the audience. It was so tremendous of him to come. He certainly didn't need to feel guilty, you know—MLA made him drop our panel because he already had two others he was doing. So I took the opportunity to ask him to follow up on some of Bruce's comments—you'll have to read Bruce's paper, it's called 'Virtual Intellectuals,' really cutting-edge politics-of-the-Internet stuff. Well, you know how mesmerizing Homi can be, even when you can't quite follow what he's saying, and he was *so* complimentary, too, you'll have to admit, Bruce."

Bruce gave a modest smile. "What I really liked, Jen," he replied, "was the way Judy Butler tied your work in with Bourdieu's. Pretty heady stuff! I'm envious, of course, particularly now she's inviting you to Bellagio, but that was the least she could do after that bravura performance of yours."

How many MLA panels had I attended over the years at which I was in—or was addressing—a listless audience of twelve? And this was the one I had to miss. It didn't even help that Jennifer was so relaxed about my absence, though I decided to chalk this up to her generous good nature. I made some excuse to decline their invitation to join them for a late lunch, and left the hotel.

Not knowing what to do, I took a cab down to the Oriental Institute at the University of Chicago, to visit their famed Egyptian galleries, hoping that I might feel enlivened by contrast. There, I ran into Dov and Vic—the first time I'd seen them out and about together of their own volition. Greeting them, I remarked that it was no surprise to see Dov in this wing of the museum, but I hadn't known of Vic's interest in such art.

"Sarcophagi and I go way back," Vic said. "To the MFA, actually, you know, in Boston. The Egyptian curator there, Kelly Simpson, was a friend of my father's; I think they met through concert circles when my father was on the Boston Symphony's board. I always wanted to be like Kelly when I grew up: a World War II flying ace turned Egyptologist, I kid you not. He did literature, art, archaeology, curated his collection and taught at Yale, too. A real intellectual and a man of the world—and a handsome, handsome man at that. I was even inspired to study hieroglyphics in college for a while, and here I am today. Just look at the purity of line on the naked goddess inside this coffin lid—what was her name, now, Ma'at? No, Nût; has anyone ever done death with such panache?"

"Certainly the Egyptians were the least morbid of all people," Dov remarked, "though the popular conception of their culture may fail to grasp this. They could not imagine that life as they knew it could ever end, even beyond the grave. One might say, indeed, that they had the *least* sense of death of any major ancient culture. The Babylonians are far more interesting on death, for they took it seriously. Do you recall the chilling scene in *The Descent of Inanna*, when Inanna dares to go visit her sister Ereshkigal, queen of the underworld, and Ereshkigal has her stripped naked and hung from a hook?"

"To me, dear Dov," Vic replied, "that scene seems all too *life*like, altogether too close to early D. H. Lawrence. It is the Egyptians who really felt the transcendent otherness of eternity and molded their art in its image. They even succeeded in holding their art almost constant for two and a half millennia. Just look at that seated scribe over there—unless you studied him closely, could you really say whether he was done in the Sixth Dynasty or the Twenty-sixth?"

Some culture, I felt sure, must have a paradise in which I could know more than my friends did, at least about something, though of course this would be hell for them; here on earth, I resigned myself to touring the galleries with them. I found myself gradually drawn in, at once soothed by the serenity of the carvings and stimulated by my companions' commentary. It was six o'clock when the museum closed and we emerged, having seen only half of the Egyptian galleries. We were supposed to have dinner later on, and I prepared to peel away on my own for the intervening hour, but Vic—whether out of genuine friendship, or simply from the love of an attentive audience—urged both of us to join him in meeting Marsha for a predinner drink.

"She wants job-hunting advice," he said, "and three head-hunters will be better than one. Then we can have the dinner hour clear for loftier things."

We went with him to the bar where he and Marsha had agreed to meet, a cozy, dimly lit establishment mercifully free of sports TV. Away from the bar, there were some conversational groupings of armchairs; when Marsha arrived, we occupied a set of these and settled in for some serious job discussion. It soon emerged, however, that we had little substantive advice for Marsha, given her anomalous situation and the way that her writing had largely been halted during her years of immersion in Bennington's teaching-intensive culture. I was relieved when Marsha herself gave a more general turn to our discussion of incompatible academic cultures.

"What *is* culture, anyway?" Marsha asked. "Here we are talking about academic cultures, cultural studies, intervening in the culture, but I don't think we know what we mean by the term itself. Even if we make the obvious distinction between culture as a set of social practices, and culture as a kind of artistic sensitivity and refinement, it's still a pretty open question how we as cultural critics are supposed to mediate between these different kinds of culture."

"Culture," Vic said, "is a vast image-repertoire, and criticism now shares with art itself the task of bringing these images to life. Sometimes (I'll grant you, Marsha) for social purposes, sometimes for the pure pleasure of it, stimulating us to consciousness of the play itself. That's what I so love in

Barthes, his playfulness with his texts, his mockery of his own mania for systems. 'My universe in crumbs,' as he says so aptly when he looks back on his career in *Roland Barthes par Roland Barthes*."

"That's just what I find hard to take in Barthes," Marsha remarked. "He makes gestures toward a liberating mode of writing or reading, but what's his liberation consist of? 'Cruising' the text? 'A faint plication' of the page? Isn't that a little too cute, a little pat? Walter Benjamin really meant something serious when he spoke of 'brushing history against the grain'—I'll take that over Barthes' *faint plications* any day, and you can keep his crumbs too. Culture's more than cake."

"Not cake," Vic replied. "Couscous." He reached into a side pocket of his camel-hair blazer and took out a book. "I've been rereading *Sade, Fourier, Loyola*—delightful conference reading, all about discipline, entrapment, multiple sessions. . . . Barthes reads Sade as though he were Saint Ignatius, and reads Loyola as though he were the wicked Marquis, but his real hero is the anarcho-communalist Fourier. He begins his Fourier chapter by analyzing his discomfort at being asked, in Morocco, to eat couscous prepared with rancid butter according to local peasant custom. I'll spare you the way this incident illustrates Fourier, but Barthes adds a delightful footnote, which I will share with you: 'Fourier would, I am sure, have been enraptured at my friend Abd el Kebir's entry into the couscous tournament, in defense of the Rancid side, in a letter I received from him.' He then gives us the letter, in which this fellow el Kebir claims, and I quote, that 'the apparent instability of the Moroccan peasant's culinary system proceeds, dear friend, from the fact that rancid butter is made in a strange underground hearth at the intersection of cosmic time and the time of consumption. Rancid butter is a kind of decomposed property, pleasing to interior monologue. Dug out in handfuls, rancid butter is worked in the following circular rite: a huge and magnificent ball of couscous is ejaculated into the throat to such an extent that the rancidity is neutralized. Fourier would call it a double-focus ellipse.' Old Abd goes on in this vein for a while more, then closes his letter with a fine flourish: 'The high price put on couscous—a truly enigmatic material—obliges me to sign off and to send you my friendly wishes.' Now, Dov, could you ask for a better image of culture, a more pleasing illustration of cultural analysis?"

"I cannot give couscous that much credit," Dov answered. "Maybe I've had too much of it in my life. Barthes's poetic friend is biting off more than I, for one, am willing to swallow. Or perhaps less: cultural activity should be more than a parable for homosexual sex."

"No Queer Theorist worth his or her salt would rest content with such an obvious reading," Vic retorted. "I will be disappointed if you persist in such a reading yourself, old chum, as your homophobia is preventing you from seeing the real point. What Barthes means by printing el Kebir's letter is to evoke an image of culture as friendship, as mutual understanding, as an endless circulation of pleasure. Certainly in part the pleasure of oral sex—though I would hardly have thought that was a gay prerogative alone—but above all the pleasure of the mind's play over the world's sensuous immediacy."

"Fine," Marsha interjected. "But how much sensuous play can most people afford? And anyway, isn't there an undercurrent of *in*tolerance in Barthes, with all his haughty send-ups of the bourgeoisie, not to mention his blanking-out of working-class culture whenever he can't poeticize it? I think it's the peasants who seem rancid to Barthes. He's intolerant of society as it is—and of anyone who'd be so crass as to try to make things better."

"I shouldn't have allowed myself," Vic said, "to be pushed by Dov's prescriptive comments on sexuality into understating the sexual charge in the passage I read you. Even I would agree that running through Barthes's work there is a slyly understated theme of transgressive sexuality as a political force—something I should never have expected you, of all people, Marsha, to deny."

Marsha was studiously examining her fingernails (purple today, I noticed), and didn't reply.

Vic pressed on, with an edge in his voice. "In Nara, for example—"

"Oh, shut up!" Marsha said. "*Can* it!"

An awkward silence ensued. Presently, Dov spoke up again, from the overstuffed armchair in the corner where he'd drawn in on himself, crossing his stocky legs beneath him, sitting lost in thought. "I think both of you are far too optimistic about culture, or I would say about our position in culture. Barthes and Benjamin were both wrong. Culture is not a pliable fabric we can brush or fold, it's not so tractable as that—and we do not sit above it, brush in hand: we are *in* it." He leaned forward, elbows on his knees, speaking with growing urgency.

"What is culture? Culture is a turbulent stream in which we are submerged, like fish. Now and again someone succeeds to swim, briefly, against the current—we call these swimmers prophets, artists—and sometimes they may even engender something new, like salmon who have fought their way upstream. But their products will mostly be swept away again, as will they themselves, and be dashed to death against rocks or against each other. A few bits of flotsam may eddy around for a while in some backwater or tide pool, say a university, then all but a very few pass out into the sea, where they vanish.

"As for gaining a viewpoint outside? To stick the head above water means, indeed, to breathe a purer, freer form of oxygen—literally freer, it is loosely bound with nitrogen, not tightly bound with hydrogen as it is below the surface. But to breathe this purer, freer air for any length of time means, simply, death to the unhappy fish who beaches up on a shoal: a death only slower and more tantalizing than the death awaiting those unfortunates who get snatched out of the stream by some deadly Fisher King. Why do you think 'The Waste Land' got so popular? Not for its bleakness, for its optimism! Eliot thinks he's the Fisher King, we want to think so too, but we're really the fish."

Vic nodded slowly, and tapped his fingers against his pursed lips. I might have replied, but I found myself thinking about a small flounder I'd caught as a boy, one summer afternoon in Maine, after it had eluded my hook for some time; how I beat its head against the dock as if it deserved to be punished; how remorseful I felt once it was dead. It was Marsha who took issue with Dov.

"I have to say, Dov," she said, hesitantly, "I think your views have been skewed by the Holocaust. Or maybe even earlier, by the collapse of your grandfather's faith that the Czar's regime would be followed by something better, by your parents' suffering under Stalin—all reinforced these days by your own disillusionment with Israel. Aren't you drawing universal conclusions from a set of worst-case scenarios?"

"Adorno did, and with good reason," I put in, hoping to take the personal edge off Marsha's remarks. But Dov shook his head.

"Adorno went too far, blaming the Enlightenment for the Holocaust, savaging his own tradition while at the same time shrinking in horror from the mass culture that would eat it up. I take your point, Marsha, but then I must change my metaphor. What all those failed revolutions tell me is that the river doesn't flow turbulently onward at all: it's frozen solid. Art's best chance, as Kafka said so well, is to be the axe that we take to our frozen hearts."

"Kafka's icy soul is a little too interior for my tastes," Marsha put in. "Too self-oriented. I'd rather take Woolf's frozen river. Do you remember the bum-boat woman in *Orlando*, frozen deep in the ice of the Thames? The king and his court go out skating, they look down at her as some kind of curiosity and then forget her. But Woolf knows we'll remember that weird image of the common woman with the noblemen skating over her head."

"Trust you to zero in on a class-and-gender set piece," Vic said, "but I think Woolf's only fitfully interested in the class angle. If there is any hope for social change, she'll usually cast it in very personal terms. The only time I recall the ice actually getting cut in that novel, or melted a bit, is when Orlando makes love outdoors with the Russian noblewoman Sasha, and the heat of their bodies begins to melt the frozen lake beneath them."

"But that's not all, either," I added. "Woolf has a whole gallery of icy scenes, and where do they all lead? It sure isn't a happy situation when the icy river begins to break up and motion is restored. What we get is the terrifying scene of the ice-floes—a whole society swept toward destruction on little rafts of ice, each peopled by an arguing couple or cluttered with a bit of cultural flotsam. She could have written that scene for Dov."

"But it's only one possible choice, and maybe an arbitrary one, to take that scene as the key to the whole story," Marsha rejoined. "It's the worst sort of mimetic self-indulgence to identify with a single character or a single scene and think it gives the author's 'message,' especially with a writer as shifty as Woolf. It bugs the hell out of me when leftist critics do it, and it's even harder to forgive in a liberal like yourself, who's supposed to make a point of seeing every side of every question. When Woolf wrote *Orlando* in '28, she was starting the deconstruction of the patriarchy she completed in *Three Guineas*, which is about as strong a cultural-political intervention as you could ask for."

"Was not that ten years later, Marsha?" Dov asked. "Now it seems to me it is you who see one moral everywhere."

"The thing that puzzles me," Marsha replied, "is how a Bible scholar like you can be so blind to political questions. Isn't the whole Bible a huge blueprint for nation-building? Aren't those prophets of yours the real pioneers of an engaged public poetry?"

"Sure, sure," Dov answered, "and they also wove the first hair shirt for the cultural critic as alienated outsider—a mantle neither Adorno nor Woolf could resist donning. But how much positive is there in their message? What hope do they hold out short of wholesale divine intervention? Sages before them, in Thebes, in Babylon, had played the constructive critic, condemning evil kings, praising virtue, standing up for the ever-popular widow and orphan; but the Hebrew prophets are the first in history who can claim the credit to hate their entire culture!"

"Come on, Dov," I said. "That's a ridiculous exaggeration."

Dov shrugged. "'My heritage has become to me like a lion in the forest,' Jeremiah says; 'my heritage is to me like a speckled bird of prey: *therefore I hate her!*' See what fine touchstones you pick up on the playground of a good school in the suburbs of Tel Aviv? Even the several writers who became that composite figure 'Isaiah' display a deep disgust with their culture, even as they elaborate their apocalyptic hopes. The prophets' hatred of culture isn't my idea anyway, it's Schneidau's point in *Sacred Discontent*. But let's not speak only of hatred. Call it a perverse kind of optimism: they really thought that maybe, just maybe, the whole culture could be transformed by God's mighty arm, root and branch, so that everyone would turn to God and forsake human ways. Show me the Egyptian sage who thought that: not Amen-em-ope, certainly not the depressive Khakheperre-sonbe. Compared to the prophets, the Egyptian sages are all fatalists. They exhort their listeners to live up to their culture's standards, to be sure, but those standards are eternally given, not to be questioned, unjust and oppressive though they may be. Of course, the prophets too have their own special fatalism: that the society *can* change its very nature but it never *will*. That's the joke on Jonah—that all Nineveh might actually put on sackcloth and ashes just because he tells them to, and no one is more astonished than Jonah when this happens. Early Jewish humor! But it never did happen, not in reality; it was just a joke after all. The truth is what God tells Jeremiah, early on: 'You shall speak all these words to them, but they will not listen to you. You shall call them, but they will not answer you.'

"The Egyptian sage's message may be more limited, but he expects to be heard and obeyed, and not only because he belongs to the ruling class himself. He speaks from that hidden place deep within his culture where the will of the gods sustains the fatal course of history. The Hebrew prophet speaks from outside his culture, from the desert, where he prays for the destruction of cities as he sweetens his locusts with wild honey."

"Aren't you extrapolating again from a period of trauma?" I asked. "Little wonder the prophets feel an edge of despair as the country begins to fall to outsiders, as they're taken off to exile in Babylon. You couldn't make the same point with the great narratives from the time of nation-building."

"Try me," Dov replied. "The Torah is a gallery of misfits, outsiders—Abraham, Joseph, Moses, strangers in a strange land, never more alien than when the land is their own. Even in Eden! Look at what the Jahwists made of the plant of immortality they found in their Mesopotamian sources, the one the serpent stole from Gilgamesh. The Jahwists copied whole tablets from that great epic when they were making their own version of primeval times, but they weren't content with the Babylonian serpent's single plant. They split it in two: the tree of life—call it culture—and the death-dealing tree of the knowledge of good and evil—call it the critical spirit, at first nomadic, then prophetic, finally scholarly in the age of Talmud and midrash."

"Is it a coincidence," Vic asked, "that your little culture history makes you, Mr. Midrash, the hero of your own tale?"

"Maybe I am—as who is not?—but I have only a modest sense of my chances as a culture hero. Clinging to the branches of the tree of knowledge, the cultural critic can look down his beak at the garish productions of the tree of life. But who pays any *attention* on the other tree? And are not the fruits of the tree of knowledge a little . . . bitter? Is there not a certain longing in the critic's mocking gaze?—But look, already I repeat the error of Benjamin and his clothes-brush. I talk as if we have some independent purchase or perch, as though we could fly back and forth at will between the two trees, or go somewhere else altogether. No! Midrash may stand for midrash, fine, but Dov is not a dove. We don't get to eat the fruit of either tree: we *are* the fruit. Wherever we happen to be, our fate is the same: we grow on our little branch; we ripen in the sun; then we fall, into the waiting jaws of Death."

Silence ensued. Midrash ceased, and sat apart, indistinct and silent, in the pose of a meditating Buddha. Nobody moved for a time, until Vic said, "All this talk of fruit. . . ." Without further ado, we all got up and went off to dinner.

I HAD made us a reservation at a quiet Vietnamese restaurant, good for relaxing and talking, though in our present mood it was unclear whether we could take advantage of the congenial atmosphere; its very congeniality, indeed, seemed almost to exacerbate the general feeling of malaise. At least we had moved beyond the confrontational mode of the previous evening, but we seemed unable to find any firm ground on which to take our conversation in a more positive direction. Everyone looked depressed, and Dov's last speech clearly still weighed on all of us. As we ordered, I tried to break the ice by purposefully deciding against ordering fish; no one smiled, and Marsha actually winced.

We ate in silence for some time, until Marsha looked up from her Buddha's Delight and addressed Dov.

"Okay, Dov," she said. "Let's talk this one through. I understand your skepticism about the utopian optimism so many of us on the left secretly or openly cherish. But maybe critics are like most people, we *need* some belief in a better future, just to get through the present. Otherwise, aren't you left with nihilism at worst, or some dogged positivism at best, you know, I'll just plug along on my little studies of these films here, hoping against hope that my students' students will some day make a better world out of all of this? Take hope as a necessary fiction, if you like. I'm not going to waste my breath trying to persuade you that some things in our culture are actually getting better, as any thinking woman, at least, in this country must know, just looking at the job opportunities we have now."

My eyebrows involuntarily rose in surprise; Marsha gave an ironic grimace in reply, acknowledging her own precarious employment situation. "Well, *some* people have job opportunities now," she went on. "And more women would, if this winner-take-all economy wasn't making things worse for three-quarters of the population of both genders. Just because things should be better than they are, it's critically important that we lay the groundwork for a better way of thinking, living, interacting. But your view is so fatalistic, Dov, what's the point of trying to do anything?"

"Often I fear that I no longer know," Dov replied. "All my emphasis on tradition comes to nothing if the tradition is so corrupted that it is no longer viable. Or was it always already this corrupt? I look at my sons, and I wonder."

"You mean they're abandoning Judaism?" I asked.

"Ari, yes, he is at university now, one semester he wants to be a computer genius, the next semester he would be a rock star. He is only drifting from one thing to the next, and never does he care for anything more than two years old. But okay, this is adolescence, what can one expect? His brother Ben is the one who worries me more. He has suddenly become almost a fanatic. He gets up at five in the morning to study Talmud, he neglects his classes even though he has his entrance examinations for university in the fall. Well, it is his choice, but he argues constantly with me about every-thing I've ever written on the Bible—I should take the whole Torah liter-ally! He condescends to me on the rare occasions he can spare a few minutes from his studies to come to the telephone. Even his mother, who is Ortho-dox and proud of his commitment, says he is withdrawn, hard to talk to. His only social life consists of arguing Sabbath-law interpretations with three or four equally self-righteous young exegetes. This is my son? *This* is my tradition?"

The thought crossed my mind that his sons' divergent adolescent diffi-culties might have less to do with tradition than with Dov's own shortcom-ings as a long-distance father—an increasingly peripatetic one at that, and now with a two-year-old daughter by his new American wife. I dismissed this explanation immediately as unkind, and belied in any case by Dov's palpable distress.

"Of course," Dov continued, "I blame myself first and foremost. What kind of father have I been? Even when I was still living in the household, was I not withdrawn into my books much as Ben is now? Was I not always making up for lost time as I drifted, like Ari, from one field of study into another? Strange justice, to punish me for my derelictions by visiting my own personality upon my children! And then, too, the boys' problems have been redoubled by my migrant life these past dozen years, to say nothing of the sudden appearance of their new American semi-sibling. . . ."

"I admire your self-awareness," I commented. "It must be painful per-sonally, but at least it means you don't need to be so hard on your cultural traditions."

"Why the hell not?" Dov asked in annoyance. "The whole point of a tradition should be to serve as a check on our human failings, to mitigate the griefs that families and other natural disasters regularly bring upon us. My boys should be glad they have not had a *worse* father—many do. So why has our tradition not helped them to put up with me better?"

Marsha gave a soft snort of exasperation. "A person would have to be a saint to live with you, Dov," she said, "and you guys don't even *have* saints."

"I for my part can live without the Catholic one-upmanship," Dov testily replied, "especially from someone who prides herself on her own apostasy."

"Come on, Dov," Marsha said; "I was just trying to lighten things up. But I think you're asking too much from your tradition anyway. Or maybe too little, if you're just using it as some kind of avoidance mechanism. Suppose the whole Judaeo-Christian thing has had its day—let's *let* it *go*. We don't need some hopeless holding action, we need to invent new ways to orient ourselves toward the world. You should really read Haraway, she's completely beyond the false dichotomy of 'human' versus 'animal,' 'culture' versus 'nature.' She might help you take seriously your own comparison of people to fish—we have to see cultural processes in the broader context of natural process."

"Sure, sure," Dov said, as he pushed away his half-empty plate of caramel beef. "All my problems will be solved if I only read the manifestos of the latest trendy in-group! My oneness with bugs!"

"Good grief!" Marsha exclaimed. "You've as much as admitted you're stuck in a rut with your head up your ass, and you just want to sit there enjoying the *view*? Ecocriticism's new, still finding its feet, but it offers a broad vision of life and our place in nature. It could help you out of the bind you're in now, caught inside a self-enclosed definition of culture that only mirrors your own obnoxious little self-regarding angst-ridden egomaniacal crypto-smugness!"

Engaged in filling his pipe, Dov barely acknowledged Marsha's comments; he merely cast a sharp glance at her, whether cryptically or crypto-smugly I couldn't decide, as he slowly put pinches of tobacco into the bowl of his pipe. Vic now spoke up.

"Life?" he asked, an edge in his voice. "Our place in nature? Look here, Marsha dear, and I will show you what life is." He drew his date book from an inside pocket of his blazer, opened it to the day's page, and pointed to the final entry: "Dinner, whole sick crew. *Saigon Lagoon*."

"Now look." He took out his Mont Blanc fountain pen and underlined the phrase. "Watch as I make this line under our dinner date here, how the ink catches the light for a few seconds, then fades. Until it dries, that is life:

wet, easily smudged, shining briefly. When it dries, it dies, but it also achieves a kind of, shall we say, contingent permanence: that is art, and that is the best we have. Give up the New-Agey cosmic harmony of all life! Culture is a *refuge* from life in nature, not a part of it, and art's purpose finally is not to reconcile ourselves to life but to death. Death, after all, is the dominant term. You wish Dov to move beyond his self-regarding anthropocentrism? Very well: but let us also move beyond the larger vanity of *zoo*centrism. Imagine looking down at the world from a cosmos made of empty space dotted with dark matter, mostly frozen gasses with a few clumps of icy rock. Then every few million light years a glowing astral furnace floats by, its very heat rendering it even more inhospitable to life than the *bit*terly cold surfaces of the most isolated comets."

"But why should art have anything to do with such desolation?" I asked.

"Desolation is in the eye of the beholder," Vic replied. "Suppose the goal of art is not creature comfort but beauty, simply beauty. Lifeless the universe may essentially be, yet its beauty is undeniable, as we regard the spinning dance of planets and whole galaxies. On earth itself, we can reconstruct the majestic ebb and flow of magma and tectonic plates over the eons. On a microcosmic scale, we can even trace the randomly ordered oscillations of protons and electrons in every atom of rock. Why should art not aspire to this intricate, impersonal harmony, rather than merely mirror the confused struggle of conflict and decay that we call 'life'? If the God who has made this universe looks down at our blue-green earth, what does he, she, or it see? Perhaps all our animate life is nothing more than the mold on the rind of an orange, an unwanted by-product that the farmer polishes off at harvest-time. Let us celebrate the whole earth, as Marsha proposes. Yet let us do so in the awareness that the earth, in all its massive sublimity, is *life*less from its molten core to its outer crust, and this life of ours may be no more than a momentary extrusion—late-appearing, soon evanescing, utterly beside the point."

Vic put the cap on his pen and replaced it in his jacket pocket along with his date book. Dov lit his pipe. Marsha used her chopsticks to nudge a few last grains of rice around her plate. As she did so, I tried to come to grips with the depressing turn the conversation had taken. I would have been hard put to say which I found more disturbing—Dov's sense of futility, Vic's vision of universal lifelessness, or the sheer eloquence with which they both expressed themselves. Whenever I got that depressed myself, the best I could do was think about the Carter administration, and none too eloquently at that. Nor did my discomfort end there. I was, after all, serving in some sense as the host for this gathering; and no host can feel truly at ease when his guests are falling one by one into seemingly suicidal despair.

I decided to press Dov on his fatalism. "Come on, Dov," I said. "You have to believe in some kind of progress, however ironic. After all, Hegel's your life!"

"Hegel is my life?" Dov replied morosely. "I have Hegel instead of a life! Or I have so many lives I have none at all: one family in Israel, another in California, and a girlfriend in Geneva"—this was news to me; I glanced at Marsha, who was glancing at Vic—"is this any way to live? Maybe I am on the cutting edge of some poststructuralist collapsing of categories: I am breaking down the difference between marriage and divorce. Professionally as well, I have achieved fame for my work on the hermeneutics of meaninglessness, and this research has gained me not one but two prestigious chairs at once. Yet what have I achieved by my constant commuting across nine time zones? I have brought on myself a collapse of the distinction between night and day, between tenure and joblessness—between freedom and entrapment on the very airplanes that are the agents of escape— between thought itself and a coma: I read almost nothing now but airline magazines!"

Dave Barry's revenge, I thought to myself with a flash of satisfaction; then shame came over me as I realized that I was still smarting from Dov's dismissal of my paper at our first meeting, four years earlier. Shame, but not remorse. Was there no way I could express my concern for Dov's very real problems and also wring the pompous little bastard's thick neck? Realizing what I was thinking, I was surprised by the violence of my reaction. I am rarely, except in faculty meetings, overcome with homicidal impulses; yet here, talking quietly with my friends at the end of a good dinner, I could not manage to muster any real sympathy with Dov—or with Mr. Universe, as I found myself thinking of Vic, who was drumming his fingers on the table, clearly hoping the check would arrive soon and release him from our company.

It was Marsha who rose to the occasion. "Look, guys," she said. "I'm not a licensed radio therapist or anything, but I think you might feel a little better about criticism's place in the cosmos if you'd take a little initiative in your own lives. Here's my unasked-for two bits of advice, and I won't even charge you the two bits: Dov, either start making the most of your two jobs or give me one of them, whichever, but the main thing—whatever you do about your love life—is, you should get your boys to come spend the summer with you in California. It may go well or it may go badly, at least you'll be in there trying, and I think they'll appreciate that. Vic, dear, we've been in Chicago three or four days now, and I haven't heard you've been to the hospital yet; isn't it about time? And David, stop looking so goddam *glum*! So you forgot your session today and nobody missed you. . . ." (Was that the impression I'd given her? Was that the *correct* impression for her to have gotten?) "The thing is, you're in a typical post-book slump, you should stop obsessing about the reviews, just get your act together to start a new project, for Christ's sake!"

Neither Dov nor Vic had registered any reaction at Marsha's comments to them, but they immediately warmed to the idea of telling me what to do next.

"Something on Gilbert and Sullivan, perhaps," Vic suggested. "I think you might have an affinity for that sort of light satire." This sounded a little insulting, and I was about to reply sharply, when Dov spoke up.

"I myself have written on the splitting of the ego in several of their operettas," he said. "Their tone is always light, to be sure, but the substance is there. Pooh-Bah is of course the most elaborate case, though my personal favorite is the King of Utopia, who rules his country by day and writes the opposition newspaper by night: 'A bad king but a good subject,' he calls himself. All in all, I believe that Gilbert helped to pave the way for Freud, and certainly for the warm English response to Freud. I have just completed a monograph on the reception of Freud in the Middle East—*Totem and Tabouleh*, I am calling it. There I discuss the English connection for the introduction of Freud in Egypt and Palestine. In my first chapter—"

"You may have something there about Gilbert," Vic interrupted. "I too have been drawn to G&S, though I would link them sooner to Wilde than to Freud. Do you know Sullivan's early operetta, *Cox and Box*—please, don't drag Freud back in to interpret those names—in which two roommates share a single bed, one working at night and sleeping by day, the other vice versa? My interest in the operettas has always been more in the music than in the lyrics; I have thought a good deal about Sullivan's witty self-revisions during the years of his developing collaboration with Gilbert. Finding that he never could escape from Mendelssohn's influence, he trumped his own limitations by perfecting a form of *self*-plagiarism. If you want models of collaborative work, David, you might do well to look there. On his own, Sullivan could rarely float freely on the heights of frivolity. All too often, he plodded onward with his Christian Soldiers along the broad highway of High Seriousness. I believe it was the influence of Gilbert's personality that brought Sullivan, in spite of himself, to do his best work. I've been meaning to write this up for some time now."

Taking Vic's collaborative clue, and recalling Marsha's early essay on *Pinafore*, I proposed that we might actually do a book of essays together. "It could be academically serious and also reach out to a broader audience," I remarked; "there's quite a grass-roots G&S public all around the country. My father used to direct the operettas in his parishes, as his father did before him. My great-grandfather Frank and his brother Walter, in fact—"

"I doubt that any publishers would be very interested in your little family history, David," Vic interrupted, rather gratuitously. "They will want to know who would really buy the book. Your contribution would probably be something literary-historical. My theme would mostly interest musicologists, Dov's article would be much more theoretical, and Marsha's rather brilliant old essay is almost a period piece; it would hardly do now."

"Maybe if my life settles down a bit I could do something new," Marsha said. "Though it's hard to make any commitments at this point."

"Moreover, David," Dov said, "from your book I think you would want more than some disconnected jeux d'esprit. It would take a concerted effort to make something coherent. This would remove Vic's objection. But really for the four of us to write a book together, disparate as we all are in personality and approach. . . ." His voice trailed skeptically off.

"Let's first see if anything ever comes of Damrosch's old idea of writing up our conference discussions," Vic interjected. "I can't say that our track record to date is any too inspiring, as we approach the end of another of our inconclusive deliberations."

This was pretty discouraging. I'd gone to a good deal of effort to make these meetings happen, and I did have a ream of notes by now, shoved into several folders back home; I had made some scattered jottings during the current conference as well. Yet it was evident that the real work of shaping an eventual written product would fall heavily on my shoulders—we clearly weren't yet at a point of readiness for fully collaborative work. Would we ever be? In principle, I could envision a range of projects that we could tackle, multifaceted topics too often treated in a limited fashion from one or another single perspective. Unlike Dov, apparently, I had become increasingly confident that the diversity of our perspectives was a real strength, and on the other hand the unexpected conjunction of our interests in Gilbert and Sullivan suggested that we did actually have more in common than we ourselves might expect.

Dov's comment about our personalities bothered me more, and this doubt was underscored by Vic's palpable restlessness—he seemed ready to bolt from Chicago on the next plane to Tahiti. Even Marsha could hardly be encouraged by our companions' mutual tendency to lecture her about the naivety of any positive outlook on the social value of criticism. If we couldn't finally connect at a basic level of sympathetic mutual interest, let alone understanding, it was hard to feel that we could ever build working relationships strong enough to hold our deep disagreements in a state of productive tension. Looking at the crumpled napkin before me, I decided that we'd all had enough.

"Should we just stop meeting?" I asked.

This suggestion was greeted with a shocked silence. Marsha looked stricken; Dov looked a little embarrassed; Vic looked annoyed.

"Just hold on, now," Marsha said. "I've got enough instability in my life without losing the only free-floating group I can count on seeing from time to time, with no special pressures or set agendas. You know, I love Tom dearly—except when he's with his middle brother, Sterno, we call him that because he's in the camping supply business, big bucks, he's much more commercially minded than either Tom or their big brother Eliot, where was I? Yes, but, you know, Tom and I have to interact so much about daily life, and it's not like you can have really scholarly conversations about *tomatoes*. Of course, Cassie's as wonderful as she could be, but still she's only five and a half. I don't really have regular colleagues these days, either, most full-time faculty treat adjuncts in their midst kind of like ectoplasm—they just sort of look through you. Then there's the old Bennington crowd, but it's a little funereal getting together with them, even when we aren't strategizing about our lawsuit against the trustees. So I've got to say I'd rather we met a little more often, not less."

"For my part," Dov said, "I feel that I owe all of you an apology for imposing my self-inflicted problems on you, and I fear that I have been less attentive to the rest of you than Marsha kindly supposes. I shall try to do better."

"I'm not quite ready for a little love-fest here," Vic said, "but I certainly don't want you to wimp out on us now, Damrosch. Buck up, man! Don't forget, you're the duly elected Navigator of the Aquatic Activities Caucus: where are you taking us next?"

"I'm not really—" I began, but, as often, Vic was already answering his own question.

"But *please*, David, not Indiana again! Why can't you persuade the comparatists to try something a little more imaginative? Europe? But we have to consider costs for the graduate students. The problem with the Caribbean is that the best resorts on the islands are too exclusive for a large group. The rest are the worst sort of tourist trap. Now Mexico, though . . . . Acapulco? No, overbuilt. Manzanilla? Already passé. Ah, but Puerto Vallarta:

you could probably get the ACLA to think of going there. True, it would be a lot of work for you, twisting arms and making all the plans, but that's what you're so good at. Lovely colonial town, some surprisingly good restaurants; dramatic bay ringed with mountains; fabulous parasailing, good air connections for our far-flung colleagues, *Night of the Iguana* connection for Marsha: yes, I think that's the ticket, don't you?"

"Well. . . ." I began.

"Good, that's settled," Vic went on. "And here's our check, don't be silly, I owe it to Marsha for the psychological counseling alone, not to mention to Dov for the psychopathology. And as for David—well, we are eternally in his debt, speaking prospectively, for Puerto Vallarta, are we not? Farewell, all: see you at the swim-up palapa bar!"

4 PUERTO VALLARTA

Critical Confessions

I have wanted to speak to you of my desire to be finished with, and to somehow terminate, a series of researches that have been our concern for some four or five years now. . . . They are in the final analysis just fragments, and it is up to you or me to see what we can make of them. For my part, it has struck me that I might have seemed a bit like a whale that leaps to the surface of the water, disturbing it momentarily with a tiny jet of spray, and lets it be believed, or pretends to believe, or himself does in fact believe, that down in the depths where no one sees him anymore, where he is no longer witnessed or controlled by anyone, he follows a more profound, coherent and reasoned trajectory. Well, anyway, that was more or less how I at least conceived the situation; it could be that you perceived it differently.

> Michel Foucault, lecture at the Collège de France, 7 January 1976

Who can say how many pseudostylic shamiana, how few or many of the most venerated public impostures, how very many piously forged palimpsests slipped in the first place by this morbid process from his pelagiarist pen? . . . and now, forsooth, a nogger among the blankards of this dastard century, you have become of twosome twiminds . . . anarch, egoarch, hiresiarch, you have reared your disunited kingdom on the vacuum of your own most intensely doubtful soul.

> James Joyce, *Finnegans Wake* 1.7

UNTIL IT TURNED into a nightmare, arranging to hold a convention in Mexico proved to be surprisingly easy. It helped considerably that the upcoming Comparative Literature Association meeting in March was in fact scheduled to take place in Indiana, for the second time in four years—not by any plan, but simply because our rather feckless organization would meet wherever someone happened to be willing to have us. Notre Dame was of course a very different locale from Indiana University, as the giant mosaic of Jesus blessing the football field could attest, but even so I'd heard a number of people express a wish to try something different in kind. The time was certainly right to explore Vic's idea. I was then on the ACLA board, and knew that no location had yet been arranged for the following year, 1997. Eugene Eoyang, now the group's president, was enthusiastic at the suggestion of Mexico, possibly because he himself had been teaching at Indiana for twenty years or more.

I made inquiries in the week following the Chicago MLA, and managed to hook up with Tuscawilla Travel, a Florida agency run by an academic turned conference-travel agent. We soon had draft contracts from three likely possibilities. Eoyang and his wife generously agreed to spend a February weekend inspecting the sites, and returned with a strong endorsement of Puerto Vallarta—"determinedly cobblestoned," as Eugene put it. We settled on a luxury hotel that billed itself as "the crown of the coastline," or words to that effect, and our board gratefully approved the idea at our meeting in South Bend. The best of all possible worlds, we thought: a place just the size for our group of three hundred; elegant accommodations made affordable by a good exchange rate; and a lavish brochure that stressed the ecological sensitivity with which the hotel's designers had sited and built the hotel and its three swimming pools, several tennis courts, restaurant, bar, and disco. The whole complex even looked out on the beautiful bay featured in *The Night of the Iguana*, and more recently, as my graduate students informed me, given renewed fame as the backdrop for *The Love Boat*.

Some of our membership thought that the whole idea seemed somehow unserious, but I had been to several of my wife's legal conventions in places like Hawaii and the Virgin Islands, and they'd always seemed to get as much work done as we ever did in New Jersey or Indiana. Were literary scholars secretly uncomfortable at being paid to work on books that give such pleasure, and was it therefore important to meet in as mundane a location as possible, lest we actually enjoy our work? How else to account for the MLA's penchant for disrupting everyone's holiday season in order to meet at the end of December in one snowbound northern city after another?

Less interested than Vic in water sports, in fact queasy at the very idea of parasailing, I liked Puerto Vallarta for pragmatic reasons. I suspected that we would get more people for our meeting if we chose a location to which people might actually want to come; we did, in fact, receive a record number of abstracts in response to our call for papers, and we had a minimal drop-out rate from the people we accepted. Even so, I worried that the setting would be too distracting once people arrived. I stewed over this for some time, and finally called Vic to express my concern.

"Have no fear!" he replied. "Attendance at sessions will surely be high. Consider, dear boy: how much *fun* can academics stand to have? I use the word 'fun' advisedly, to suggest something different from high-toned cultural enrichment. Put professors in a major city, replete with museums, plays, and second-hand bookstores, and you may never see them again after their own session is over. But how many of our colleagues can really bear a beach for more than half an hour a day? They are far too compulsive just to lie there; they have to bring a book. And of course nothing resembling 'beach reading,' heaven forbid! Probably a late Henry James novel or some sparkling little potpourri of essays on Kafka. They'll be back indoors within the hour, looking for a session to attend."

Only partly reassured by this, I determined to structure the conference in such a way as to engender some real work, while also clustering the work time in the first half of the day. Hoping to avoid the common convention pathology of disconnected drifting from session to session, I arranged for all the papers to be grouped in twelve-person seminars, with four papers to be presented each morning for the three mornings of the conference. Then we'd have a plenary session or two, and turn people free by early afternoon. The seminar structure would have the further advantage that everyone attending the conference could be a presenter. Marsha praised this plan for breaking down the invidious distinction between star performer and plebeian attender; pleased at her approval, I didn't mention that my main idea had been to enable more people to have their deans pay for the trip. I worked with several colleagues through the fall of 1996 to select and group the papers, and by January of 1997 we were able to send out a very satisfactory program. This was later than I'd intended—I'd been talked into chairing my department, which would have been a heavy time commitment even in a cordial and unified department—but at last the conference was finally set. I breathed a sigh of relief, and looked forward to a few weeks of relative calm before the conference itself.

Then came the nightmare. "The Crown of the Coastline"—I prefer not to recall their actual name—sent me a brief fax expressing their regret that they had just sold half our rooms to another convention. They would, however, find comparable accommodations elsewhere for our displaced persons and would bus them back for the sessions. Knowing that the hotel occupied an isolated beach miles away from the city, I was horrified at the disruption that our communal experience would suffer, and I was hardly confident that the "comparable" accommodations would compare favorably to the rooms that were being taken from us. I insisted that our contract should be honored, a response which seemed to hurt the hotel people's feelings: didn't I understand that they were doing their best to help us out in this difficult situation? They indicated that a government agency had actually *ordered* them to resell the rooms, and so their hands were tied.

Tuscawilla Travel swung into action, and soon letters were being faxed in several directions. We learned that the conflict had arisen when an association of travel agents had asked for the space; the prospect of future business seemed to be more the issue than governmental intervention. I began to see the advantage of meeting in locations no one else would want to go to. We engaged a lawyer, and after several nail-biting weeks, we finally succeeded in getting the hotel to relinquish our entire group and forward our deposit on to the Sheraton, the only hotel in town that happened still to have enough rooms for all our people. Disaster had been averted, but we would be in a place we hadn't seen; I crossed my fingers and hoped for the best.

I hoped as well that things might be improving for my friends. I knew that at least Marsha's situation had taken a notable turn for the better. In the spring of 1996, I had run into an acquaintance of mine, Peter Sellers— not the director of much the same name, and of course not the deceased actor, but a mathematician at the University of Pennsylvania. He had originally contacted me after I had published an article he liked on P. G. Wodehouse; a true devotee, Sellers had the distinction of owning two complete sets of Wodehouse's ninety-eight novels. He kept one set at home in Philadelphia, the other at his summer place on Mount Desert Island in Maine, where he had become involved with the College of the Atlantic—a young, innovative college that was making its mark by emphasizing marine biology and coastal studies. I ran into Peter at the Columbia faculty club, where he was lunching with a chemist with whom he regularly wrote papers—the sort of collaboration that humanists find so fraught but that seems to be natural in the natural sciences. He mentioned that he was about to fly up to Bar Harbor for a trustees' meeting at the College of the Atlantic. Did I know anyone in literature, he asked in passing, whose interests could dovetail with the college's ecological mission? They'd had a search under way for some time, but their favorite candidates had both ended up accepting offers from larger schools in less isolated locations.

What I'd seen of Marsha's recent work made for an obvious match, particularly given her own rural preferences. Sellers followed up on my recommendation the next day, Marsha visited the campus the next week, and she had the job sewn up before her visit ended. She and her family moved to Mount Desert in the summer, and she sent me happy e-mails during the fall and winter. ("We even found a place to rent on Echo Lake, that's really its name," she wrote. "Of course I'm planting narcissus all along the shore. We got Cassie her first camera, too, and she's taking amazing pictures of reflections. And the COA kids are a trip to teach, even if they do come to class smelling like kelp.") I was looking forward to a firsthand report in Puerto Vallarta.

Neither Dov nor Vic had given me much in the way of personal news since Chicago, but at least they were prompt in responding to e-mails and active in helping to refine the plan for our work together in Puerto Vallarta. After floating various ideas, we settled on confessional criticism as the topic for our seminar. Memoirs had become the darlings of the best-seller lists and of book reviews, and even in academia scholars were starting to speak

openly about their lives—their backgrounds, their prejudices and predispo-
sitions, even their youthful sexual experiences, if any—as a way of locating
their critical perspectives and orienting their readers. How to sort out the
most useful tendencies in work that could readily fall into triviality, anecdotalism, narcissistic self-display?

We divided up our work. Dov decided to take a historical view, looking
at self-revelation and concealment in (puzzlingly, I thought) Matthew Arnold. I agreed to bring the discussion forward by taking up the work of a
major twentieth-century critic, Frank Kermode, who had just published a
highly regarded memoir. Marsha proposed to look at recent feminist confessional criticism, and Vic surprised me by renouncing his usual stylistic
approach and deciding to talk about AIDS literature and its criticism. I
succeeded in finding a number of other proposals that seemed likely to work
well with ours, including submissions from our friends Susan Suleiman and
Hymit Bathtöi, and our seminar was set.

I was curious, and a little apprehensive, to see how it would unfold. While
I hadn't mentioned this to the others, my own motivation for endorsing the
topic had been my continuing uneasiness about the personal disparities
among the four of us. In Chicago our recurring incompatibilities had nearly
led our group to collapse, and I felt that we needed to work through the
whole issue of personality if we were ever to operate effectively together.
Perhaps I should have been chastened by our difficulties in coming to
agreement in our previous discussions on culture and cultural studies, but
those very difficulties gave new urgency to the question of personality. It
was time for a decisive move forward, if we were ever to go beyond a pattern
of sporadic conversations with no concrete results. Puerto Vallarta would
be a new beginning—or a last hurrah.

THE trip down was uneventful, though all the way from Texas the
airplane flew through thick and often turbulent clouds. Someone who combined Dov's analytical bent with my fears might have enjoyed the interesting mix of claustrophobia and acrophobia I experienced. The clouds began
to break only as we approached Puerto Vallarta, sporadically revealing

jagged mountaintops that appeared and vanished nearer and nearer to the windows. Finally, the plane banked sharply between two peaks—all the fun of parasailing, I thought grimly—and landed. My pulse had returned to normal well before I arrived at the Sheraton, where I was greeted by Irasema Campos, the hotel's resolutely competent conference coordinator. She would be ubiquitous during the following days, walkie-talkie in hand. She ordered me to relax and leave everything to her, which I did.

The Sheraton turned out to be a lucky find, opulent by comparison with the dormitory-style accommodations to which we were usually treated by our typical university hosts. As the day went on, I saw various knots of comparatists wandering around, looks of guilty pleasure on their faces. The Sheraton's only problem was that it didn't have as many conference rooms as we needed for our many seminars, and some groups had to use patios and other odd corners. Still—apart from a few irate people who had never gotten word of the change of venue and had trekked down to the Crown of the Coastline by mistake—people seemed prepared to make do with some disruptions to normal academic routine.

Given my high hopes for this meeting, the first evening was a little anticlimactic. Not happening upon any of my usual conference companions, I ended up going out to dinner with one of those vague, ad hoc groupings of people with nothing else to do and no one else to do it with. Everyone was in that slightly manic start-of-conference phase: wanting to relax but still keyed up after the struggle to break free from campus and get to the airport; wanting to feel universally sociable, but a little regretful not to have hooked up yet with some old friends—or with someone important who would be a pleasure to get to know, or seem to know, in the mode of temporary equality that conferences foster, as long as the important people haven't yet managed to hook up and head off with still more important people.

Thrown together as we were, we made the mistake of following the concierge's advice to go to a nearby restaurant, for which he gave us discount tickets for a free drink—never a good sign, but we were drawn by our own inertia and the lure of "comida típica méxicana." In a way it was, down to the canned peas in the salad, but the tortillas were soggy, the beer was lukewarm, and the salsa was watered down to the presumed taste of the tourists who filled the place. At least the music was too loud to allow any talking; we'd had enough forced heartiness just on the walk to the restaurant.

My room, however, was large and quiet when I got back to it, high above the beach and with a plate glass window giving a panoramic view of the Pacific. As I looked out, a large pelican swooped by just at eye level. Or was it an albatross? Time would tell, I decided, and went to bed.

I saw Marsha and Vic at the breakfast buffet the next morning. They had arrived a day before me, and had spent the whole previous day sailing, with pauses to snorkel through coral reefs.

"On our return, we ended up at the most charming little restaurant over-looking the Catedral," Vic added, "Mexican nouvelle cuisine, not a contra-diction in terms at all—the chef was *ut*terly brilliant, a master of subtle combinations of exotic spices. And the wine list: superb. What's the matter, David?"

I decided to ask how we should proceed in our seminar. I had been awakened that morning by a gravelly call from Dov. He had arrived the previous night, feverish and with a bad sore throat, made worse by the stale air on the plane. He had been slated to go first, but hoped that someone could take his place, so now I sounded out the others.

"I wouldn't have minded leading off," I said apologetically, "but I still need an hour to finish my presentation."

"And I need an hour to *start* mine," Vic put in brightly.

"Okay, guys, I'm on," Marsha said. "Of course I'm sorry about Dov's throat, but it's kind of nice if we don't start by genuflecting to *Matthew Arnold* as some grand progenitor. The Best that Has Been Thought and Said, for Christ's sake! Give me a break!"

On the whole, I was just as glad that Dov hadn't come down to breakfast.

Our group gradually assembled at our patio location—fortunately, at this early hour no one was yet using the nearby volleyball net—and Marsha led off our session with a paper she had titled "Professors as Confessors: The Prose and the Cons."

"It's a great time to be miserable," she began. "Or better, to have had a miserable childhood, an oppressive adolescence, and a dysfunctional adulthood. You used to have to pay a therapist to hear about all this stuff; now, people will pay you to read all about it. And academics can jump right on in. We can shelve that half-written monograph on Joyce and delve into ourselves, maybe even interest a general public with the enticing tactics of self-display. It's American as Whitman's "Song of Myself." What's more, women have an equal share of the stage for the first time in dog's years. As a matter of fact, the whole emphasis on the personal these days comes out of the consciousness-raising sessions of late-sixties feminism, working in synergy with the civil rights movement's recovery of the older testimonials by African-American women and men alike from the days of the struggle against slavery.

"For academics, one of the pros of this form is that we *are* pros, as writers and analysts. So many memoirists are really amateurs: we have the writerly skills and the intellectual resources to capitalize on our investment in our own lives. I want to celebrate this new openness, but I also want to look carefully at its consequences. My title alludes to the pros of the personal voice but also the cons, one of which is that any self-recording is bound to *be* a con game of a sort. I want to see how we can deal productively with this problem. If we can't, we might as well retreat into the safer pseudo-objectivity of faceless commentary that literary criticism has usually taken as its special little bailiwick.

"I was put in mind of the con game aspect by a sharp article by Linda Kauffman called 'The Long Goodbye: Against Personal Testimony, or An Infant Grifter Grows Up.' In that essay she compares memoirs to the shady sales pitches she used to help put across as a child, going door to door with her traveling-salesman dad. Having allowed that 'our intellectual work as feminists is clearly related to our personal histories,' Kauffman goes on to ask: 'So what's my beef?' She answers her own question—as memoirists always get to do, by the way—by warning that too often the personal approach is like a grifter's spiel, putting something over on people who have no way of judging the truth of the matter. As Kauffman nicely puts it, 'My checkered past is too easy to transform into a Nixonian Checkers speech of bathos. By insisting on the authority of my personal experience, I effectively muzzle dissent and muffle your investigation into my motives.'"

Marsha paused and thought for a few seconds, then smiled. "And you see what her own language does here? She's using her metaphors to give us a sub rosa sales pitch *against* the memoirists' manipulations: memoir readers are muzzled, like Checkers himself, and we're muffled to boot, like the ever-loyal Pat in her 'Republican cloth coat.' Kind of interesting—maybe a seemingly straight-ahead analysis style can close the sale just as smoothly as a sob story can? Let's agree with Kauffman that subjectivity's no guarantee of authenticity, but it's not like the 'objective' mode's a piece of cake either. Either way, after deconstruction we're on to our own games more than we were, and we academics may be able to negotiate the treacherous shoals of falsehood and self-deception better than less critically aware memoirists may be.

"But falsehood isn't Kauffman's only gripe. She also argues that feminist testimony is mostly a matter of preaching to the choir, retelling versions of the same conversion narrative to an audience of fellow converts. Her essay is a kind of challenge to the book in which it appears—a whole volume of feminist testimonials edited by Gayle Greene and Coppélia Kahn, called *Changing Subjects: The Making of Feminist Literary Criticism*, recently out from Routledge. This volume is filled with essays by fifty-something feminists, many of whom trace similar trajectories through sixties New Left politics, the first failed marriage, and the conversion to feminism. As Kauffman asks, 'Are "we" feminist scholars solipsistically talking only to ourselves?'

"In one sense, that's just the point: to build sisterly solidarity through a fund of common experiences. As Elizabeth Ermarth says in her essay in the same volume, the great revelation of those early consciousness-raising groups was that *she wasn't alone*: 'We had infinite variations to tell but it was always the same story. What a relief, what a mutually enabling moment it was.' In her important book *Beyond Feminist Aesthetics*, Rita Felski sees this as a fundamental difference between men's and women's autobiography. In contrast to the unique story of the classic Great Man, she says, feminist memoir builds on 'the feminist recognition that it is the representative aspects of the author's experience rather than her unique individuality which are important.'

"For Felski, in fact," Marsha went on, "the deceptions of individuality that bug Kauffman mean that the best memoirs shouldn't really be individual at all. Instead, they're sort of sociology writ small, a node or meeting-point for readers to negotiate their own experience. Felski is dead set against bourgeois individualism altogether—the sort that men's autobiographies bank on. 'The current fascination with intimacy and self-discovery,' she says, 'engenders an ever more frantic pursuit of a kernel of authentic self which continually eludes one's grasp.' For Felski, the assertion of individual subject positions is just a useful phase that members of an oppressed group can pass through as they find their way into writing."

Marsha glanced over her shoulder; an impromptu volleyball game was forming at the net thirty feet away. She returned to her talk.

"All too often, Felski's right that memoirs tend to heighten individuality and mute any solidarity. Certainly this is true for a book like Frank Mc-Court's *Angela's Ashes*, now in its sixth straight month on top of the best-seller lists in the U.S. Its boy hero makes his way up and out of Ireland, en route to a fresh start in America, and he does this all on his own. And not just on his own: he has to *reject* the evil influences of politics and religion, which join forces to oppress the Limerick poor, working hand in glove to keep people in their places—frozen in mystical piety or in impotent nostalgia for the days of the struggle for independence. All we see is the hard-heartedness of the Saint Vincent de Paul Society, making Frank's poor mom wait in the cold for her pittance, just as the Irish political club turns away his dad as an alcoholic good-for-nothing, not worth their coppers.

"But is McCourt really being fair to either group? In a situation of grinding poverty, with Ireland not yet able to reap the benefits of its independence thanks to the worldwide crisis of capitalism called the Depression, church groups like the Saint Vincent de Paul Society were doing their level best to provide the safety net that the government couldn't or wouldn't give. And they and the old Fenians alike mixed moralism and realism in trying to keep their scarce resources from being pissed away by Frank's drunken dad. Between them, the Fenians and the Church were the only real forces both for solidarity *and* for moral transformation going in Limerick. McCourt would have none of it, and in telling his tale he mirrors his dad's stubbornness, rejecting any group whose price of admission would involve living up to some collective norms and values. Little wonder he'd rather make it in an America where he could find himself—or fantasize himself— free of all attachments, all commitments."

Marsha smoothed her papers, which were being ruffled by a gust of wind, and continued.

"Okay," she said, "we can see the dangers here, and—in her third beef with most women's memoirs—Kauffman has good reasons for wanting feminists to give up the whole novelistic 'Ms. Horatio Alger' plot, as she calls it: the deceptive coherence of a triumphant march from fifties repres- sion to sixties liberation, institutional infiltration in the seventies, and ten- ure in the eighties. The question is whether autobiographical criticism can find a viable alternative to this all too cozy plot.

"David Simpson's dubious. In his new book *The Academic Postmodern and the Rule of Literature: A Report on Half-Knowledge*, he has a field day with what he calls 'the virtual stampede into autobiography on the part of literary critics.' Simpson argues that 'the gesture of making present, of bringing to life, tends to function . . . as an alternative to methodological doubt, and as a celebration of living without doubt.' He tells us later on that 'the now monotonous reiteration of who one is and where one is coming from is accompanied by an almost audible sigh of relief, as if one is thereby exoner- ated from responsibility or culpability.'

"As if this weren't bad enough, this kind of self-justification is just the tip of the autobiographical iceberg. Simpson sees this new wave of personal criticism as part of a larger problem, a turning away from real attention to broad historical patterns and forces. Even 'new historicists' like Steve

Greenblatt, he says, have substituted anecdotes and reports of conversations for genuine historical analysis. This is a serious issue, especially for those of us who are involved in collaborative work. Is there any way a conference like this one, for example, can yield something more than the separate little papers we all wrote before coming here—or *while* coming here? Wouldn't we really learn more if we just stayed home and spent even a couple of hours in the library—let alone several whole days? Shouldn't we give up the charade of communication and just go join that volleyball game over there?"

I looked around the table. Everyone seemed uncomfortable, probably because several of our group had, in fact, been looking rather longingly at the enviably tanned and minimally clad volleyball players not far away. Despite Dov's flu, on the other hand, he was the only person to have come to the patio wearing a necktie. He was visibly perspiring, and it was clear that he would have preferred to be curled up in bed with some back issues of the *International Journal of Phenomenology.*

"The people I've been quoting are all pretty down on confessional criticism," Marsha went on. "But they don't seem to agree on the nature of the underlying problem. In fact, they have two quite opposite views: so we have an impasse wrapped in a contradiction."

This caught Dov's attention; he loosened his tie and leaned forward, scratching his beard thoughtfully.

"For Simpson," Marsha continued, "the problem is what he announces by his title: 'the academic postmodern' has given up on coherence and teleology alike, so it has to content itself with 'half-knowledge.' The personal becomes the pathology of least resistance"—Vic smiled at this—"and by resistance I mean political resistance to the status quo. Atomized, ironic anecdotes replace any common ground for progressive action. But if Simpson sees too much postmodernism, both Kauffman and Felski see little or none. It's naive realism, not self-consuming irony, that Kauffman complains about. What's more, to continue in Kauffman's vein, when the triumphant, linear view of progress is thwarted, as in many ways it began to be in the Reagan-Bush years, the critic is left floundering, with nostalgia the main reaction to the collapse of the straight-ahead march of history. Several of the essays in the *Changing Subjects* volume could illustrate this all too well, as a matter of fact.

"Now, postmodernism arose as a way of coming to terms with the deferrals and ambiguities of historical process, but Felski doesn't see postmodernism as an available mode for women today. In her view, modernism was always a mostly male ploy to retain critical dominance over popular and women's writing. 'It is difficult to see how the linguistic experiments of male avant-garde artists bear *any* direct *or indirect* relationship to the liberation of women, however broadly conceived,' she tells us, and you'll note the absolutes I've emphasized in reading this quote.

"So everyone agrees we're at an impasse, but apparently for opposite reasons: do we have too much postmodernism, or none at all? Is personal testimony a compelling way to recover history after the collapse of those oppressive old grand narratives, or is it just a symptom of the collapse? Is the critical confession just another expression of Christopher Lasch's 'culture of narcissism,' as Felski fears? Or is the problem not solipsism at all, but a too easy group solidarity with no real staying power in the face of opposition? Finally, can the problems with autobiographical criticism be solved simply by abandoning the whole genre, or do they inhere in any sort of historical work today? For all his admirable commitment to rigorous historicizing, David Simpson doesn't seem too sure it'll lead him anywhere any more either. As he tells us in his concluding chapter, 'What has been lost— or at least I have lost it—is any firm faith that, in the words of one believer, "historical knowledges" are "necessary for the social struggle against oppression," or that the "struggle over theory" will produce "emancipatory knowledges." I certainly hope that this might be the case, but I have no solid conviction that it is.' "

Marsha glanced down at her feet, which had just been bumped from behind by a stray volleyball that had rolled up between the legs of her chair. Hardly pausing, she gave the ball a swift rearward kick and continued her presentation.

"Let's assume that Simpson is deliberately being ironic here when he makes the very move he spends his book critiquing—advancing his personal loss of faith as anecdotal emblem of a universal loss. This loss is ignored only by a 'believer' here and there who may still hope that historical knowledge can help us make the world a better place. It's no accident, I think, that the deluded believer here is a feminist, Teresa Ebert. He's quoting her article on 'Ludic Feminism.' It's kind of odd that he makes her his straw girl, since she's as hard on anecdotalism as he is. She's deeply concerned that feminists have been having too much *fun* doing po-mo riffs on desire when we should be struggling against workers' oppression. I think we have to acknowledge that the new voices in the room have brought their bodies with them, and we have to work through all this and not shrink from it: we'll do better to go through the personal, not around it, toward broader analysis and larger forms of collective understanding.

"It's a false opposition to say we should stop wasting our time on anecdotes and get back to analyzing texts. Any given text is a kind of anecdote within the broad narrative of literary history, and an interpretation is a story we tell about that story. We can agree that a poem is more complex than your typical personal anecdote. But even so, it's a difference in degree, not one in kind, as with popular art generally. What's more, anecdotes really never reach print as such, except in the minimal form of a newspaper's gossip column. Academics' anecdotes ought to bear more weight than that, just as the texts we use to exemplify some trend need to be framed within a developed analysis. A complex understanding of a simple anecdote may be worth a lot more than a simplistic interpretation of a great book. That's why I like *The Psychopathology of Everyday Life* better than Freud's one-dimensional readings of *Oedipus Rex*.

"Maybe neither Simpson nor Felski has looked closely enough at what's really going on in feminist personal criticism. They both concentrate so strongly on giving a broad overview that neither of them goes into any particular text in any detail. Now, granting that 90 percent of personal criticism is pretty forgettable—this compares with about *98* percent of criticism in general—the real question is how things work in the 10 percent of really good stuff. I'd like to take one short autobiographical text as a case in point: my 'anecdote,' if you like, which to me exemplifies the kinds of really interesting confessional writing that we started to see once feminism began to break out of its heavily middle-class seventies mode. I'll deliberately go back a bit, to the early eighties, before personal criticism became the flavor of the month and was still a very risky thing to try, at least in print. It was a specially tricky matter if you were going to challenge the assumptions of the white, bourgeois commonality of mainstream feminism. The first great salvo in this debate was a 1981 collection, *This Bridge Called My Back: Writings by Radical Women of Color*, edited by Cherríe Moraga and Gloria Anzaldúa. The editors and their contributors tried all sorts of things, from historical analysis to prose poetry. The individual pieces are wildly heterogeneous, you could say uneven, but the volume as a whole had a tremendous impact, and its message was carried as much in how everyone wrote as in the specific arguments they put forth.

"Here I'll just talk about one of the essays in that volume, Gloria Anzaldúa's 'Speaking in Tongues: A Letter to 3rd World Women Writers.' This piece shows the major features of feminist confessional writing that Felski identifies. For instance, Anzaldúa champions the speaking voice over a distanced prose style, rejecting abstract theorizing and instead using the genre of the letter to emphasize directness of address to an audience she wants to get as close to as she can. Here's how she begins her piece: '21 mayo 80. Dear mujeres de color, companions in writing—I sit here naked in the sun, typewriter against my knee trying to visualize you. Black woman huddles over a desk in the fifth floor of some New York tenement. Sitting on a porch in south Texas, a Chicana fanning away mosquitos in the hot air, trying to arouse the smouldering embers of writing. Indian woman walking to school or work lamenting the lack of time to weave writing into your life. Asian American, lesbian, single mother, tugged in all directions by children, lover or ex-husband, and the writing.'

"As you can see, Anzaldúa wants her own experience to relate structurally to working-class minority women's experience in general. But she does this by laying her individual body on the line. She describes the social barriers to making her voice heard, as a multiply marginalized working-class Chicana lesbian, and she also emphasizes the very personal resistances she has to surmount before she can write: 'The problem is to focus, to concentrate. The body distracts, sabotages with a hundred ruses, a cup of coffee, pencils to sharpen.' Examples like those are general and decorous enough; but she goes farther, into a 'ludic' feminism that both asserts her unique individuality and sends it up: 'Eating is my main distraction. Getting up to eat an apple danish. That I've been off sugar for three years is not a deterrent nor that I have to put on a coat, find the keys and go out into the San Francisco fog to get it . . . . anything just to put off the writing.'"

I noticed Vic rolling his eyes at this; so did Marsha, but she grinned. "This writing's out-and-out *embarrassing*, isn't it?" she went on. "But that's just the point: at one and the same time, Anzaldúa draws us in and holds us off by this stark personalism, a dynamic she reinforces linguistically by freely mixing Spanish into her English. Throughout her essay, she shifts back and forth between the general and the personal. She resists a totalizing linear narrative, and yet she really isn't Felski's helpless postmodern searcher for an ever-vanishing core of self. She displays her very palpable self for us, naked before her typewriter, forcing us to visualize her as she tries to visualize us. She's vividly individual and also socially constructed, separated from many people and deeply linked to others through the determinants of class, gender, ethnicity, and sexual preference, and her body itself is a social presence as much as a somatic one. 'Your skin must be sensitive enough for the lightest kiss,' she says, 'and thick enough to ward off the sneers.' As Elizabeth Ermarth has put it, 'The personal voice is not definable as one, essential thing; it is more like a power to vary between what is uniquely individual and what is general and public; it is a power crucial to sociality, and a power that must be learned.'"

Marsha glanced at her watch, cleared her throat, and resumed.

"Anzaldúa has found her voice, and harnessed its power, in two ways: by talking with her community of friends, and by reading. It's interesting that her writing owes a lot, in fact, to the great modernist tradition of Woolf,

Joyce, and Proust. I'll give you the example of Proust, in the denouement of Anzaldúa's apple danish quest. 'Returning after I've stuffed myself,' she writes. 'Writing paragraphs on pieces of paper, adding to the puzzle on the floor, to the confusion on my desk making completion far away and perfection impossible.' So far, this looks like Felski's receding self: the apple danish hasn't done anything for Anzaldúa. It's no madeleine, her past remains inaccessible to her even though she covers her floor with fragments like Proust's Marcel does as he struggles to write the *Recherche*: 'I cut and paste and line the floor with my bits of paper,' Anzaldúa goes on: 'My life strewn on the floor in bits and pieces and I try to make some order out of it working against time, psyching myself up with decaffeinated coffee, trying to fill in the gaps.' Like Marcel, Gloria struggles against encroaching time, and she even fortifies herself with coffee, though hers is decaf, a less potent brew than his famous café au lait.

"The story doesn't end here, though: as in Proust, a social intervention makes the work cohere. But now, the embodiment of this social nexus isn't a Proustian servant, but a figure of feminine equality: 'Leslie, my housemate, comes in. Gets on hands and knees to read my fragments on the floor and says, "It's good, Gloria."' Leslie's affirmation triggers the involuntary recollection the apple danish had failed to produce, and Anzaldúa is flooded with her past even as she's freed from it: 'And I think: *I don't have to go back to Texas, to my family of land, mesquites, cactus, rattlesnakes and roadrunners. My family, this community of writers. How could I have lived and survived so long without it. And I remember the isolation, re-live the pain again.* "To assess the damage is a dangerous act," writes Cherríe Moraga. To stop there is even more dangerous."'"

Marsha took off her glasses, letting them hang from her neck by their cord, and looked around the table. "Did you notice the interplay between speech and writing here?" she asked. "The recollection of Texas is framed by Leslie's speech and Moraga's essay, with which Anzaldúa is in dialogue, and with *whom* she's having conversations that will result in their work together on the collection in which this essay now appears. 'This book will change your life,' Moraga tells her, as the book's preface tells us in turn. You can see that Anzaldúa's essay goes far beyond the paralyzing dichotomies of solipsism versus group identity, anecdote versus history, personal speech versus theoretical analysis, realism versus postmodernism. And she does all this in just nine pages! I'll stop here, but as Anzaldúa says, it's dangerous to stop with analysis alone. The point is to see how we can use our lives—and our life histories—to build a more vital social and intellectual community. Anzaldúa shows it can be done: the challenge for us is to see if we can do as well ourselves."

The members of our group straightened up and looked around, coming out of the various hunched postures each person had unconsciously adopted while listening closely to Marsha's talk. There was even a little burst of applause from some people standing nearby, though this proved to be directed at the winning volleyball team, the game having just ended.

Hymit Bathtöi spoke first. "A splendid paper, Marsha," he said. "Perhaps there is one further dichotomy that we might deconstruct a little—the one you cite from Rita Felski on the difference between men's triumphalist autobiography and women's less ego-laden writing. You showed so well how Anzaldúa used Proust's autobiographical masterpiece. The *Recherche* is certainly a self-consciously great work; and yet, think how tentatively Proust inscribes his own name into it. His clearly autobiographical hero remains unnamed for a full two thousand pages, and then only fleetingly is he referred to as 'Marcel,' and that in the *most* ambiguous of ways. Do you recall? Albertine wakes from sleep, sees the narrator in bed beside her, suppresses a frown of annoyance, and then addresses him by his 'nom de baptême'—'ce qui, en donnant au narrateur le même prénom qu'à l'auteur de ce livre, *eût fait* "mon Marcel, mon chéri Marcel."' American critics often miss the point and merely call the narrator Marcel—you are far from alone in this— but note the past conditional tense: 'which, to give the narrator the same name as that of the author of this book, *would have been* Marcel.' Are any identities, male or female, so very stable in Proust? Does this hegemonic male narrative really exist?"

"I don't know if that's such a compelling exception to the dynamic Felski identifies," Marsha replied. "Certainly Anzaldúa wants to ally herself with a range of marginalized groups whose gender, class, or ethnicity sets them askew from mainstream values. I don't think her use of Proust is random at all here: he's inspiring to her precisely because he shook up the norms of nineteenth-century realism. Wasn't he led to do this partly because—gay or mostly gay, half-Jewish, floating in between the aristocracy and the bourgeoisie—Proust didn't fit in to the mainstream either?"

Bathtöi skeptically stroked his long moustaches with a thumb and index finger; as he did, I had an involuntary recollection of my own. "Look, Hymit," I blurted out, "I remember you coming out of a seminar we were in together in graduate school, on realism. We were reading *Old Mortality*—you remember, Walter Scott. As we came out, you stroked your moustache and said sadly, 'But it isn't Proust.' Weren't you reacting against Scott's use of the realist mode he helped create, which Proust broke with and which has more and more broken down since? Hasn't it broken down most dramatically for women and other groups who were never fully included in it to begin with?"

I stopped, a little surprised to have spoken so forcefully, and uncomfortable at having made such a point of a twenty-year-old anecdote. After all, I only still remembered the episode because of the embarrassment I'd felt at the time at never having read Proust. When I finally did read the *Recherche* the following fall, it was too late to work up some sharp rejoinder to Bathtöi, who in any event had stopped talking by then to anyone less theoretically sophisticated than himself.

Happily, he had mellowed, or his standards had lowered, since 1977. He smiled genially.

"Did I say that?" he asked. "How childish we were then! Now, of course, I see that Proust was telling us as much about fin-de-siècle Paris as about the rhetorics of reading that our honored professor de Man loved to deconstruct. Conversely, too, had I not been so young and brash I would have reflected on Scott's own resistance to the fixities of authorial identity. Why else did he write anonymously for so many years, strewing his prefaces with sly mockeries of the attempt to unravel the 'true' identity of 'the Author of *Waverley*'? In that book you recall us as reading, Old Mortality himself loses his own name, gaining his deathly nickname from his ceaseless quest to *counter* the erasures of time, as he travels from graveyard to graveyard, re-cutting the names that time has blurred on tombstones! Was Proust per-haps thinking of that very book when he described his novel as a cemetery in which the real names on the tombstones have been effaced?"

Marsha was undaunted by this rapid sequence of thought. "It seems to me, Hymit," she replied, "now you're implying Scott *was* Proust—early, proto-Proust. It's kind of a nice idea, but if you just check out some of the costume dramas like *Rob Roy* that Hollywood's been putting out lately, you'd see how readily Scott can be recuperated for a pretty linear history. I'm willing to allow there isn't any *absolute* difference between men's histo-riography and women's, but I'd still want to say there's usually been a con-siderable difference in degree. Agreed?"

We all agreed. I mentioned that time was getting on and so we should move to our next speaker. Two excellent papers followed, one by Dart-mouth's Marianne Hirsch on the ambiguities of Holocaust testimonial and one by Lois Zamora, of Houston, on the suppression of dialogue in Eliza-beth Burgos-Debray's recording of the life story of Rigoberta Menchú. Finally, Maarten van Delden gave an illuminating paper that used the criti-cal writings of Carlos Fuentes to challenge Benedict Anderson's concept of "imaginary communities." In his paper, called "Imaginary Disunities," van Delden emphasized the effects of the early split in Fuentes's life, divided between years in the United States and in Mexico. Mexican national reality itself, he argued, was far more divided than Anderson's model would sug-gest, and print culture was as much a centrifugal force in Mexico as a cohe-sive one. Van Delden concluded with a few wry remarks tying his topic into his own life: as a Dutch citizen working in America, now on the point of moving with his Korean wife from NYU to Rice University in Houston, he was probably secretly hoping to do as well as Fuentes in managing personal and professional dislocations.

All three papers produced some good discussion, though the presentations had not cohered as well as I had expected from the abstracts. Everyone's tone, moreover, was a little tentative. Time would tell whether things would jell further as the conference proceeded.

THE afternoon, however, was reserved for relaxation. Marsha, Dov, and I all needed to go into town to find presents to take home to our children, and Vic was eager to add to his collection of Mexican masks. We walked into central Puerto Vallarta after lunch, but the cobblestones seemed determined only to lead us past resort-wear shops, agencias de viaje, and jewelry establishments too far up the scale for the average academic, even with the favorable exchange rate. We did eventually find some adequate toys for my kids and for Dov's and Marsha's daughters, but beyond that we were disappointed. Dov wanted to find some particularly impressive hand-carved chess set to give to his sons, but we didn't see any worth a second look. We did encounter a few masks in an artesanía, but Vic dismissed them as "airport art."

"What I want," he said, distastefully setting down a cutely scowling tiger mask, "is the real thing. Genuine masks are never made to hang on a wall, and their beauty has nothing to do with conventional 'prettiness.' They're used in dances, but this *tigre* here doesn't even have eye holes for a wearer to look through. In preconquest times, warriors dressed as jaguars danced in the temple courtyards before they went out to the slaughter. Returning home, they would dance through the streets, wearing the flayed skin of one of their opponents: the true Dance of Death, now distantly remembered in the Christian festival of the Día de los Muertos. Even in their present form, the Indians' dances go back to early colonial times, with themes like the expulsion of the Moors from Spain—a most interesting transposition of their own conflicts of Spaniard against Indian, is it not? And they still make splendid masks of Death; I have some chilling ones from Oaxaca and some rather comic ones from Guerrero. They are strangely invigorating."

"You don't say?" Marsha commented. "If it wasn't you talking, Vic, I'd think your interest lay as much in the masks' use value as in their artistic designs."

"I shall not deny the effects of your corrupting influence," Vic replied with a smile. "Of course, for me the reward remains aesthetic. Use alone cannot consecrate a mediocre design, and in fact most of the people who use the masks in dances today probably care more about a comfortable fit than about subtleties of carving. Even so, the masks' 'use value,' as you call it, does focus a village's passion on them, thus providing the social conditions within which the true artists among carvers can create extraordinary things. Not one mask in a hundred presents the combination I seek: exceptional technical skill, originality in the use of formulaic motifs, and a unifying sensibility of mordant irony. The casually knocked-off specimens in this shop show nothing of this. But perhaps la Patrona knows where we might look."

Vic went to the front of the store and had a rapid-fire conversation with the shopkeeper. "Bueno," he said, returning to us. "La Patrona has a cousin, Ángel by name, who gets masks from Indians in the back country. A very distant cousin, she insists—I suspect he is a mestizo, they are usually the middlemen in such transactions—but she gave me his address. Just across from the road up to a beer garden in the hills, a few miles south of town. Sounds intriguing; shall we?"

We hailed a taxi. The driver said he knew Ángel, though he warned us that he might or might not be at home; if not, we might find him having a beer up at the cervecería. Finding no one at the house, we followed the sign across the road that pointed the way to El Jardín de Eden, as the place was called, a kilometer's walk up a dirt road winding into the wooded mountains ringing Banderas Bay. The afternoon was hot and sunny, but vine-covered trees gave shade, and a rushing stream could be heard in the underbrush off to our right as we climbed up through the narrow valley. Dov actually took off his tie, and professed to be feeling better.

"My throat will not yet let me smoke, however," he commented, "and so we should talk. I was surprised by your discussion of *Angela's Ashes*, Marsha: I would not have expected you to defend that miserable Saint Vincent de

Paul Society. I should rather have thought you would identify with Mc-Court's rejection of the Church and all its works."

"You know, Dov," Marsha answered, "I've been thinking some about my attitudes toward religion since we talked in Chicago, I'm trying to catch myself when I fall into some posture of simplistic dismissiveness. I mean, forget the belief system, but still, as a social phenomenon there's an awful lot going on with religion. A while back, I would have chuckled along with all of McCourt's little digs at religion and just gotten annoyed by his reductiveness about politics, actually that *was* my reaction for about the first half of the book. But then I began to notice how similar the two topics are in his account, and I started asking myself what's really behind all that anti-Catholicism. He's even got to wheel out a kill-joy Catholic priest in the very last scene, remember? Once he's landed in America and is about to screw one of that group of bored housewives who are looking for a little anonymous sex, so they can act out their frustration at being trapped in dead-end marriages. It's a cute ending in a way, he gives the padre the slip and gets the girl who's, you'd have to say thrusting, herself on him, but it's been the moral of his story all along. Everyone for themselves alone. It's not enough to say the priest doesn't want anyone to have any fun—he also represents the forces of social cohesion that are trying to support families, build community, lessen the war of all against all. McCourt makes this kind of move all through the book."

"I suppose I should be pleased that you give religion some sort of credit," Dov said, "if only as a social service agency."

"It's more than that," Marsha said. "Or both more and less. There's always some weird set of conflicting agendas in a church group, at least there always was in my mother's parish, the whole thing kept degenerating into bickering, and the resources were pretty small potatoes. I mean, Mom and her friends would spend months planning some bake sale to benefit the IRA, in the end they'd maybe raise five hundred bucks. But it meant a lot to all of them, and it was hard cash they raised. I don't know that my dad's Marxist discussion group ever accomplished as much. Maybe in the early days, but they kind of imploded over the invasion of Hungary in '56 and never really recovered after that. At least they got me to Mexico once, it was in '61, after the Bay of Pigs. They wanted to do something in solidarity—they felt they'd become too theoretical, too distant from the actual scenes of struggle. They couldn't go to Cuba, so they finally chartered a bus and came down to Mexico City, families and all. We had a pilgrimage to Trotsky's favorite café. I guess politics and religion were always mixed up in my household."

We passed a sign: *Jardín de Eden: 1 km.* "Funny," Vic remarked. "Back at the bottom of the road the sign said the same thing. Aren't we getting anywhere?" The road was steep and dusty, the sun was now beating down on us as we climbed higher, and each bend in the road looked much like the last. We trudged on in silence for another ten minutes or so, whereupon we came to another sign: *Jardín de Eden: 1 km.* This was getting discouraging. Dov wanted to turn back, pleading that his throat was beginning to bother him again.

"Come on, Dov," Marsha replied; "just listen to the stream, it sounds like we're getting toward some rapids, maybe a waterfall. We must be almost there, and we haven't passed anyone the whole way up. We could be the only people in Eden!"

We trudged on, and after a hundred yards or so we suddenly came to a large clearing, marked by a faded sign: *El Jardín de Eden.* A newer sign next to it proclaimed that this had been the setting for scenes in the 1988 action film *Predator.* In front of us we saw a small waterfall plunging down into a large pool; a shed stood along one side, ornamented with a rusty Coca-Cola sign. There was a cement patio, where two or three pairs of tourists were seated on white plastic chairs, drinking beers, fanning themselves, and staring vaguely at the waterfall. They had ridden up by another path, on several listless-looking ponies that were now cropping such grass as they could find in the dusty clearing. A couple of Mexican guides were relaxing in the shade on the far side of the clearing, waiting for the tourists to finish their beers.

Inquiries at the shed revealed that Ángel had been there earlier in the afternoon, but had left. We bought bottles of beer beneath a signed publicity still of Arnold Schwarzenegger.

"So this is Eden," Dov said, as we stood out on the cement patio. "I might have known. Et in Arcadia Schwarzenegger!"

"Appropriately enough," Vic remarked. "It's Death who is the *ego* in Arcadia in the Renaissance tag, and the Terminator is only his modern guise."

"More like his post-modern guise," Marsha added. "Arnold isn't the heavy in this one anyway. The Predator's this weird teenage mutant Godzilla cyborg. A walking A-bomb, too, with a Darth Vader headpiece—he's really an anthology of movie monster history. And to defeat him, Arnold has to do a back-to-nature Tarzan thing, plastered in mud—bows and arrows, no less."

"Don't tell me you think there's some little eco-moral here!" Vic exclaimed. "Mr. Steroids Hugs a Tree?"

"You never know with Schwarzenegger," Marsha replied. "It's always some unstable mix of parody, self-parody, and straight action. But the ecological gestures in *Predator* are just silly. The only real political message is social. Arnold brings this whole Mission Impossible team with him—his long-time collaborators. When the CIA pig who's hired them dismisses his crew as 'expendable units,' we get Arnold's longest speech in the whole flick. 'My men are not expendable units,' he growls. Eloquent, huh? Of course, the Predator offs them one by one anyway."

"He always does," Vic said soberly.

Still thinking about death, I reflected. I'd hoped Vic's mood had improved since Chicago. I thought of asking how his friend there was doing, but decided that the connection might be too obvious.

"Still thinking about death?" Marsha asked softly. Vic smiled.

"More than that, dear Marsha," he replied: "I have come to see death as a *research opportunity*! It was my former lover Bill who gave me the idea, indirectly. When I went to see him in the hospital, I found him reading the *Duino Elegies*—Rilke was always a common passion of ours. He now credits the elegies as much as the medications for seeing him through that difficult period. When I saw him, he told me that for the first time he was drawn to the tenth elegy, the one in which Death takes the poet to the land of Laments, pointing out the great constellations: The Mother; The Burning

Book. As Bill and I talked, I became intrigued by Rilke's recourse to medieval allegory in order to talk about death. I began to think that death might be a thread to follow, a way to link some of my disparate medieval and modern interests. I shall call the project *Death: A Biography*. It will be a look at the shifting ways poets have imaged the unimaginable."

"I hope you will go back to the Bible," Dov said. "There Death is doubly repressed, as the Jahwists were reluctant to admit so powerful a rival to the divine court. So you have a figure who is, shall I say, unimagable as well as unimaginable. All the more interesting, then, to see his hooded face peek out at times—even associated to love. In the climax of the Song of Songs, for example: *'azzah ka-Maweth, 'ahavah; qashah ki-she'ol, kinah.* 'Love is strong as death, passion cruel as the grave,' as the translation goes, though the translators have preferred to forget that Death is a proper name."

"You bring to mind Wagner's fascination with the idea of the Liebestod," Vic replied. "Again with medieval sources, most notably Gottfried's *Tristan*. Gottfried even spells Isolde at times as Isôt, to rhyme with *tôt*, 'death.' It was to read Gottfried that I first studied Middle High German. Such a poet! The anagrammatic play with Tristan/Tantris, the acrostic weaving of the poet's own name into his opening stanzas, his sardonic irony, comedy both high and low, and always the ineluctable blending of love and death. A theme all too fully realized in Gottfried's own early death! Think of that incantatory French couplet Tristan sings near the poem's premature end—to the wrong Isolde, it's true, bit of a mix-up there, but all the more haunting to see his love spiraling out of control—*'Isôt ma drûe, Isôt m'amie, / En vûs ma mort, en vûs ma vie!'* "

Our beers finished, we began the walk back downhill. It was now late in the afternoon; when we would glimpse the sun ahead of us, out over the Pacific, it seemed to be hanging in the sky, preparing for its sudden plunge into the ocean. A hushed stillness pervaded the woods around us.

"Suppose the world outside Eden ended while we've been here?" Marsha asked idly. "What would we do if we find we're the only ones left, and this forest is all there is? Could we re-create some degree zero of culture?"

"We could play chess," Dov said. "Like the gods in the Prose Edda. After the end of the world they sit around Valhalla, playing game after game. We still have not found a chess set, so we will have to make our own, but we will have all the time in the world to perfect our skill."

Marsha shuddered. "What a grim vision of the future—endlessly replaying our battles, like Napoleon on Elba."

"Able was I . . ." I remarked absently, my mind largely incapacitated by the sun and the beer. "A man, a plan, a canal—"

Vic interrupted me, none too soon.

"I see the Edda's ending differently," he said, as we emerged from the woods and came in sight of the paved road. "What could be more delightful than to sum up all earthly experience in the perfection of a game? Symbolic violence instead of bloodshed, conversation replacing the transitory securities of weapons and fortresses. Surely this is Snorri Sturluson's own dream, as he composes the Edda, retelling the old pagan stories after decades of feuding have led to Iceland's loss of independence to Christian Norway. Do you remember his bravura frame-tale? . . . No? A traveling king, Gylfi, comes upon an enchanted castle. There, he hears all the old myths, told to him by a parodic Holy Trinity: Har, Jafnhar, and Thridi—'High One,' 'Just-As-High,' and 'Third.' Then at the end, in a sudden coup de théâtre, the entire castle vanishes into thin air. 'Make of it what you can,' the spirits tell Gylfi as they melt away—whether in mockery or in encouragement I could never say. We could do worse than spend eternity re-enacting our own version of that sublime scene of instruction. The conference to end all conferences!"

"And how would we apportion the roles?" Dov asked.

"You'd have to be High One, of course," Vic said. "I'm sure you could pull off the requisite pomposity if you really tried. The eternally egalitarian Marsha would be Just-As-High. I myself would opt for Thridi—I believe he is really my hero Loki, the trickster-god, in disguise."

"What about me?" I asked.

"You'd be the perfect Gylfi, David," Vic answered. "Audience par excellence, recorder of the event, actually the title character—that entire section of the Edda is named after you, I mean him: 'The Deluding of Gylfi.'"

I wasn't sure I liked this idea, but we were now back at Ángel's house. We were encouraged to hear salsa music coming from a radio inside. Ángel answered the door, and welcomed us into the front room of his two-room house. The walls were covered with masks, and—to Dov's delight—a shelf was lined with a dozen chess sets, hand-carved from wood with tops made of bone. Ángel told us that his brother made them from local wood and oxen bone (Vic suspected dog), and after some bargaining—silently supervised from the inner doorway by Ángel's wife María—Dov bought the most elaborate set, whose bone finials and heads had been carved into lacelike traceries.

"My boys are devoted to chess," he said. "It is almost the only thing the three of us can agree on. I will have this for them when they come to stay with me again this summer."

"So they did visit last summer?" Marsha asked.

"In fact yes, I took your advice," Dov replied. "It was awkward at first. Ari would be practicing his guitar late at night, then Ben would rise early to do his Talmud. He would always drop something in the kitchen and wake his little sister Zena, whose room is just beside. Even so, by the end of the summer they had finally become more comfortable with my wife Amy, and Ben had some long talks with Bob Alter when he came down from Berkeley to visit. Bob put him in touch with a very interesting biblical scholar in Jerusalem, Ilana Pardes, a feminist interested in text history. Ben sat in on her seminars this year, and apparently he was impressed by a session in which she critiqued my book on the erotics of biblical narrative. This was the work in which I argued that the theme of polygamy in the patriarchal narratives serves to work through the authors' hidden anxiety about the multiplicity of their sources. Ben writes me long e-mails now in which he tries to show me the error of my ways from both the Talmudic and the feminist perspectives at once. If he can pull this off, he may become a real scholar, and at least our arguments are interesting now."

Vic, meanwhile, was studying the masks on the wall above the chess sets.

"Quién es?" he asked Ángel, pointing to a delicately carved mask of a woman's face, her blue eyes and pink complexion contrasting strangely with two beribboned horns protruding laterally from her temples.

"Es una Malinche," Ángel replied. "Muy fina."

"I thought as much!" Vic exclaimed in delight. "Here, Marsha, she is for you." He took the mask from the wall and handed it to her. Marsha held it to her face, momentarily transformed, then took it off. "She's beautiful," she said. "Who is she?"

"Cortés's native mistress and interpreter," Vic replied. "A crucial figure of cultural contact and conflict. Interesting to find her here. She was obviously made down in Guerrero, old Aztec territory, still the center of Nahuatl language and culture. But see—the modern carver has given her the features and the complexion of a Hollywood starlet. Yet she still bears the horns of power of a pre-Columbian divinity, with ribbons in the colors of the four sacred directions. Two love goddesses in one—Xochiquetzal meets Marilyn Monroe!"

We paid for the chess set and the mask and left, with Marsha and Vic amicably arguing whether the Malinche mask was a sign of cultural defeat or a triumphant index of resiliency.

"All the Aztecs' art is about survival," Vic remarked, "as this mask's uncanny power attests. Do you remember my favorite of the old poems, Marsha?" He began to recite, softly, as we walked along the road.

> *In zan iyollo ya quinequi, in Ipal Nemohuani*
> *in cozcatli, in quetzalli*
> *in quipuztequiz oncan.*

I didn't know why he expected Marsha to follow this, but I certainly couldn't. Seeing my quizzical look, Vic translated.

"'The one heart's desire of the Giver of Life is jade, is quetzal plumes: to tear them apart.' *In quimmonequiz*—the poet continues—*quimontepehuatiuh in cuauhtin, in ocelo:* 'This is his desire: to scatter apart the eagles, the jaguars.' A song of resignation and defeat, in lesser hands; the eagles and jaguars are companies of warriors. 'How many jewels, how many quetzal plumes, have been destroyed? Ah, though it was jade, though it was gold. . . .' Yet the poet gives his theme an unexpected turn. His poem itself is a cloth, perhaps a shroud—it's an obscure word—in which the likenesses of the eagles and the jaguars are woven; we will wear this cloth when we go to join them. 'So may you now be happy, my lords,' he concludes; *ayac, ayac, mocauhtiaz in tlalticpac*. 'No one, no one, is left behind on earth.' "

By now, dusk had descended and was rapidly becoming night. Just ahead of us, we saw a sign for the *Ristorante del Paraíso*. The sign touted the restaurant's dramatic location on a bluff overlooking Banderas Bay, adding that it had been the setting for the film of *The Night of the Iguana*.

"How can we pass this up?" Marsha asked.

"Cómo no?" Vic declared, and in we went.

Despite its self-promoting billboard, the restaurant proved to be a charming and low-key establishment, almost deserted at this (by Mexican standards) predinner hour, and with frosted Margaritas to precede the meal.

As we looked out at the stars filling the sky over the ocean, I sipped my Margarita with satisfaction. Everyone seemed exceptionally mellow; even Dov had surely stopped thinking about Heidegger for the time being.

"That mask of yours," he remarked to Marsha, "brings Levinas to mind. He makes much of 'the face,' which he sees as the meeting place of self and other. This expresses his concept that ethics precedes ontology: we come into existence through our interactions with others. But I wonder—do not identity politicians like your friend Anzaldúa place their ontological status first, making any ethics secondary to their preordained selfhood?"

"I don't think so at all," Marsha replied. "Actually Anzaldúa herself has done an anthology called *Making Face, Haciendo Caras*. It's kind of like Levinas, the face is just what isn't your own private possession. She plays on *caras*, faces, and *máscaras*—masks—as our protection against hostile gazes and also the bearers of all the marks that society puts on us. 'We're written all over,' she says, 'carved and tattooed with the sharp needles of experience.' "

"Not my cup of tequila at all," Vic observed. "You can take me or leave me, but what you see is what you get. As much as I enjoy our little get-togethers, the fabric of my being hardly depends upon them. I was perfectly real, thank you, before I ever met any of you, and I am quite sure that you were too, Marsha: you are so vividly *present*. Now Damrosch, on the other hand, I am less sure of. Tell me, David," he asked, turning to me, "when you pass a mirror, can you see your reflection?"

This got to me. "You tell me this, Vic," I answered sharply. "When *you* pass a mirror, can you see anything *else*?"

"Touché, dear boy!" Vic replied. "I shall concede your existence after all. I really meant to praise you as the one among us who most clearly sees the value in getting people together. Whatever inspired you to set out on this mad quest for community?"

"It might have been C. S. Lewis," I answered. "At least he was one of the inspirations, when I first read him as a teenager, along with Tolkien and Charles Williams and the others in that discussion group of theirs, 'the Inklings.' What you're saying about faces reminds me of an image that's stayed with me ever since I first read his book *Till We Have Faces*. Lewis, or his narrator, has a vision of a banquet in hell. The damned are seated around a table laden with exquisite dishes, but they're all starving—they've been cursed with fused elbow joints, so they can't eat the food they have before them. Then the narrator is shown a banquet in heaven. Similar dishes, even the same physical disability: the blessed too have elbows that won't bend. Yet they're all well-fed, talking happily together. The narrator's astonished. He asks his angelic guide how they can manage to feed themselves. The angel replies: 'They feed one another.'"

"That's sweet," Marsha said. "But it sure is an Oxbridge idea of heaven, isn't it? Fine if you're one of the plump professors at the high table, you know?"

"Lewis never thought of himself that way at all," I protested. "In fact, his background was more like Anzaldúa's. He was hardly to the manner born—half Irish, half Welsh, half-orphaned by his mother's early death. A scholarship student, out of his element in England. And marked from birth as dramatically as Anzaldúa, by his physical debility."

"Lewis was handicapped?" Dov asked.

"Fused thumb joints!" I replied triumphantly.

Marsha looked at me like I'd gone out of my mind. "You really mean to equate a totally trivial problem like *that* with pervasive racial injustice like Anzaldúa faced in Texas?"

"It's Lewis himself who reports the profound effects of his handicap. In his memoir, *Surprised by Joy*, he traces his whole sense of the world to that problem. He was always clumsy, he could never do well in sports—that key to acceptance in his boy's school. He says his disability bred 'a settled expectation that everything would do what you did not want it to do.' He was left with 'a deeply ingrained pessimism,' a sense that 'the universe is evil.' Insecurity and a feeling of estrangement run through all his work, fiction and criticism alike. That's why joy is such a surprise if it comes to him. I'm sure that scene of the fused elbows in *Till We Have Faces* reflects the deep problems caused by his fused thumbs. Hell as his childhood experience, with heaven being the community he longed to have."

Our own food arrived. I was a little surprised to see that Marsha had joined the rest of us in ordering fish.

"I thought you were a strict vegetarian," I remarked.

"Sometimes," she replied. "I keep going back and forth. These days, I'm following Cassie's lead. 'I feel sorry for the animals,' she tells me, 'but I *like* to eat them.' I guess I don't think it's our cultural duty to repress this basic side of our animal natures."

"And besides," Vic interjected, "where would your movies be without meat? Could Mrs. Waters have seduced Tom Jones over tofu?"

"On the other hand," I remarked, "think of *Night of the Iguana*. We admire that defrocked priest for cutting the iguana loose so the lover boys can't cook it up."

"Yes," said Marsha, "but there's also the scene where the women get to know each other while they cut the heads off the fish they're going to fry for dinner. It sets up the moral of the whole story, when that grifter-portraitist tells the defrocked Reverend Shannon she's finally discovered something to believe in. 'Broken barriers between people. A wanting to help each other. On a verandah, outside their separate cubicles.'"

"Of course, it can also be delightful to have a door connecting the cubicles," Vic said, addressing the group as a whole but with a quick glance at Marsha.

A hint of a smile crossed Marsha's face. "You always did go in for ancient history, didn't you?" she said.

"Autres temps, autres murs," Vic replied, half to himself.

At the mention of history, we fell to speculating about the dinners we'd most like to have attended in the past. I voted for the Last Supper: partly for the spiritual experience, of course, but also because I'd always wanted to know just what words Jesus used in formulating the Lord's Prayer. I explained to my companions—at more length than I'd intended to—that in college, when I was still expecting to go on to divinity school, I'd taken a New Testament course for which I'd written a term paper about a single word in the prayer: *epiousios*, translated as "daily" in the phrase "give us this day our daily bread." No one really knew what the word meant, though; the evangelist had coined the term to translate some obscure Aramaic phrase. The lost Aramaic may really have meant "our bread for the coming age," referring to a heavenly banquet, in which case the petition would be part of the prayer's opening wish for the world to end, rather than a turning to the needs of daily life. In my paper, I'd found that as they weighed the evidence, Protestant scholars universally concluded that Jesus did mean a sacred banquet at the imminent end of the world; Catholic scholars, reluctant to endorse an interpretation that might have Jesus mistaken about the future, always ended up finding that the word really did mean "daily" after all.

Silence greeted my conclusion.

"You sure went meta early, David," Marsha remarked politely. "If I had my druthers," she went on, "it would have to be dinner at San Simeon, William Randolph Hearst's castle, you know? I'd go for the weekend he invited Buster Keaton to come up, it was in around '26. There were probably a couple of senators there too, the glamorous Marion Davies, of course, and assorted hangers-on. We'd gather in the baronial dining hall, waiting for the curtain to rise when Hearst would finish reading all his newspapers for the day. He'd be up in his room in his bathrobe, walking around with the papers spread out all over the floor, turning the pages with his toes. Finally he'd get dressed and come down in his private elevator—a private elevator in his *own house*, mind you!—and dinner could be served. A fabulous banquet, and that surreal setting, Renaissance tapestries in a poured concrete castle. . . . And the conversation would be pretty wild, too, at least until Buster got too drunk to be coherent. What about you, Dov?"

"Bread and cheese with Nietzsche," Dov replied immediately. "Wine too, of course, on an alpine hillside overlooking the hut where he was composing *Die fröhliche Wissenschaft*. Simple fare, to be sure—Nietzsche was morbidly attentive to his poor digestion, as you know—but he had a sort of genius for friendship, assuming he felt the presence of a kindred soul."

"Yourself, for example," Vic commented; Dov nodded.

"Let us stipulate," Dov went on, "that Nietzsche has had a successful afternoon, wandering the hills and composing ironic epigrams. Their bitter lucidity has for the moment banished all thoughts of suicide from his head; he is ready to relax, to regale his visitor with absurd tales from his days as Professor of Philology in Basel: 'Life among the dwarves,' he calls it. The sun begins to set, mists arise from the valleys below us, Nietzsche even starts to wax poetic, and this is just the moment for a decisive intervention: I persuade him to abandon work on *Thus Spake Zarathustra*."

We looked at Dov in surprise.

"I never could abide that bathetic book," he said in explanation. "The heavy 'poetic' style, the burgeoning Messiah complex that will lead to the fantasy of the *Übermensch*. . . . Better he should have written another brilliant compilation of aperçus like, what is it in English, *Daybreak*. Do you know the beautiful ending of that book? He compares the philosopher to a sea bird who flies far from land, always in search of some farther shore, some further truth. This ultimate shore constantly recedes, he can never find it. Finally he must return home, land for a time on some quite ordinary cliff overlooking the sea, rather as we do here. Yet his heart still pounds with longing to be out again flying *wo alles noch Meer, Meer ist*—'where all is still sea, sea,' with a lovely suggestion of *noch mehr*: more, always more."

"Nietzsche could do worse than dine with you," Vic commented. "For my part, I am divided. As we've been speaking of memoirs, I think of those magnificent dinners that Giacomo Casanova would continually put on to impress his aristocratic friends, if friends they are, lavishly spending the money he has won from them at cards. We are in Turin, let us say. Mid-1760s, Casanova in his mid-forties—by now a consummate master of self-creation. He regales his guests at dinner with stories from his recent travels in France and the German territories. The climax of his narrative comes in Augsburg, where he is called in for questioning by the local magistrate, who has heard unsavory tales. Just who *is* this adventurer who has the effrontery to style himself 'Chevalier de Seingalt'? 'Is Herr Casanova aware,' the Magistrate asks icily, 'that it is against the law in Augsburg to assume a false name?'

"Casanova retells this story with great gusto at dinner, pausing dramatically before he reveals the reply that silenced the Magistrate: as Casanova himself has *invented* the title of Chevalier de Seingalt, he is perhaps the only person on earth who knows that his name is genuinely his. Indeed, the Magistrate himself can never be certain of his own name—he might have been the product of an illicit affair, and bears his mother's husband's name only by default. A risky reply, no doubt, but Casanova wins his wager: instead of arresting him for his effrontery, the Magistrate merely smiles thinly. He wishes Casanova a pleasant—but brief—stay in Augsburg, and shows him out.

"How I would love to hear Casanova tell that tale, and to watch the modulations of reaction among our fellow dinner guests: the irritated glances of the impoverished nobility whose own ancient names have lost half their value; the nervous laughter of the other adventurers at table, their nagging fear of exposure trumped by Casanova's splendid self-assurance; the puzzled blush of this week's mistress, fifteen years old, only yesterday a simple tailor's daughter, now seated in honor across from Casanova, wondering how she should react.

"But no," Vic went on. "Casanova has already left us an incomparable record of his dinners and their conversational seductions—and the conversations, dear friends, are the real point of his memoir. We have the twelve volumes; why need we be there in person? Far better to experience a banquet that has truly been lost to us. Is not this the scholar's great responsibility and greatest pleasure—to bring the lost past to life? Let us go, then, to the royal palace at Knossos, fifteen hundred years before David's Last Supper. In the cool of the evening, the sea breeze wafting in through the polychromed lotus pillars, we have retired to eat after watching the sacred bull-jumping acrobats—men and women alike, stripped to the waist, grasping the bull literally by the horns and flinging their lithe bodies with abandon across the courtyard."

"Aren't there pictures of those scenes?" I asked. "Does this really meet your criterion of a lost banquet?"

"All this we know, of course, from the frescoes preserved at Knossos and at Phaistos. And we have images too of the flute players and the tambourinists who serenade us as we eat our honeyed meal. But *their songs*—how I long to hear them! What haunting music did those flutes play? And the lyrics? What a disappointment that the long-sought decipherment of Linear B yielded only lists of chariot parts! The lovely Greek lyrics we have, so often fragments themselves, are a thousand years later in date. Suppose they were but echoes of what came before? The royal court at Knossos reached a height of culture perhaps unprecedented in antiquity, if the art and architecture are anything to go by: *those* are the poems, utterly lost to us today, that I would give anything to have heard."

Our meal was done. We asked the waiter to call us a cab; we had to be up for our seminar in the morning.

Dov, his throat now fully recovered, was scheduled to begin the session.

"Oh good," Marsha whispered to me as we settled into our patio chairs. "Now we get to hear about *Matthew Arnold*."

I didn't share Marsha's impatience with the very idea of a talk on Arnold, but I was unsure whether Arnold was really relevant to a seminar on autobiographical criticism. Had Dov merely plugged in something he happened to be working on anyway? I remembered a line from *Culture and Anarchy* in which Arnold wittily described himself as a renegade Philistine, "a traitor to the ideas and the tea-meetings of my own class," but this seemed a fairly slender thread from which to hang a whole topic.

"You may suppose," Dov began, "and from the expression on her face, I suspect our colleague Marsha *does* suppose, that Matthew Arnold could have little to say to a confessional critic like Gloria Anzaldúa. Such critics, after all, advance the personal as antidote to the repressive impersonality of the Arnoldian tradition. Indeed, Arnold has too often been used in support of a monolithic conception of tradition as an edifice built of touchstones, a monument to 'the best that has been thought and said' throughout a culture's history. It is interesting, however, to discover just how fully Arnold put himself into play as he advanced his ideas, and it is especially intriguing to see how he divided himself up in the process. Even his touchstones are little pieces only, those scraps of poetry that persist in memory after we have forgotten almost the whole of the poem from which they come. You see, Arnold may be closer than we realize to the fragmented sensibility of modernism.

"My focus here, however, will not be on those proto-modernist works *Culture and Anarchy* and the *Essays in Criticism*. Rather, I wish to draw to your attention a much more radical work, *Friendship's Garland*. I believe this book to be Arnold's masterpiece, though it is rarely discussed, and is not in fact in print today. Possibly its neglect is a sign of its radicalism: it has been too hard to assess, certainly for those who prize Victorian earnestness. It is a memoir of a sort, and so it fits within our seminar's theme. It is the record of Arnold's antagonistic 'friendship' with a German philosopher of culture named Arminius. This Arminius wrote long letters to the editor of a London newspaper at irregular intervals in the late 1860s, criticizing Arnold's ideas; Arnold wrote letters in response to defend himself, and later collected these letters under the ironic title of *Friendship's Garland*.

"Arminius, however, did not in fact exist—he is Arnold's own creation. Even as he was completing his monumental *Culture and Anarchy*, Arnold was casting about for ways to bring his ideas to the attention of a broader public, and at the same time to answer the various criticisms his ideas had been receiving. So he created a Prussian philosopher, Arminius von Thunder-ten-Tronckh. All very well, you may say, but what is original in this obvious pastiche of *Sartor Resartus?*" Dov looked over at me for confirmation. I couldn't repress a helpless gesture of puzzlement.

"*Most* of you will recall," Dov continued, "Carlyle's inspired creation, his German professor Diogenes Teufelsdröckh, philosopher of clothing, putative author of *Die Kleider: Ihr Werden und Wirken*, published in Weissnichtwo, Germany, by the firm of Stillschweigen and Company. A delightful fiction! But Arnold decided to go Carlyle one better, not only by linking his writer to Voltaire's philosophical romance *Candide* but by bringing his creation directly into the world. He caused his imaginary interlocutor to write actual letters to the *Pall Mall Gazette*—the equivalent of a middlebrow American journal like *Newsweek*. In his first letter, Arminius takes up Arnold's championing of Continental ideas, in essays that had criticized the parochialism and the polemical narrowness of English culture. Arminius insists that Arnold has actually stolen his own ideas, and gotten them wrong in the process: the Enlightenment values symbolized by the term *Geist* are far loftier and more complex than Arnold's feeble brain can grasp. He writes as follows: 'To the Editor. Sir: An English friend of mine, Mr. Matthew Arnold, seems to have rushed into print with an idea or two he picked up from me when I was in England, and to have made rather a mess of it; at least, he sends me some newspapers which have answered him, and writes me a helpless sort of a letter at the same time, asking me how he is to parry this, and what he is to say in reply to that. Now, I have a regard for this Mr. Matthew Arnold, but I have taken his measure, and know him to be, as a disputant, rather a poor creature.'"

Dov paused, and once again glanced my way. Why was he looking amused? In any event, he immediately returned to his paper. "Arminius scorns especially Arnold's wish to see issues from his adversary's point of view. By contrast, Arminius writes, 'I, Sir, as a true Prussian, have a passion for what is *wissenschaftlich*; . . . I love to proceed with the stringency of a philosopher, and Mr. Matthew Arnold with his shillyshallying spoils the ideas I confide to him. Therefore I write to you myself. . . .' He then goes on to expound a version of Arnold's own critique of British provincialism.

"To this first letter, a wounded Arnold replied in the next issue, recounting something of his first acquaintance with Arminius, criticizing his friend's prideful polemics even as he clarifies the terms that his own critics had failed to understand. This fictive correspondence serves several purposes. First, it creates a dialogic situation for the playful testing and elaboration of ideas, much as did Anzaldúa's choice to write her essay in the form of a letter, as we have just heard. Second, by blending fact and fiction—now a frequent tactic of feminist memoir, my friend Marsha Doddvic tells me—Arnold challenges his readers' solid sense of self, suggesting that their own certainties may rest on a shifting and shiftable ground.

"Best of all, Arnold can have his rhetoric both ways: he himself can be the mild-mannered figure of reasonable compromise, while Arminius can indulge in savage critiques of British philistinism. These attacks Arnold can advance under the pretense that they are directed at himself rather than his readers. Even as he earnestly protests against Arminius's polemics, indeed, Arnold subtly reinforces them. When Arminius dismisses a popular British newspaper, the *Daily Telegraph*, as 'incorrigibly lewd,' Arnold cries out: 'No, Arminius! I hope not *incorrigibly*!' Insisting that the *Daily Telegraph* can be redeemed, he only underscores its present lewdness."

Dov went on to detail the substance of Arnold's plea for the spiritual and intellectual renewal of British culture, giving particular attention to the progressive development of an imaginary industrialist named Bottles, and to the valedictory scene of the death of Arminius, described in Arnold's final letter to the editor—putatively written not by Arnold himself but by a reporter friend who is in France, covering the Franco-Prussian War of 1870. "According to this letter, this friend has come upon Arminius, fatally wounded by a stray bullet while serving on outpost duty. The friend mentions Arnold's name. 'Poor fellow!' Arminius murmurs. 'He had a soft head, but I valued his heart. Tell him I leave him my ideas—the easier ones.' His fingers feeling instinctively for his tobacco-pouch, Arminius dies. A touching scene! Perhaps the Arnold of *Friendship's Garland* is in fact an early post-modernist," Dov concluded. "The problems of identity that he treated with such melancholy self-awareness in his poetry here become the basis for a sparkling comedy of ideas. The construction of his antagonistic friend finally frees 'the Scholar Gypsy' from the burden of self-consciousness, enabling his now multiplied self to advance a broad-based cultural critique from two opposing positions at once—both of which he in some sense holds himself."

Hymit Bathtöi followed Dov's paper with a discussion—yet again, I must say—of Paul de Man's suppressed anti-Semitic wartime writings. Still, Hymit gave the issue a compelling twist. He read de Man's subsequent work on Rousseau's *Confessions* as an elaborate "but always already futile" deconstruction of the need for a confessional criticism. "This is a deconstruction," he concluded, "that demonstrates the ineluctable reality of the events it refuses to confess. Even as de Man unpacks and neatly folds Rousseau's intellectual baggage, he reveals that there is no transcendental wardrobe in which Rousseau's purloined ribbon—or any textile or text—can be shelved, hidden safely away from the winds of history. Is not the autobiographical text finally a *chemise en abîme*, blown about like Benjamin's Angel of History in a space whose essence is not the emptiness for which de Man longed, but rather an ineluctable materiality?"

A slightly stunned silence followed Bathtöi's presentation. Had Hymit said the last word on the subject, or had he said nothing at all? There seemed to be little foothold for further discussion in either event. I went directly into my own paper, an analysis of Frank Kermode's recent memoir, *Not Entitled*. I compared this to his earlier book *The Sense of an Ending*, in which Kermode had employed an urbane, conversational voice that made him seem vividly present to the reader without, in fact, locating him anywhere in particular at all. By contrast, at the literal end of his career, in *Not Entitled* the now seventy-five-year-old Kermode looked back at his childhood and youth, revealing that he had been born to a working-class family on the Isle of Man and had always felt out of place and even fraudulent throughout his career in England, less and less "entitled" to the more and more prestigious posts he held in the years following the publication of *The Sense of an Ending*. I concluded that Kermode's open locating of himself gave his work a new depth and honesty, even as it made it more difficult for him to advance grand, sweeping theories.

The counterpointing of Arnold, de Man, and Kermode proved fruitful, and a lively discussion followed, building on the themes of concealment and self-revelation that had emerged across the three papers. We reluctantly adjourned when we saw lunch was being set up on the terrace off to our left. Vic and Bathtöi left together to go parasailing—I had a momentary image of Hymit suspended, like Dalí, by his moustaches, but I assume that he ended up using more conventional gear. I then went to lunch with Dov, who indicated that his life was taking a more satisfactory turn.

"I have decided it is too much to change continents every semester," he told me. "So we will try a year-by-year alternation for a while. This should be better for little Zena, as she begins preschool. She can have a whole year in Geneva, and for next year Amy has a grant to write a book on Voltaire and Mademoiselle de Scudéry. Do you know de Scudéry? No? I commend to you her great novel *Clélie*, with its map of the 'Royaume d'Amour.' The map shows the archetypal pattern of desire in the form of a circular path. It begins at the Plaine d'Indifférence, proceeds through Inquiétude to the Heights of Jouissance, then descends to Satiation and the lowlands of Faible Amitié. Finally one reaches Inclination Nouvelle, 'où l'on recommence le circuit d'Amour.'"

"And so, going back to Geneva. . . ." I said hesitantly.

"No, no," Dov replied, with a wave of his hand. "It is not as you suppose. That situation has resolved itself in a natural fashion—my intimate *amie* there completed her sabbatical year and is now teaching back in her native Finland. I mean rather that Amy and I can renew our romance on new terms. Actually this is the inverse of de Scudéry: instead of traversing the same terrain with a new love, we revisit our love in a new setting. Switzerland will be refreshing, after the cloying, superficial friendliness of California. Strangers in Irvine keep telling me to have a nice day! What is it to them if I do? In Geneva, thank God, no one even *wants* you to have a nice day, and your experience is your own business, not theirs. But first, France. We shall take a villa in Ferney for the summer, Amy will read Voltaire *in situ*, and I have only two books to finish, no other commitments. It will be a true idyll."

"Two books at once?" I asked.

"Both small," he replied. "First, a monograph on conjunctions in the modern essay."

"Juxtapositions and connections, you mean?"

"No, actual conjunctions. Critics too often limit their discussion to more obvious features of an essayist's work. Nouns, for example. Even"—Dov gave a scornful grunt—"*verbs*. Okay, such words do contribute to the meaning, but less than many suppose. Great writers like Nietzsche and Arnold—very similar thinkers, incidentally—carry their argument forward above all through the rhythmic modulation of their sentences. Conjunctions give a good index of this."

"You're focusing on the nineteenth century?" I asked.

"I end with Virginia Woolf. It was Marsha, actually, who drew my attention to the very different uses of 'but' in the crucial opening pages of *A Room of One's Own* and *Three Guineas*. I have extended this insight, and progress to conclude with a discussion of Woolf's subtle uses of ellipses. This provides a nice frame for my opening chapter, on Kierkegaard, from whom I derive my title: *Both/And*."

"I like those conjunctions," I remarked. "And the project sounds intriguing."

"It is really only a prolegomenon to a much more ambitious book," Dov replied. "The semiotics of the semicolon."

"You think a single volume will be enough?" I asked, unable to resist needling him a little. Dov, however, merely pondered my question for a moment.

"I hope so," he replied. "But the topic has so many ramifications. . . . The semicolon!" he exclaimed softly, leaning back in his chair, arms folded, as he gazed into the sky above my head. "Pivotal figure at once of connection and disjunction! I dream of writing its cultural history, as it plays out within the shifting semiotic field of punctuation in general. The colon, of course, and obviously the comma and the period as well. But I plan to explore the broader reaches of the parenthesis, too, and especially—he smiled in anticipation—the dash."

"So this will be your second project next year?" I asked.

"No, no, it will take five years at least once I start it. The other book I am finishing now is a more popular work, intended for a general audience. This I am calling *Hegel Is My Life*. Our conversations in Chicago gave me the idea, in fact. It is kind of a parody of self-help books, but serious as well—the desperate meliorism of modern culture could gain much from the analytical rigor of Hegel at his best. So I present a day of my life, one chapter per hour, showing how one's choices can be guided by frequent reflection on the *Phänomenologie des Geistes*. Menu planning, for instance."

"Menu planning?"

"Take breakfast," Dov replied. "How would Hegel have us resolve the spiritual crisis of our choice of sustenance? Do we choose eggs, say, or oatmeal? Taking eggs as our thesis, we observe they are colorful, perfectly formed, an animal product—not too healthy, but pleasurable to the palate. Oatmeal is of course their antithesis: vegetable product, virtually colorless; shapeless and tasteless as well, but very good for you. You can read my book to see the full reasoning by which I arrive at the synthesis of a buttered croissant. And then I must drink something: do I opt for coffee—hot, black, stimulating—or its antithesis: cold, white, soothing milk? Finally I synthesize these as café au lait and enjoy a good meal."

"I have to say the whole thing sounds a little exhausting," I commented. "At least you must work up an appetite in the process."

"True, it may almost be lunchtime before one gets a bite, if the analysis is done properly. Happily, you Americans have solved this problem by the synthesis you call 'brunch'—a true Hegelianism!"

Dov Midrash, mass-market guru? I found this hard to believe. "So you really think there's an audience for something like this?" I asked.

Dov shrugged. "Who knows. Still, I feel it is time for me to locate myself more directly in the American culture I seem to be adopting. There was a certain self-indulgence—was there not?—in the cultural despair I allowed myself in these last years. Perhaps this experiment will appeal to few, but that is finally the publisher's affair, not mine. One never knows with these trade publishers. At least they have an incentive to sell the book, as they have paid me a six-figure advance. My agent is quite optimistic. She keeps using words that end in prepositions, which are apparently good for books. Spin-offs. Tie-ins."

We spent the balance of the lunch discussing Americanisms. In the afternoon, I settled the conference accounts with the hotel and then relaxed by the pool with Nabokov's *Pnin*. Later, I dined in town with my friends Gail Finney, of U.C. Davis, and Charles Bernheimer, of Penn. Charlie regaled us with stories about decadent representations of Salomé, on whom he was working. We began discussing Wilde's epigrammatic style, which Charlie saw as an Irish artist's defense mechanism in London literary society. Gail, however, insisted that pithy wisdom was a universal occurrence, and she illustrated her point with a series of lines from recent Country/Western songs, of which she turned out to have an encyclopedic knowledge.

Toward midnight, they headed off to find a fusion jazz-salsa club they'd heard about; I headed off to bed, still pondering the line "I've been drowning in the water you walked on."

THE next morning we had the final meeting of our seminar. The highlight of the session was Vic's presentation. He gave—or extemporized—a brilliant paper on AIDS memoirs, sketching the outlines of a poetics of *thanatography*, as he called it: the writing of death, used as a means of coming to terms with life. He built splendidly on Marianne Hirsch's earlier paper on Holocaust testimonial, and Susan Suleiman followed him with a moving account of her return, after many years, to her childhood home in Hungary. The discussion that ensued was at once theoretically sophisticated and highly personal, intense and friendly. Unable to bring ourselves to stop the conversation after two and a half hours, we went together for lunch.

My pleasure at this success was somewhat dampened by several chance conversations while I was on line at the buffet and then as lunch was ending.

Several people came up to complain of problems with their panels—one had a chair who dominated the whole discussion, another had endless snafus with audio-visual equipment, a third just never got any good discussion going. I had the impression that my interlocutors were inclined to blame me personally for these problems. In the afternoon, tired of sightseeing, I spent my time fretting over what I'd been told. Then in the evening, we had our annual banquet, where nothing seemed to me to go as well as I'd expected. Had there always been so many little prizes to award? Had the nominating speeches always gone on so long? Had the food been so bland earlier in the week?

I realized that I'd begun to crash—after all the anxieties of planning the conference and getting through the seminar sessions, I was feeling numb. I probably should have gone to bed, but I lingered on once the banquet had finally dragged its slow length to an end. We'd hired a band for dancing; though I was too tired to dance myself, I thought the merriment might cheer me up.

It didn't. The band was lively, and everyone around me was dancing happily, displaying the slightly desperate exuberance of people who know this is their last night of freedom before they return to grading papers. Vic had skipped the banquet—"David, *please* . . ." he had said, when I'd asked him earlier if he was going—but he now came in with Bathtöi, and they began dancing up a storm. They seemed to be engrossed in each other, and Vic was even letting Hymit lead; could he be in love?

I knew that Marsha was looking forward to the arrival of her companion, Tom, the next morning; they were going to spend a week together in the Yucatan. For his part, Dov had indicated that he would be going back to his room after dinner to pack, as he was eager to leave promptly the next day to get home to his wife and daughter in Los Angeles. I was a little surprised, then, to see him sweep by me as I sat beside the dance floor, tightly entwined with a young post-Freudian in a slinky black dress. I caught his eye as he passed; he gave a quick shrug, and they spun off again in the crowd.

Across the dance floor, I saw Marsha doing some kind of free-form macarena with Gail Finney and Charlie Bernheimer. Their infectious friendliness was if anything more depressing than the more romantic pairings I'd been observing. Where did they get the energy? Why was I, alone, alone in this crowd, and with my birthday coming up the next day? Nothing to look forward to except the closing business meeting, then the long flights back to Dallas and then New York. It would be almost midnight by the time I'd get home. Then it would be Monday, back to the joys of chairing my department, an activity that has rightly been compared to herding cats.

I got up to head off to bed. Seeing me, Marsha came over and urged me to join her and the others. I begged off.

"I can see you're really tired," she said. "So go and get some rest, but you've got to hang around after the business meeting tomorrow, okay? Dov and Vic and I have a present for you, it was supposed to be a total surprise, but I want to be sure you don't miss us."

A nice gesture, I thought to myself as I headed for my room, not that I'd seen anything in the local shops that had really appealed to me. So fine, things had gone pretty well at this conference, and perhaps we would really be able to work together after this; but I could just see my life devolving into low-level administration—arranging conferences for my friends, getting parking spaces and research assistants for my departmental colleagues, answering endless copyediting queries for my eleven coeditors on a British literature anthology I was now engaged on. With the anthology running to fourteen thousand pages of copyedited manuscript, it was looking as though I'd never get back to my own writing in the foreseeable future. And tomorrow was going to start with the business meeting, at which I'd be treated to complaints from everyone whose session had gone badly. Some birthday.

IRASEMA CAMPOS, the conference coordinator, was waiting for me the next morning when I got to the ballroom, the dance floor now covered with orderly rows of chairs for our business meeting. She asked me to follow her to a small room off to the side; not knowing what new hassle had arisen, I went along reluctantly. There I found Eugene Eoyang and the rest of the ACLA board, all standing around a table. On the table was a large cheesecake, bearing the legend, *Felicidades, Profesor Davíd!*

"We have so much enjoyed having your group," Irasema told me, "and so when I heard it would be your birthday, I wanted to have this made for you."

Eoyang presented me with a genuine Chinese "scholar's hat," complete with a long, braided queue, which he had picked up for me in Hong Kong after reading my scholarship book. On behalf of the board, Gail Finney gave me a book called *The Hidden Meaning of Birthdays*. "Check out April 13th," she urged. "You *are* your birthday!" I found the place. "Bold, powerful, reforming," I read, oddly flattered by this commendation from a small paperback whose author could hardly have been thinking of me personally. I was less pleased, to be sure, by the remaining traits listed: "Reclusive, sensitive, odd."

"We were thinking more of the description below the traits," Gail said. "Look: 'You are a reformer, willing to toil long and hard to effect the changes you consider vital. Your novel ideas may cause coworkers and acquaintances to regard you as an oddball at first, but later they will recognize the wisdom of your reforms and may even come to appreciate your slightly harebrained approach to problem solving.' Truer words were never written, pal."

It was time for the business meeting, where I was pleasantly surprised to find that the overall response to our new structure was very positive. The few unsuccessful seminars I'd earlier heard about had been the only real disappointments. The great majority had gone well—a notably higher proportion than under the more typical conference format—and the meeting concluded with a unanimous vote to continue the new structure for future years.

Charlie Bernheimer had been sitting beside me; he gave me a hearty slap on the back as the vote went through. "I thought I'd just be coming here for a vacation," he remarked, as people began to leave the ballroom. "You know, the leisure of the theory class? I needed a break, but it's been a lot more than that. My seminar kept missing lunch, we were having such good discussions, and we're going to do a follow-up next year. I can't wait!" He picked up the tennis racket he had stored under his chair, and left, whistling.

Marsha, Vic, and Dov were waiting for me at the back of the ballroom. "Our fearless leader!" Vic exclaimed.

"We owe it all to you," Marsha added. "So here's our little thank-you." Dov handed me a manila envelope.

Probably some etching of Puerto Vallarta, I thought as I opened it. Inside I was surprised to find only my own curriculum vitae. Elegantly printed on cream-colored bond, to be sure, but still . . . was my own self-presentation really so inept that I needed their design services?

"Look at the publications, dear boy," Vic said.

Glancing down, I saw my narrative book and my scholarship book, my forthcoming British literature anthology—and a book I didn't recognize, also listed as forthcoming: *Meetings of the Mind.*

"We wanted to show you our commitment to our conference conversations," Dov said. "We mean to work with you in the coming year to make the book a reality."

"Of course, we still expect you to do the actual writing," Vic put in. "Your prose style is so beautifully . . . prosaic, you can get the thing drafted rather rapidly. Then we will improve it for you."

"We hope you like the title," Marsha added. "But keep looking, there's more."

I turned the page; nothing special there, just my occasional articles. But toward the bottom of the page, I again found things I didn't recognize.

"What's this article on 'The Aesthetics of Conquest: Aztec Poetry Before and After Cortés'?" I asked. "I don't get the joke—you know perfectly well I don't know anything about Aztec poetry, and you've even got this listed as though it's actually appeared in *Representations.*"

"It has," Vic replied. "Here it is."

He handed me an offprint from a recent issue of the Berkeley journal. Not only did it appear to be an actual reprint; I was given as its author.

"Here's the deal," Marsha said. "We know how much time you've put into all the shitty little arrangements it took to get our whole thing going over the years, and we know the burden's mostly going to fall on you to write our book up. So we thought, what could we give you to help make up for lost time? It's not like we could give you a life, you've already got that together better than most of us, but we thought we could give you a sexier intellectual profile. I mean, those articles on Wordsworth and on Wode-house are lovely, really, but we knew you'd be doing something a little more ambitious by now if you'd had time. So here you are."

"But this is dishonest—it's plagiarism!" I exclaimed.

"Not at all," Vic replied. "Quite the opposite. Rather than stealing your work, we are *giving* you work."

"You should think of our articles as examples of the great tradition of pseudepigraphy," Dov remarked.

"Of what?" I asked, feeling increasingly bewildered.

"Pseudepigraphy: a common custom in antiquity. Later tradition would often attribute an anonymous work to some famous sage. Even a text's own author might attach an honored name to his work in preference to his own. Do not suppose this was always a matter of falsehood. I am sure it was often a mark of loyalty and respect, less a deception than a way to orient the reader, linking the new work to a chosen tradition. Pseudepigraphy has also reappeared in modern times, as an expression of friendship: Samuel John-son used to refresh his mind in this way, putting aside his major projects and writing essays for his friends to publish under their own names."

"I assume he did so with their knowledge," I replied tartly, and I meant it to sting. "You didn't and don't have my permission to do this. It's ab-surd—this Aztec article has nothing to do with me at all!"

"It has everything to do with you," Marsha responded. "We couldn't have done it without you. Vic and I wrote the Aztec piece together, when you read it you'll see. I could never unravel the formal complexities of those poems the way Vic can, and of course I don't know the language either, but I could bring the whole post-colonial perspective to the argument."

"I had meditated on those poems for years," Vic added, "but they were a kind of private vice. I had no way to talk about them to someone outside the charmed but rather small circle of Mesoamericanists, most of whom care little for literature at all. Together, Marsha and I were able to pull it off. I must show you the acceptance letter Greenblatt sent you at my—I mean, your—summer address on the Vineyard: it is quite complimentary."

"But really, I can't accept this," I said.

"Just who do you think you *are*, trying to deny work for which you were the prime inspiration?" Vic asked. "I don't suppose you have much choice in the matter anyway, as three of our four joint articles are already out."

"Here is our second effort," Dov said, handing me a reprint titled "The Ethnic Ethnographer: Judaism in *Tristes Tropiques*." This too was headed with my name, and had also been published in *Representations*. "I have been on this journal's board for some years now," Dov went on. "As you may know, Greenblatt and Alpers established an editorial collective to evaluate papers. Submissions not infrequently come through one or another member of the editorial board, and I merely introduced our manuscripts in the natural course of business. Addams here suggested this topic to Marsha and to me. It was a good idea, as it combined her anthropological interests with mine in Judaism. We found that for years we had both been thinking in a general way of working on Lévi-Strauss."

"You'll also quite like your article on allegories of love in Egyptian poetry and the Song of Songs," Vic interjected. "Dov and I learned a lot ourselves writing it. We were even planning a sequel when you glom—stumbled onto us at the Oriental Institute in Chicago."

"The fourth piece isn't out yet," Marsha put in, "the one on technologies of the self in Buster Keaton? Stuart McDougal's going to use it in a collection of his on meta-cinema, but apparently some of the other contributors are holding it up. At least you did give it a couple of years ago at the Cinema Studies Association."

"I did?" I asked dubiously.

"Actually I delivered the paper for you," Vic said cheerfully. "No one seemed to know the difference. I take it you don't know many people in the academic film community. I was prepared, if asked, to say you'd been taken ill and I was reading the paper for you, but in fact the question never came up. I simply arrived and told the moderator I was there to give the Keaton paper, and she showed me to my spot on the podium. I assume she thought I was you. She did seem puzzled that I didn't know a colleague of yours in French, but I merely mentioned what a large and disjointed place Columbia is, and she let it pass."

"But what am I supposed to *do* with this fraudulent CV?" I asked.

"First of all, stop using ridiculous terms like 'fraudulent,'" Marsha said. "Are we living in the late twentieth century, or what? Second, maybe you can take it as kind of a challenge, see if you can live up to your resumé now it's a little livelier itself."

"I should think that in theory there is no problem for 'Damrosch' to encompass these various interests," Dov remarked. "Anyone with a modicum of linguistic talent and the requisite restlessness might gain the various knowledges necessary to write these works. The better question is to ask *why* someone might choose to work on such disparate materials. Imagine you have indeed written these pieces, then ask yourself how you can best build on these beginnings for the future. This could yield interesting results."

"But first, dear boy," Vic said, "you have our book to write. We have given you a new lease on scholarly life: now you must do the same for us. If you can have a draft of the first chapter by September, say, that would be convenient—you can send it to me in Venice. Before then I will be at Hymit's summer place in the Dardanelles. I must e-mail you the address."

"Take your time, David," Marsha said reassuringly. "What we're saying is, we'll be there for you whenever you're ready for us. And we think this'll just be the beginning of some extended collaborations in the future. . . . But for now, we've got to get out of here, they're holding Sunday Mass in this room. I hear some church around here is being renovated."

Sure enough, Irasema and her crew were draping the rostrum with clerical-looking cloths. People in their Sunday best were beginning to file into the room, and a priest and two altar boys were waiting with polite impatience for us to leave.

I had brought my bag down with me, as I had my plane to catch. My friends walked me to the hotel door. Dov nodded farewell as he took out his pipe, Vic kissed me on both cheeks, and Marsha gave me a quick hug. "Take care of yourself, now," she said. "Till we meet again!"

BIBLIOGRAPHY

Adams, Hazard. *The Academic Tribes*. New York: Liveright, 1976.

Addams, Vic d'Ohr. "'The Aztec King David'?: Nezahualcóyotl, Fabricated Poet." *Estudios de Cultura Azteca* 22:4 (1987), 1–25.

———. "Cruising." *American Yachtsman* (Summer 1989), 3–9.

———. "Cruising." *Grand Street* (Fall, 1994), 1–15.

———. *Death: A Biography*. Forthcoming from W. W. Norton, fall 2001.

———. "'His Name Means Bliss': The Aesthetics of Naming in Ananda-vardhana and Abhinavagupta." *Sanskritique* 18:1 (1986), 55–80.

———. "'I Am Not a Man but a Woman': The Hermeneutics of Gender in Bernard of Clairvaux." *Saeculum* 104:2 (1991), 220–40.

———. "'I've Heard the Music's Din Afore': Self-Parody in *The Pirates of Penzance*." *Echolalia* 2:2 (2000), 24–42.

———. "Just One of the Buoys: Adrift in the Indian Ocean." *Yachting Today*, October 1990, 11–18.

———. "The Prism-House of Language." *Autoregard* 3:4 (1990), 2–3.

———. "The Scones of Venice: Proust at the Café Ruskin." *Bulletin des petites-amies de Marcel Proust* 95:2 (1983), 22–24.

———. "Silence Be—It Was the Catamaran." *Yachting Today*, August, 1994, 30–38.

———. "Sixteen Ways of Looking at a Blank Bard: A Reply to Miguel León-Portilla." *Estudios de Cultura Azteca* 24:4 (1989), 56–66.

———. *The Utility of Futility*. New Haven: Yale University Press, 1989.

———. "'What Madness to Think a Cloud Can Speak': Floating Signifiers in Kalidasa's *Meghaduta*." *Jadavpur Journal of Comparative Literature* 12 (1990), 122–33.

Adorno, Theodor. *Minima Moralia*. Tr. G.F.N. Jephcott. London: Verso, 1978.

Adorno, Theodor, and Max Horkheimer. *Dialectic of Enlightenment*. Tr. John Cumming. New York: Continuum, 1988.

Anzaldúa, Gloria. *Borderlands*. San Francisco: Aunt Lute Books, 1999.

———. *Making Face, Haciendo Caras: Creative and Critical Perspectives by Women of Color*. San Francisco: Aunt Lute Foundations, 1990.

———. "Speaking in Tongues: A Letter to 3rd World Women Writers." In Cherríe Moraga and Gloria Anzaldúa, eds., *This Bridge Called My Back: Writings of Radical Women of Color*, 165–74.

Apter, Emily. *Continental Drift: From National Characters to Virtual Subjects*. Chicago: University of Chicago Press, 1999.

———. *Feminizing the Fetish: Psychoanalysis and Narrative Obsession in Turn-of-the-Century France*. Ithaca: Cornell University Press, 1991.

Arnold, Matthew. *Culture and Anarchy*. New Haven: Yale University Press, 1994.

———. *Friendship's Garland*. New York: MacMillan, 1913.

———. "The Function of Criticism at the Present Time." In *Lectures and Essays in Criticism*. Ann Arbor: University of Michigan Press, 1980, 258–85.

———. "The Study of Poetry." In *Matthew Arnold: Poetry and Prose*. ed. John Bryson. Cambridge: Harvard University Press, 1954, pp. 663–84.

Arnott, Nancy. *The Hidden Meaning of Birthdays*. Kansas City: Andrews and McNeal, 1996.

Auerbach, Erich. *Mimesis*. Tr. Willard R. Trask. Princeton: Princeton University Press, 1968.

———. *Scenes from the Drama of European Literature*. Gloucester, Mass.: P. Smith, 1973.

Bakhtin, Mikhail. *The Dialogic Imagination*. Tr. Caryl Emerson and Michael Holquist. Austin, Texas: University of Texas Press, 1981.

Barnes, Djuna. *The Ladies' Almanack*. New York: New York Press, 1992.

———. *Nightwood*. New York: New Directions, 1961.

Barry, Dave. *Dave Barry Turns Forty*. New York: Fawcett Columbine, 1991.

Barthes, Roland. *The Empire of Signs*. Tr. Richard Howard. New York: Noonday Press, 1989.

———. *Mythologies*. Tr. Annette Levers. New York: Noonday Press, 1972.

————. *The Pleasure of the Text*. Tr. Richard Miller. New York: Hill and Wang, 1975.

————. *Roland Barthes by Roland Barthes*. Tr. Richard Howard. New York: Hill and Wang, 1977.

————. *Sade, Fourier, Loyola*. Tr. Richard Miller. Baltimore: Johns Hopkins University Press, 1997.

Bashō, Matsuo. *Back Roads to Far Towns: Bashō's Travel Journal*. Tr. Cid Corman and Kamaike Susumu. Fredonia, N.Y.: White Pine Press, 1986.

————. *The Essential Basho*. Tr. Sam Hamill. Boston: Shambhala, 1998.

Bathtöi, Hymit. "Bahdaffi, c'est moi? À la lecture de *Borrowed Lives*." *Tlön* 12:3 (1997), 40–56.

————. "Blacklist and Insults: Hirsch on Midrash on de Man." *Glyph* 8:3 (1986), 566–90.

————. "'If Everybody's Somebody, then No-One's Anybody': Gilbert ve Sullivan'ın Gondoliersunda Kimlik Meselesi." *Uqbar* 22:6 (1998), 1–22.

Beerbohm, Max. "Enoch Soames." In *Seven Men and Two Others*. Oxford: Oxford University Press, 1980, 1–44.

Bénabou, Marcel. *Why I Have Not Written Any of My Books*. Tr. David Kornacker. Lincoln: University of Nebraska Press, 1996.

Benchley, Robert. *Twenty Thousand Leagues Under the Sea: or, David Copperfield*. New York: Henry Holt, 1928.

————. "Why We Laugh—or Do We?" In *The Benchley Roundup*, ed. Nathaniel Benchley. New York: Delta, 1962, 277–80.

Benengeli, Cide Hamete. *Cervantes y Yo: Obra como vida*. Ed. G. de Pasamonte. Salamanca: Orbis Tertius, 1620.

Benjamin, Walter. *Moscow Diary*. Ed. Gary Smith. Tr. Richard Sieburth. Cambridge, Mass.: Harvard University Press, 1986.

————. "The Storyteller." In Hannah Arendt, ed., *Illuminations*. Tr. Harry Zohn. New York: Schocken, 1969, 83–109.

————. "Theses on the Philosophy of History." In *Illuminations*, 253–64.

Bernheimer, Charles. "The Decadent Subject." *L' Esprit Créateur* 32: 4 (1992), pp. 53–62.

———. *Flaubert and Kafka*. New Haven: Yale University Press, 1982.

———, ed. *Comparative Literature in the Age of Multiculturalism*. Baltimore: Johns Hopkins University Press, 1995.

Bloom, Allan. *The Closing of the American Mind*. New York: Simon and Schuster, 1987.

———. *Giants and Dwarves*. New York: Simon and Schuster, 1990.

Bloom, Harold. *The American Religion*. New York: Simon and Schuster, 1992.

———. *The Anxiety of Influence: A Theory of Poetry*. New York: Oxford University Press, 1997.

———. *The Western Canon*. New York: Harcourt Brace, 1994.

Borges, Jorge Luis. "Borges y Yo." In *Other Inquisitions, 1937–1952*. Tr. Ruth L. Simms. Austin: University of Texas Press, 1964.

———. "Pierre Menard, Author of Don Quixote." In *Ficciones*. Tr. Anthony Kerrigan. New York: Grove Press, 1963.

———. "Tlön, Uqbar, Orbis Tertius." In *Ficciones*.

Bourdieu, Pierre. *Homo Academicus*. Tr. Peter Collier. Cambridge, England: Polity Press, 1988.

Bradbury, Malcolm. *My Strange Quest for Mensonge: Structuralism's Hidden Hero*. London: Andre Deutsch, 1987.

Bromwich, David. *Politics by Other Means*. New Haven: Yale University Press, 1992.

Brooks, Peter. *Body Work: Objects of Desire in Modern Narrative*. Cambridge: Harvard University Press, 1993.

———. *World Elsewhere*. New York: Simon and Schuster, 1999.

Burke, Kenneth. *The Philosophy of Literary Form: Studies in Symbolic Action*. Berkeley: University of California Press, 1973.

———. *Toward a Better Life: Being a Series of Epistles or Declarations*. Berkeley: University of California Press, 1973.

Byron, George Gordon, Lord. *Don Juan*. In *Complete Poetical Works*, ed. Jerome J. McGann. New York: Oxford University Press, 1980–.

Calvino, Italo. *Invisible Cities*. Tr. William Weaver. New York: Harcourt, Brace, Jovanovich, 1978.

———. "The Pen in the First Person: For the Drawings of Saul Steinberg." In *The Uses of Literature*. Tr. Patrick Creagh. San Diego: Harcourt, Brace, Jovanovich, 1986, 291–99.

Carlyle, Thomas. *Sartor Resartus: The Life and Opinions of Diogenes Teufelsdröckh*. New York: Oxford University Press, 1982.

Casanova, Giacomo. *History of My Life*. 12 vol. Tr. Willard R. Trask. Baltimore: Johns Hopkins University Press, 1966.

Clendinnen, Inge. *Aztecs: An Interpretation*. New York: Knopf, 1995.

Coleman, Eliot. *Four Season Harvest: How to Harvest Fresh Organic Vegetables from Your Home Garden All Year Round*. White River Junction, Vermont: Chelsea Green, 1999.

Coleman, Elizabeth. "Leadership in the Change Process." *Liberal Education* 83:1 (1997), 1–4.

Coleman, Tom. *The Whole Tool Catalog*. Burlington, Vermont: Earthworks Collective, 1991.

Combe, William. *The Tour of Doctor Syntax, in Search of the Picturesque*. Philadelphia: W. Charles, 1814.

Conrad, Joseph. *Heart of Darkness; and The Secret Sharer*. New York: Doubleday, 1997.

Cornford, Francis MacDonald. *Microcosmographia Academica: Being Advice to the Young Academic Politician*. London: Bowes and Bowes, 1978.

Corngold, Stanley. "On Paul de Man's Collaborationist Writings." In Werner Hamacher, Neil Hertz, and Thomas Keenan, eds., *Responses: On Paul de Man's Wartime Journalism*. Lincoln: University of Nebraska Press, 1989, 80–84.

Corngold, Stanley, and Irene Giersing. *Borrowed Lives*. Albany: State University of New York Press, 1991.

Crews, Frederick. *The Pooh Perplex*. New York: Dutton, 1963.

Damrosch, Barbara. *The Garden Primer*. New York: Workman Press, 1988.

Damrosch, David. "Auerbach in Exile." *Comparative Literature* 47:2 (1995), 97–117.

Damrosch, David. "Literary Study in an Elliptical Age." In Charles Bern-heimer, ed., *Comparative Literature in the Age of Multiculturalism* (Balti-more: Johns Hopkins University Press, 1995), 122–33.

———. *The Narrative Covenant*. San Francisco: Harper & Row, 1987. Repr. Cornell University Press, 1991.

———. "'Peter Bell' Revised." *The Wordsworth Circle* 4 (1980), 232–38.

———. "P. G. Wodehouse." In George Stade, ed., *British Writers Supple-ment III*. New York: Scribners, 1996, 447–64.

———. "'You *Are* Rather Triangular': Mimetic Desire in Gilbert and Sullivan's Middle Period." Forthcoming in *Girard Studies Annual*, 2001.

———. *We Scholars: Changing the Culture of the University*. Cambridge: Harvard University Press, 1995.

———. *What Is World Literature?* Forthcoming from Princeton University Press.

Damrosch, David, et al., eds. *The Longman Anthology of British Literature*. 2 vols. New York: Addison Wesley Longman, 1999.

———. *The Longman Anthology of World Literature*. Forthcoming from Ad-dison Wesley Longman, 2003.

'Damrosch, David' (attrib.), "The Aesthetics of Conquest: Aztec Poetry Be-fore and After Cortés." *Representations* 33, 101–20. Repr. in Stephen Greenblatt, ed., *New World Encounters* (Berkeley: University of Cali-fornia Press), 139–58.

———. "Allegories of Love in Egyptian Poetry and the Song of Songs." *Stanford Literature Review* 5:1, 25–42.

———. "The Ape behind the Camera: Subject and Object in Buster Kea-ton." Forthcoming in Stuart McDougal, ed., *Metacinema*.

———. "The Ethnic Ethnographer: Judaism in *Tristes Tropiques*." *Represen-tations* 50 (1995), 1–13.

Damrosch, Frank, *Some Essentials in the Teaching of Music*. New York: G. Schirmer, 1916.

Damrosch, Frank, Jr., *The Faith of the Episcopal Church*. New York: More-house-Gorham, 1958.

Damrosch, Leo. *God's Plot and Man's Stories*. Chicago: University of Chicago Press, 1985.

———. *The Sorrows of the Quaker Jesus*. Cambridge, Mass.: Harvard University Press, 1996.

Damrosch, Walter. *My Musical Life*. New York: Charles Scribner's Sons, 1923.

Dante Alighieri. *Commedia*. Milano: Editel, 1994.

Deleuze, Gilles, and Felix Guattari. *Anti-Oedipus: Capitalism and Schizophrenia*. Tr. Robert Henley, Mark Seem, and Helen R. Lane. New York: Viking, 1977.

Deleuze, Gilles, and Claire Parnet. *Dialogues*. Tr. Hugh Tomlinson and Barbara Habberjam. New York: Columbia University Press, 1987.

De Man, Paul. *Allegories of Reading*. New Haven: Yale University Press, 1979.

———. *Blindness and Insight*. Minneapolis: University of Minnesota Press, 1983.

———. *The Resistance to Theory*. Foreword by Wlad Godzich. Minneapolis: University of Minnesota Press, 1986.

Derrida, Jacques. *Glas*. Tr. John P. Leavey, Jr., and Richard Rand. Lincoln: University of Nebraska Press, 1986.

———. *Of Grammatology*. Tr. Gayatri Chakravorty Spivak. Baltimore: Johns Hopkins University Press, 1976.

———. *The Postcard: From Socrates to Freud and Beyond*. Tr. Alan Ross. Chicago: University of Chicago Press, 1987.

———. "Suis-je Shatner? L'arti-fils biographique de *Jacquesbaby*." *Plomb* 3:3 (1996), 902–88.

Diderot, Dennis. *Jacques le Fataliste et son maître*. Geneva: Droz, 1976.

Doddvic, Marsha. *The Hole Truth: The Social Fabric of Film*. New York: Subverso, 1993.

———. "Jacques the Fatalist and his Mastery." http://www.jacquesbaby.com.

———. "L'Oeil-Mort in a Pinafore: The Specular Jouissance of 'Dick' Deadeye." *Cygnes* 2:4 (1984), 18–40.

Doddvic, Marsha. "Portrait of a Lady as a Young Man: James/Joyce and Gender." *Modernisms* 2:2 (1992), 2–22.

———. *Reflections on Echo Lake: Explorations in Human/Nature*. Photographs by Cassandra Coleman-Doddvic. Watertown, Conn.: Persephone Press, 2000.

Doddvic, Marsha, and Dov Midrash. "Sign and Sight: Saturday Night at the Movies with Heidegger." *Metacritical Inquiry* 19:2 (1999), 55–77.

Ebert, Teresa. *Ludic Feminism and After: Postmodernism, Desire, and Labor in Late Capitalism*. Ann Arbor: University of Michigan Press, 1996.

Eliot, Thomas Stearns. "Tradition and the Individual Talent." In David Damrosch et al., eds., *The Longman Anthology of British Literature*, 2:2447–52.

———. "The Waste Land." In *Collected Poems, 1909–1962*. New York: Harcourt, Brace and World, 1970, 51–76.

Eoyang, Eugene. *Coat of Many Colors: Reflections on Diversity by a Minority of One*. Boston: Beacon Press, 1995.

Fanon, Frantz. *Black Skin, White Masks*. New York: Grove Press, 1991.

Felski, Rita. *Beyond Feminist Aesthetics: Feminist Literature and Social Change*. Cambridge: Harvard University Press, 1989.

Fielding, Henry. *An Apology for the Life of Mrs. Shamela Andrews*. Los Angeles: University of California Press, 1956.

———. *The History of Tom Jones, Foundling*. New York: Modern Library, 1994.

Finney, Gail. *Look Who's Laughing: Gender and Comedy*. Langhorne: Gordon and Breach, 1994.

Fodor's 91. *Japan: With Tours of Old Japan and Advice for Business Travelers*. New York: Fodor's Travel Publications, 1991.

Foucault, Michel. "Two Lectures." In *Power/Knowledge: Selected Interviews and Other Writings, 1972–1977*. Ed. Colin Gordon. New York: Pantheon, 1980.

———. "What Is an Author?" In *Language, Counter-Memory, Practice*. Tr. Donald F. Bouchard and Sherry Simon. Ithaca: Cornell University Press, 1977, 113–38.

Freud, Sigmund. *Beyond the Pleasure Principle*. Tr. James Strachey. New York: W. W. Norton, 1989.

———. *Civilization and Its Discontents*. Tr. James Strachey. New York: W. W. Norton, 1989.

———. *Fragment of an Analysis of a Case of Hysteria ("Dora")*. Tr. James Strachey. New York: Simon and Schuster, 1991.

———. *The Psychopathology of Everyday Life*. Tr. James Strachey. New York: W. W. Norton, 1989.

Frye, Northrop. *Anatomy of Criticism*. Princeton: Princeton University Press, 1973.

———. *The Great Code: The Bible and Literature*. San Diego: Harcourt, Brace, Jovanovich, 1983.

Futuri, Franco. *Learning from las Vegas de Bloomington*. Forthcoming from MIT Press: Zone Books, 2001.

Gadamer, Hans-Georg. *Wahrheit und Methode*. Tübingen: Mohr, 1972. Tr. by Garrett Barden and John Cummings as *Truth and Method*. New York: Seabury Press, 1975.

Garibay K., Ángel María. *Poesía Náhuatl*. Mexico City: UNAM, 1964.

Gilbert, William Schwenk. *Original Plays*. London: Chatto & Windus, 1920.

Godzich, Wlad. *The Culture of Literacy*. Cambridge, Mass.: Harvard University Press, 1995.

Gottfried von Strassburg. *Tristan*. Tr. A. T. Hatto. New York: Viking Penguin, 1960.

Graff, Gerald. *Beyond the Culture Wars: How Teaching Conflicts Can Revitalize American Education*. New York: W. W. Norton, 1992.

———. *Professing Literature: An Institutional History*. Chicago: University of Chicago Press, 1987.

———. "Self-Interview." In H. Aram Veeser, ed., *Confessions of the Critics*, 97–102.

Greenblatt, Stephen. *Renaissance Self-Fashioning from More to Shakespeare*. Chicago: University of Chicago Press, 1980.

Greene, Gayle, and Coppélia Kahn. *Changing Subjects: The Making of Feminist Literary Criticism*. New York: Routledge, 1992.

Grossberg, Lawrence, Cary Nelson, and Paula Treichler, eds. *Cultural Studies*. New York: Routledge, 1992.

Haraway, Donna J. *Modest_Witness@Second_Millennium.FemaleMan©_Meets_OncoMouse: Feminism and Techno-science*. New York: Routledge, 1997.

———. *Simians, Cyborgs, and Women: the Re-invention of Nature*. London: Free Association, 1991.

Hardy, Cynthia, et al. "Strategy Formation in the University Setting." In James L. Bess, ed., *College and University Organization: Insights from the Behavioral Sciences*. New York: New York University Press, 1984, 169–210.

Hassig, Ross. *Aztec Warfare: Imperial Expansion and Political Control*. Norman: University of Oklahoma Press, 1998.

Hegel, G. F. W. *Phenomenology of Spirit*. Tr. A. V. Miller. Oxford: Clarendon, 1977.

"Henry James." *Encyclopaedia Britannica*. Chicago: 15th edition, 1976. Macropaedia: Knowledge in Depth, 10:24–27.

———. *Encyclopaedia Britannica*. Chicago: 15th edition, revised, 1987. Micropaedia: Ready Reference, 6:485–87.

Hirsch, E. D. *Cultural Pre-literacy: What Every Infant Needs to Know*. Boston: Very Basic Books, 1992.

———. "Darkness Risible." *New Jersey Review of Books* 55 (April, 1985), 1–6.

———. "Gadamer's Theory of Interpretation." In *Validity in Interpretation*. New Haven: Yale University Press, 1967, 245–64.

James, Henry. *The Aspern Papers and Other Stories*. Ed. Adrian Poole. New York: Oxford University Press, 1983.

———. *The Golden Bowl*. London: Dent, 1984.

Jerome, Jerome K. *They and I*. New York: Dodd, Mead, 1909.

———. *Three Men in a Boat*. Oxford: Oxford University Press, 1998.

Johnson, Gordon. *University Politics: F. M. Cornford's Cambridge and His Advice to the Young Academic Politician*. Cambridge, England: Cambridge University Press, 1994.

Joyce, James. *Finnegans Wake*. New York: Viking Press, 1955.

_____. *A Portrait of the Artist as a Young Man.* New York: Garland, 1993.

_____. *Ulysses.* New York: Random House, 1986.

Kafka, Franz. "Josephine, the Songstress: or, the Mouse Folk," *The Transformation and Other Stories.* Tr. Malcolm Pasley. New York: Penguin, 1992, 220–36.

_____. *Metamorphosis.* Tr. Stanley Corngold. New York: Bantam Books, 1972.

Kaplan, Alice. *French Lessons.* Chicago: University of Chicago Press, 1993.

Kauffman, Linda. "The Long Goodbye: Against Personal Testimony, or an Infant Grifter Grows Up." In Gayle Greene and Coppélia Kahn, *Changing Subjects: The Making of Feminist Literary Criticism,* 129–46.

Kermode, Frank. *Not Entitled.* New York: Farrar, Strauss, and Giroux, 1995.

_____. *The Sense of an Ending.* New York: Oxford University Press, 1967.

Kierkegaard, Søren. *Either/Or.* Tr. Howard V. Hong and Edna H. Hong. Princeton: Princeton University Press, 1978.

_____. *Fear and Trembling; Repetition.* Tr. Howard V. Hong and Edna H. Hong. Princeton: Princeton University Press, 1983.

Kleist, Heinrich von. *Penthesilea.* Tr. Joel Agee. New York: HarperCollins, 1998.

Lacan, Jacques. "The Insistence of the Letter in the Unconscious: or, Reason Since Freud." In *Ecrits: A Selection.* Tr. Alan Sheridan. New York: W. W. Norton, 1977, 146–78.

Lamar, Howard. "Disciplining the Disciplines." Review of David Damrosch, *We Scholars. The Yale Review* 83 (October 1995), 95–100.

Langer, Suzanne, *Philosophy in a New Key: A Study in the Symbolism of Reason, Rite, and Art.* Cambridge, Mass.: Harvard University Press, 1957.

Lasch, Christopher. *The Culture of Narcissism: American Life in an Age of Diminishing Expectations.* New York: Warner Books, 1979.

Lem, Stanislas. *A Perfect Vacuum.* Tr. Michael Kendel. New York: Harcourt Brace Jovanovich, 1979.

L'Engle, Madeleine. *A Wrinkle in Time.* New York: Farrar, Strauss and Giroux, 1963.

León-Portilla, Miguel. *Aztec Thought and Culture: A Study of the Ancient Nahuatl Mind.* Tr. Jack Emory Davis. Norman: University of Oklahoma Press, 1971.

———. "Nezahualcóyotl de Tezcoco: Poeta, arquitecto y sabio en las cosas divinas." In *Trece poetas del mundo azteca.* Mexico City: UNAM, 1967, 40–75.

———. "Nezahualcóyotl, verdadero Davíd: Una respuesta al Dr. V. Addams." *Estudios de Cultura Azteca* 23:4 (1988), 40–50.

Levinas, Emmanuel. *Entre Nous: On Thinking-of-the-Other.* Tr. Michael B. Smith and Barbara Harshav. New York: Columbia University Press, 1998.

———. *Otherwise than Being: or, Beyond Essence.* Tr. Alphonso Lingis. Pittsburgh: Duquesne Universty Press, 1998.

Lévi-Strauss, Claude. *Tristes Tropiques.* Tr. John and Doreen Weightman. New York: Modern Library, 1997.

———. *The View from Afar.* Ed. Didier Eribon. Tr. Joachim Neugroschel and Phoebe Hass. Chicago: University of Chicago Press, 1992.

Lewis, C. S. *Out of the Silent Planet.* New York: Scribner Classics, 1996.

———. *The Screwtape Letters.* New York: MacMillan, 1954.

———. *Surprised by Joy.* New York: Harcourt Brace, 1955.

———. *Till We Have Faces: A Myth Retold.* New York: Harcourt, Brace, Jovanovich, 1985.

Lodge, David. *Changing Places: A Tale of Two Campuses.* London: Secker and Warburg, 1975.

———. *Small World.* New York: Warner Books, 1991.

———. *Working with Structuralism.* Boston: Routledge and Kegan Paul, 1981.

Longenbach, James. "What Literary Criticism Cannot Do." *Raritan* 17:1 (1997), 152–62.

Longenlost, Darcy. "Stanley and Me: A Passionate Collaboration." In T. Bahdaffi, ed., *Borrowing Back Our Lives.* Forthcoming from Princeton University Press.

Lukács, Georg. *The Theory of the Novel.* Tr. Anna Bostock. Cambridge: MIT Press, 1973.

Mallarmé, Stéphane. "The Book: A Spiritual Instrument." In Hazard Adams, ed., *Critical Theory Since Plato.* Fort Worth: Harcourt, Brace, Jovanovich, 1992, 690–92.

Malle, Louis, director. *My Dinner with André* (1981). Screenplay by Wallace Shawn.

Martin, George. *The Damrosch Dynasty.* Boston: Houghton Mifflin, 1983.

McCourt, Frank. *Angela's Ashes.* New York: Scribner, 1996.

McDougal, Stuart, ed. *Play It Again, Sam: Retakes on Remakes.* Berkeley: University of California Press, 1998.

Mead, Margaret. "Conference Arrangements." In W. Warner Burke and Richard Beckhard, eds., *Conference Planning.* La Jolla: University Associates, 2d ed., 1976, 45–61.

Mechthild von Magdeburg. *Das fliessende Licht der Gottheit. Nach der einsiedler Handschrift in kritischen Vergleich mit der gesamten Überlieferung.* Ed. Hans Neumann. Munich: Artemis Verlag, 1990.

———. *The Flowing Light of the Godhead.* Tr. Lucy Menzies. New York: Paulist Press, 1998.

Midrash, Dov, D.C.A. "Arnold e(s)t Arminius: La voix dédoublée dans *Friendship's Garland.*" *Anglomanie* 82:3 (1999), 450–501.

———. *Both/And.* Cambridge, Mass.: Harvard University Press, 1999.

———. *Hegel Is My Life.* New York and Los Angeles: Knopf/Schuster/ Disney, 1999.

———. *Narrheit und Methode.* Berne: Teufel, 1983. French translation, 1984. Japanese translation, 1985.

———. "'Over Here Where the Chief Justice Can't Hear Us': Die Zersplitterung des Ichs von *The Mikado* bis *Utopia Ltd.*" *Hinundhermeneutik* 12:1 (1985), 1–35.

———. *Textual Promiscuity: The Erotics of Biblical Narrative.* Translated from the Hebrew by Herb Marks. Bloomington: Indiana University Press, 1990.

Midrash, Dov, D.C.A. *Totem and Tabouleh: Freud in British Palestine.* London: Recto, 1995.

———. "The Unbearable Lightness of *Being and Nothingness.*" *Mentation* 22:3 (1982), 240–70.

Millar, Fergus. "The Debased Campus." Review of David Damrosch, *We Scholars. The Times* (London), *Higher Education Review*, 28 April 1995, 26.

Milton, John. *Paradise Lost.* New York: Longman, 1998.

———. *Paradise Regained.* In *The Portable Milton*, ed. Douglas Bush. New York: Viking, 1958, 549–609.

Mishima, Yukio. *Confessions of a Mask.* Tr. Meredith Weatherby. New Directions, 1958.

———. *Spring Snow. The Sea of Fertility*, vol. 1. Tr. Michael Gallagher. New York: Knopf, 1972.

Mokichi Okada Association. *MOA Museum of Art.* Kyoto: MOA Productions, 1990.

Moraga, Cherríe, and Gloria Anzaldúa, eds., *This Bridge Called My Back: Writings by Radical Women of Color.* New York: Kitchen Table, Women of Color Press, 1983.

More, Sir Thomas. *Utopia.* Ed. and tr. George M. Logan and Robert M. Adams. Cambridge: Cambridge University Press, 1989.

Murasaki Shikibu. *Murasaki Shikibu: Her Diary and Poetic Memoirs.* Ed. and tr. Richard Bowring. Princeton: Princeton University Press, 1982.

———. *The Tale of Genji.* Tr. Edward G. Seidensticker. New York: Vintage, 1990.

Mythit, Tobiah. "Bin ich Bathtöi?" *Omphaloskepsis* 88:1 (1999), 88–124.

Nabokov, Vladimir. *Ada, or Ardor: A Family Chronicle.* New York: McGraw-Hill, 1969.

———. *Pale Fire.* New York: Knopf, 1992.

———. *Pnin.* New York: Vintage Books, 1989.

———. *Speak, Memory: An Autobiography Revisited.* New York: Vintage International, 1989.

Namlerep, Sidney. "Critical Introduction." *The Best of S. J. Perelman*. New York: Modern Library, 1962, ix–xiv.

Nietzsche, Friedrich. *Daybreak: Thoughts on the Prejudices of Morality*. Ed. Maudemarie Clarke and Brian Leiter. Tr. R. J. Hollingdale. Cambridge: Cambridge University Press, 1997.

———. *Ecce Homo*. Tr. Walter Kaufman. New York: Vintage, 1989.

———. *Thus Spake Zarathustra*. In *The Portable Nietzsche*. Ed. and tr. Walter Kaufmann. New York: Penguin Books, 1976.

———. *Untimely Meditations*. Ed. Daniel Breazeale. Tr. R. J. Hollingdale. New York: Cambridge University Press, 1997.

Nimoy, Leonard. *I Am Not Spock*. Milbrae, California: Celestial Arts, 1975.

———. *I Am Spock*. New York: Hyperion, 1995.

O'Molloy, J. J. "'The Man in the Macintosh': Authorial Masks in *Ulysses*." *James Joyce Monthly* 20:11 (1990), 455–75.

Penley, Constance. *Feminism and Film Theory*. New York: Routledge/BFI, 1998.

———. "Feminism, Psychoanalysis, and the Study of Popular Culture." In Lawrence Grossberg et al., eds., *Cultural Studies*, 479–500.

Perelman, S. J. *The Best of S. J. Perelman*. New York: Modern Library, 1962.

Pirke Avot: Sayings of the Fathers. Ed. and trans. R. Travers Herford. New York: Schocken Books, 1962.

Plato. *The Symposium*. Tr. Robyn Waterfield. New York: Oxford University Press, 1994.

Price, Richard, and Sally Price. *Enigma Variations*. Cambridge: Harvard University Press, 1995.

Pritchard William. *English Papers: A Teaching Life*. St. Paul: Graywolf Press, 1995.

Proust, Marcel. *À la Recherche du temps perdu*. 3 vols. Paris: Gallimard, 1987.

———. *Contre Sainte-Beuve*. Paris: Gallimard, 1987.

Rasta, Lex. "*Cyberhegel*'s Ari Midrash: Hot New Game Was a Family Affair." *Wired*, 31 November 2000, 22–23.

Rilke, Rainer Maria. "Duino Elegies." In *The Selected Poetry of Rainer Maria*

Rilke. Ed. and tr. Stephen Mitchell. New York: Random House, 1992, 149–223.

Robbins, Bruce. *Secular Vocations: Intellectuals, Professionalism, Culture*. New York: Verso, 1993.

———. "Virtual Intellectuals." Forthcoming in *Social Subtext*, 2000.

Robbins, Bruce, and Pheng Cheah, eds., *Cosmopolitics: Thinking and Feeling beyond the Nation*. Minneapolis: University of Minnesota Press, 1998.

Ronell, Avital. *The Telephone Book: Technology, Schizophrenia, and Electric Speech*. Lincoln: University of Nebraska Press, 1989.

Ross, Andrew. *Strange Weather: Culture, Science, and Technology in the Age of Limits*. New York: Verso, 1991.

Saddam, Orchid V. "Jacques on Jacques: At the Eiffel Tower." *Jacquesbaby* 4 (1991). http://www.jacquesbaby.com.

———. "Jacques on Jacques: At the Gay Barre." *Jacquesbaby* 6 (1992).

———. "Jacques on Jacques: You're On the Air!" *Jacquesbaby* 8 (1993).

Said, Edward. "Traveling Theory." *Raritan* 1:3 (1982), 41–67.

———. "Traveling Theory Reconsidered." In Robert M. Polhemus and Roger B. Henkle, eds., *Critical Reconstructions: The Relationship of Fiction and Life*. Palo Alto: Stanford University Press, 1994, 251–65.

Scieszka, Jon. *The Stinky Cheese Man*. New York: Viking Penguin Press, 1999.

———. *Tut, Tut*. The Time Warp Trio, vol. 6. Madison: Demco Media, 1992.

Scott, Sir Walter. *The Tale of Old Mortality*. New York: Columbia University Press, 1993.

Scudéry, Madeleine de. *Clelia: An Excellent New Romance Dedicated to Mademoiselle de Longueville*. Tr. John Davies. London: Moseley and Dring, 1656.

Shattuck, Roger. *Proust's Binoculars: A Study of Memory, Time, and Recognition in "A la recherche du temps perdu."* New York: Random House, 1963.

————."Standing Up for Literature." *Civilization* 2:5 (1995), 70–72.

Shelley, Percy Bysshe. *A Defence of Poetry*. In David Damrosch et al., eds., *The Longman Anthology of British Literature*, 2:695–705.

Silence, Sylvia. "Finding Ourselves in *Finnegans Wake*." *James Joyce Weekly* 10:26 (1990), 330–34.

————. "Transgressive Performativity in Feminized Spaces." *Sighs* 1:1 (1995), 1–11.

Silentio, Johannes de. *Frygt og Boeven: Dialektisk Lyrik*. Copenhagen: Reitzel, 1843.

————. *Kierkegaard og mig*. Copenhagen: Rätsel, 1850.

Simpson, David. *The Academic Postmodern and the Rule of Literature: A Report on Half-Knowledge*. Chicago: University of Chicago Press, 1995.

Simpson, William Kelly, et al., eds., *The Literature of Ancient Egypt*. New Haven: Yale University Press. 2d edition, 1973.

Smiley, Jane. *Moo*. New York: Knopf, 1995.

Soames, Enoch. *Fungoids*. Preston, England: Preston Printing Co., 1891.

————. *Negations*. Preston: Preston Printing Co., 1890.

————. "Portrayal as Betrayal: Beerbohm and Myself." In T. K. Nupton, ed., *Inglish Litteracher 1890–1900*, revised ed. (Berne: Teufel, 1992), 235–90.

Spiegel, Maura, and Richard Tristman. *The Grim Reader: Writings on Death, Dying, and Living On*. New York: Anchor Books, 1997.

Spitzer, Leo. *Linguistics and Literary History: Essays in Stylistiques*. Princeton: Princeton University Press, 1967.

Steichen, Edward. *The Family of Man*. New York: Museum of Modern Art, 1955.

Sterne, Laurence. *The Life and Opinions of Tristram Shandy, Gentleman*. Oxford: Oxford University Press, 1983.

————. *A Sentimental Journey through France and Italy*. New York: Dutton, 1960.

Sturluson, Snorri. *Egil's Saga*. Tr. Hermann Pálsson and Paul Edwards. New York: Penguin, 1976.

Sturluson, Snorri. *The Prose Edda of Snorri Sturluson: Tales from Norse Mythology*. Tr. Jean L. Young. Berkeley: University of California Press, 1966.

Suleiman, Susan Rubin. *Budapest Diary: In Search of the Motherbook*. Lincoln: University of Nebraska Press, 1996.

———. "Criticism and the Autobiographical Voice." In Marjorie Garber, Rebecca Walkowitz, and Paul Franklin, eds., *Field Work: Sites in Literary and Cultural Studies*. New York: Routledge, 1996, 256–61.

———. *Risking Who One Is: Encounters with Contemporary Art and Literature*. Cambridge, Mass.: Harvard University Press, 1994.

Swift, Jonathan. *Gulliver's Travels; A Tale of a Tub; The Battle of the Books*. New York: Modern Library, 1931.

Thunder-ten-Tronckh, Arminius von. *Briefwechsel mit Arnold: oder, die Unbegreiflichkeit der Begriffe auf Englisch*. Weissnichtwo: Stillschweigen, 1872.

Thurber, James. "My Fifty Years with James Thurber." In *The Thurber Carnival*. New York: Harper and Brothers, 1945, xi–xiii.

———. "The Secret Life of James Thurber." *The Thurber Carnival*, 30–35.

———. "The Secret Life of Walter Mitty." *The Thurber Carnival*, 47–51.

Todorov, Tzvetan. *The Conquest of America: The Question of the Other*. Tr. Richard Howard. New York: Harper Perennial, 1992.

———. "A Dialogic Criticism?" In *Literature and Its Theorists: A Personal View of Twentieth-Century Criticism*. Tr. Catherine Porter. Ithaca, New York: Cornell University Press, 1987, 155–68.

Van Delden, Maarten. *Carlos Fuentes, Mexico and Modernity*. Nashville: Vanderbilt University Press, 1998.

Veblen, Thorstein. "The Higher Learning as an Expression of the Pecuniary Culture." In *The Theory of the Leisure Class*. New York: Random House, 1934, 363–400.

Veeser, H. Aram, ed. *Confessions of the Critics*. New York: Routledge, 1996.

Venturi, Robert. *Learning from Las Vegas*. Cambridge: MIT Press, 1972.

"Virginia Woolf." *Encyclopaedia Britannica*. Chicago: 15th edition, 1976. Micropaedia: Ready Reference, 10:743.

Voltaire, François Marie Arouet de. *Candide: or, Optimism*. Ed. and tr. Robert M. Adams. New York: W. W. Norton, 1991.

West, Cornel. "The Postmodern Crisis of the Black Intellectuals." In Lawrence Grossberg et al., eds., *Cultural Studies*, 689–705.

Whitman, Walt. "For Him I Sing." In *Leaves of Grass*. New York: New American Library, 1958, 35.

———. "One's-Self I Sing." *Leaves of Grass*, 31.

———. "When I Read the Book." *Leaves of Grass*, 35.

Wicke, Jennifer. *Advertising Fictions: Literature, Advertisement, and Social Reading*. New York: Columbia University Press, 1998.

Wilde, Oscar. "The Critic as Artist." In Richard Ellmann, ed., *The Artist as Critic*. Chicago: University of Chicago Press, 1982.

———. "The Decay of Lying: An Observation." In Ellmann, *The Artist as Critic*, 210–319.

———. *The Importance of Being Earnest*. New York: Chelsea House, 1988.

———. *The Picture of Dorian Grey*. New York: Modern Library, 1992.

———. "The Truth of Masks." In Ellmann, *The Artist as Critic*, 408–32.

Wodehouse, P. G. "The Clicking of Cuthbert." In *The Most of P. G. Wodehouse*. New York: Simon and Schuster, 1960, 385–97.

Wodehouse, P. G. *Jeeves and the Tie That Binds*. New York: Perennial Library, 1985.

———. *Pigs Have Wings*. Garden City: Doubleday, 1952.

Wolfe, Alan. "Common Concerns." Review of David Damrosch, *We Scholars*. *Washington Post Education Review*, 30 July 1995, 3.

"Woody Allen Signs Benigni, Kidman, to Star in Hegel Movie." *Daily Variety*, 31 June 2000, 2.

Woolf, Virginia. *Orlando*. Oxford: Blackwell, 1998.

———. *A Room of One's Own*. New York: Harcourt, Brace, 1989.

———. *Three Guineas*. New York: Harcourt, Brace, 1966.

———. *To the Lighthouse*. New York: Harcourt, Brace, 1927.

Žižek, Slavoj, ed. *Everything You Always Wanted to Know about Lacan (But Were Afraid to Ask Hitchcock)*. New York: Verso, 1992.

————. *For They Know Not What They Do: Enjoyment as a Political Factor*. New York: Verso, 1991.

Zum Brunn, Emilie, and Georgette Epiney-Burgard. *Women Mystics in Medieval Europe*. Tr. Sheila Hughes. New York: Paragon House, 1989.

INDEX